TEXAS MASONIC DEATHS

WITH
SELECTED
BIOGRAPHICAL SKETCHES

Michael Kelsey
Nancy Graff-Kelsey
Ginny Guinn Parsons

HERITAGE BOOKS
2019

HERITAGE BOOKS

AN IMPRINT OF HERITAGE BOOKS, INC.

Books, CDs, and more—Worldwide

For our listing of thousands of titles see our website
at
www.HeritageBooks.com

Published 2019 by
HERITAGE BOOKS, INC.
Publishing Division
5810 Ruatan Street
Berwyn Heights, Md. 20740

International Standard Book Number
Paperbound: 978-0-7884-1037-6

TEXAS MASONIC DEATHS WITH SELECTED BIOGRAPHICAL SKETCHES

INTRODUCTION

In 1828, eight years before Texas achieved her independence upon the battlefield of San Jacinto, the first Masonic Convention in Texas was held at San Felipe de Austin on the Brazos river. Attending the convention were Stephen F. Austin, the Father of Texas, Ira Ingram, the first Speaker of the Congress of the Republic of Texas, H.H. League, Eli Mitchell, Joseph White and Thomas M. Duke, each of whom figure prominently in Texas history. Since then, there have been many Texans, from all walks of life, affiliated with the Masons.

Local organizations of Masons, called Lodges, are located across the state. Each Lodge is responsible for maintaining and submitting records about their members to the Grand Lodge of Texas, the administrative body in charge of Masonry in Texas, located in Waco. The Grand Lodge publishes information from these records in their annual report.

Information from annual reports published for the years 1858 through 1882 is the basis for this book. The book is organized in three parts. The first part contains the name, number and location of the Lodge, the county where meetings were held, and the names of Lodge members who died during the year prior to submission of the report to the Grand Lodge. Part two includes biographical sketches for many of the Masons mentioned in the first part of the book. The biographical sketches were created using information from Lodge records, newspaper obituaries, and tombstone inscriptions. The third and final part of the book provides additional information about Masonry, including two articles titled "Masonry as Explained in 1853" and "Petition for First Lodge in Texas", where to write the Grand Lodge, and a glossary of Masonry terms.

Questions pertaining to this work may be addressed to Michael Kelsey or Nancy Graff-Kelsey, 1015 North 1st Street, Temple, TX 76501.

~~~~~

TABLE OF CONTENTS

PART 1

DEATHS REPORTED IN LODGE RECORDS

NOTE: Pursuant to a resolution adopted at the Annual Communication of 1874, a Grand Lodge of Sorrow was opened in Grand Lodge Hall in memory of deceased Masons. A list of names for the Lodge of Sorrow was included with the Lodge returns and is included in this part of the book. Any inconsistencies between the local Lodge returns and the information submitted for the Lodge of Sorrow are noted by including the spelling of the deceased's name as listed in the Lodge of Sorrow in "[ ]" next to the entry from the Lodge return.

PROCEEDINGS OF
THE TWENTY-THIRD ANNUAL COMMUNICATION
FOR MASONIC YEAR 1859
DEATHS

Holland Lodge No. 1--------J.B. Andrews, Jas A. Bolinger, John L. Duvall, W.D. Smith, "P.G. Lectures"
Red Land Lodge No. 3 --------J. Pinkney Henderson, Eliha Williams
Harmony Lodge No. 6 -------- J.B. Riddle, Sam M. Williams, P.G.M., J. Massa, Jno. H. Bennett
Matagorda Lodge No. 7 --------Richard E. Stewart
Milam Lodge No. 11 --------L.G. Moore, F.C.
Austin Lodge No. 12 --------Thos. Cassidy
Constantine Lodge No. 13 --------Wm. W. Porter
Friendship Lodge No. 16 --------L.E. Hatley, J.D. Williams
Washington Lodge No. 18 --------R.H. Banna
Graham Lodge No. 20 --------R.W. Fuller, W.A. Higgins
Marshall Lodge No. 22 --------W.H. Kelsey, W.C. Nebbatt
Clinton Lodge No. 23 --------Thos. R. Pitner, Jno. J.R. LeGrand
Montgomery Lodge No. 25 --------E.G. Collier, J. Worsham
Paris Lodge No. 27 --------E.J. Crook, J.F. Robertson
Palestine Lodge No. 31 --------W. Farquhar
Lavaca Lodge No. 34 --------Wm. H. Dallum
Mt. Moriah Lodge No. 37 --------W.S. Vance
Jefferson Lodge No. 38 --------C.F. Griffin, John Sentell, H.C. Yell, Thomas H. Owens, F.C.
Douglass Lodge No. 43 --------J.G. Jones, D.M. Scuggs
Alamo Lodge No. 44 --------B.C. Edwards
Euclid Lodge No. 45 --------C.M. Johnson
Liberty Lodge No. 48 -------- Peter B. Wooten, Sol Barrow, Geo. W. Wheatly
Tannahill Lodge No. 52 --------W.P. Martin, Wm. H. Keen
St. Johns Lodge No. 53 --------Louis Reuter
Grand Bluff Lodge No. 54 --------Alex Sweeten
Gillespie Lodge No. 55 --------R.P. Rice
Warren Lodge No. 56 --------Jno. Cockrell, J.P.L. Montague
Larissa Lodge No. 57 --------G.C. Moore, P.M. Boles
Boston Lodge No. 69 --------J.N. Lassita, J.W. Fort
Mt. Vernon Lodge No. 71 --------J.J. Wall, M.G. Miller
Rio Grande Lodge No. 81 --------J.P. Putignat, Abram Alsbach
Jackson Lodge No. 88 --------E. Stewart
Waxahachie Lodge No. 90 --------T.M. Lemon, E.H. Tarrant, P.D.G.M.
Tarrant Lodge No. 91 --------J.C. Sanders, B.N. Hampton, R. Millhollon, R.R. Cook, E.A.P.
Ioni Lodge No. 93 --------Charles Long
Goliad Lodge No. 94 --------S.M. Cassels

Newburn Lodge No. 97 --------J.H. Inman
Canton Lodge No. 98 --------H.D. Collier, G.W. Hill, J.W. White
Fairfield Lodge No. 103 --------W.S. Grayson
Red River Lodge No. 114 --------John Hollaway, J.C. Patterson
Travis Lodge No. 117 --------W. Coffee, Isaac B. Walker
Flora Lodge No. 119 --------F.C. McKnight, S.W. Sicduff, M. Spivey, J.E. Hodges
Mt. Hope Lodge No. 121 --------Andrew Hartgraves, Jno. W. Rotan
Texana Lodge No. 123 --------James N. Stanton
Coleto Lodge No. 124 --------Wm. G. York
Robt Burns Lodge No. 127 --------T.S. Shaddon
Camden Lodge No. 135 --------Griffith Lacey
Mt. Horeb Lodge No.137 --------Alex Vaughn
Neill Lodge No. 138 --------Isaac West , J.W. Browder, E.A.
Keechi Lodge No. 140 --------J.M. Capshan
Pierce Lodge No. 144 --------J.W. Rutherford
Truit Lodge No. 149 --------Wm. Henry
Jamestown Lodge No. 150 --------S.D. Buchanan
Eclectic Lodge No. 153 --------Sam Sneed, E.A.
Honey Grove Lodge No. 164 --------S.S. McLeary
Munroe Lodge No. 168 --------Jno. Pettit
Jas. F. Taylor Lodge No. 169 --------Jackson Smith
Bosque Lodge No. 171 --------E.J.K. Blair
E.J. Glover Lodge No. 178 --------J.M. Glover
Denton Lodge No. 201 --------A.P. Lloyd
Jas. A. Baker Lodge No. 202 --------Wm. S. Bolding, D.A. Mills
F. Sexton Lodge No. 206 --------Jno. Clabourn
Gainesville Lodge No. 210 --------Hiram Wood
Deer Creek Lodge No. 212 --------D. McFarland
Newport Lodge No. 228 --------James T. Durdin, E.A.
Lively Lodge No. 237 --------J.A. Orr

REPORTED BY THE SEVERAL LODGES
IN THEIR ANNUAL RETURNS TO
27 DECEMBER 1859
DEATHS

Holland Lodge No. 1--------John Dawson, G.W. Shetty
Red Land Lodge No. 3 --------F. V. McKee
St. Johns Lodge No. 5 --------R.M. Edwards, W.W. Williams
Harmony Lodge No. 6 --------H.L. Conner, Stephen Kirkland, J. Butler
Austin Lodge No. 12 -------E. Nash, Thos. Ward, H.W. Sublett, R. Green, H.L. Upshur
Constantine Lodge No. 13 --------Dan. Dulany, J.P. Wilkerson
Trinity Lodge No. 14 --------C.J. Saunders
Washington Lodge No. 18 --------R.J. French
Forest Lodge No. 19 --------W.W. Leach, B.A. Oliphant, W.H. Price
Graham Lodge No. 20 -------- John Estes, Wm. Norris
Lothrop Lodge No. 21 -------- Wm. F. Wall
Marshall Lodge No. 22 --------C.M. Adams, R.B. Anderson, W.P. Spencer, S.F. Taylor, Edwin Cater, E.A.
Clinton Lodge No. 23 --------J.I. Likens
Montgomery Lodge No. 25 --------F.L. Davis
Olive Branch Lodge No. 26 --------John S. Smith, W.R. Smith
Gonzales Lodge No. 30 --------J.R. Brantley
Palestine Lodge No. 31 --------Jas. Cautrell, Jno. Hassell
LaFayette Lodge No. 34 --------Wm. M. Baylor, G.W. Walker
Leona Union Lodge No. 39 --------L.O. Durst
Douglass Lodge No. 43 --------J.W. Paine, J.M. Sharp
Alamo Lodge No. 44 --------R.S. Neighbors, A.W. Bell, F. Eagan, H.F. Oswald
Euclid Lodge No. 45 -------J.F. Timmins, D.M. Waits, B.B. Cannon, John Sellers
Liberty Lodge No. 48 ----G.W. Wheatley, J.H. Johnston, G.S. Loving, A.D. Mayes
St. Johns Lodge No. 53 --------C.C. Taylor, A.O. Erwin
Grand Bluff Lodge No. 54 --------J.M. Wynn
Gillespie Lodge No. 55 --------Geo. Ellis, Jos. McAnulty
Larissa Lodge No. 57 --------W.A. Dunning
Woodville Lodge No. 62 --------F.W. Joinegan, F.S. Herrall
Chireno Lodge No. 66 --------John C. Barnett
Caledonia Lodge No. 68 --------A. Grace
Boston Lodge No. 69 --------C.A. Barbor, T.J. Heatherly
Mt. Vernon Lodge No. 71 --------B.F. Ragan
Morton Lodge No. 72 --------John Barnett, L.D. Weaver, A.H. Hodge
Springfield Lodge No. 74 --------D.F. Clendenon
Brazos Lodge No. 75 --------W.E. Howth, E.T. Bulger

4

TEXAS MASONIC DEATHS WITH SELECTED BIOGRAPHICAL SKETCHES

Cameron Lodge No. 76 --------J.W. McDonald, T.J. Waters
Murchison Lodge No. 80 --------A.T. Martin
Rio Grande Lodge No. 81 --------W.S. Lincoln, John Young
Terrell Lodge No. 83 --------John Burliegh
Indianola Lodge No. 84--------Samuel Turner, B. Segui
Pine Bluff Lodge No. 85--------John Waldrom
Tarrant Lodge No. 91--------James L. Partain, W.W. Poff, A.J. Speaker
Ioni Lodge No. 93--------N.B. Blair
Colorado Lodge No. 96--------Micajah Cole
Canton Lodge No. 98--------T.S. Harmon
Wharton Lodge No 99--------D.J. Whitten, S.J. Dyche
Unity Lodge No. 102--------S. Harrison, S. Henry
Kickapoo Lodge No. 105--------Wm. Foster, R.J. Morrow
San Jacinto Lodge No. 106--------James Springstun
Bloomfield Lodge No. 112 --------J.D. Love
Red River Lodge No. 116 --------W.A. Park
Travis Lodge No. 117 --------B.P. Smith, C.F.H. Goodryan, Nathan Coffey
Flora Lodge No. 119 --------J.M. Willis
Mt. Hope Lodge No. 121 --------Frank Castillian
Texana Lodge No. 123 --------Thos. Menifee
Robert Burns Lodge No. 127 --------T.L. Shaddon
Griffin Lodge No. 132 --------J.J. Davidson
Neill Lodge No. 138 --------Daniel McGee
Herschell Lodge No. 139 -------C.H. McNairy, J.W. Taylor, Jno. Thornton, E.A.
Keechi Lodge No. 140 --------Neil McEachern
Spring Hill Lodge No. 155 --------J. Treadwell, W.M. Roberts
East Trinity Lodge No. 157 --------M.L. Barnes
Sumpter Lodge No. 163 --------T.M. Baldwin
Athens Lodge No.165 --------C.B. Meredith, A.F. Mallard
Bosque Lodge No. 171 --------M.H. Bush, Joseph Johnston
Mound Prairie Lodge No. 173 --------W.H. Hudson
Corsicana Lodge No. 174 --------Joseph A. Love
St. Paul's Lodge No. 177 --------George Moore
Hopkinsville Lodge No. 183 --------W.B. Renvin, F.C.
Corpus Christi Lodge No. 189 --------James Mowatt, Judson C. Mann
Refugio Lodge No. 190 --------Abram H. Lea
Jack Titus Lodge No. 194 --------Thos. R. Peak
Lyons Lodge No. 195 --------James W. Nabers
Aguilla Lodge No. 196 --------Benj. Green, E.A.
DeMolay Lodge No. 199 --------Wiley Carpenter
Denton Lodge No. 201 --------S.D. Clark
Pine Lodge No. 203 --------J.T. Veazey
Walnut Creek Lodge No. 205 --------R.J. Billingslea, G.B. Givens
Frank Sexton Lodge No. 206 --------W.G. Milligan
McMahon Lodge No. 208 --------J.D. Crenshaw

Stedman Lodge No. 215 --------A.L. Stewart, P. Davis
Stanfield Lodge No. 217 --------Willis Wilson, J.M. McIlhenny
Bright Star Lodge No. 221 --------John H. Koke

PROCEEDINGS OF THE M. W. GRAND LODGE OF TEXAS
AT ITS TWENTY-FIFTH ANNUAL COMMUNICATION,
HELD AT THE CITY OF HOUSTON,
COMMENCING ON THE SECOND MONDAY IN JUNE A.D. 1861.
LIST OF DEATHS REPORTED
BY THE SEVERAL LODGES IN THEIR ANNUAL RETURNS TO
27 DECEMBER 1860

Holland Lodge No. 1 --------Jno. Dawson, R.H. Mesler
Red Land Lodge No. 3 --------Jas. Perkins
St. Johns Lodge No. 5 --------W.G. Hill, E.D. Nash
Harmony Lodge No. 6 --------Jas. Perry, Wm. Rayhouse, L.H. Smith
Austin Lodge No. 12 --------C. Coney, J.C. Hampton
Constantine Lodge No. 13 --------J.B. Chadwell
Trinity Lodge No. 14 --------Absolom Foster
Friendship Lodge No. 16 --------John McDenna
Washington Lodge No. 18 --------Thos. Price
Forest Lodge No. 19 --------Ed Earnest
Graham Lodge No. 20 --------J.H. Day, M.C.F. Barbour
Lothrop Lodge No. 21 --------J.A. Stubblefield
Marshall Lodge No. 22 --------A.D. Burris, A. Sanders, H.F. Spiley
Canton Lodge No. 23 --------J.H. Tramwell, P.B. Turner
De Witt Clinton Lodge No. 29 --------J. Falvey
Palestine Lodge No. 31 -------- J.E. Cravens, P.D.G.M.; W.A. Crawford, D.C. McMeans
Sam Houston Lodge No. 32 --------B.M. McGuffy, Mathew Carrol, B.F. Adams, E.A.
LaFayette Lodge No. 34 --------M. Clark
Jefferson Lodge No. 38 --------T.O. Alley, Joel Hughes, J.J.M. Mason
Douglass Lodge No. 43 --------Henry Wade
Alamo Lodge No. 44 --------R.J.L. Evans, A.A. Lockwood, H. Jasper
Euclid Lodge No. 45 --------S.M. Cook
Liberty Lodge No. 48 --------C. Bryan, G.S. Loving
St. Johns Lodge No. 51 --------Wm. Perkins
Gillespie Lodge No. 55 --------R.M. Conner, J.A. Cavitt
Warren Lodge No. 56 --------T.D. Woldredge
Hubert Lodge No. 67 --------R.H. Chappell, J.M. Stranger, C.E. Travis
Caledonia Lodge No. 68 --------J.H. Robson, J.G. Louge
Boston Lodge No. 69 --------R.M. Lindsey
Mt. Vernon Lodge No. 71 --------Martin Binion
Oasis Lodge No. 79 --------Spencer Migpen
Murchison Lodge No. 80 --------Joseph Garner
Rio Grande Lodge No. 81 --------T.J. Dirgan
Terrell Lodge No. 83 --------Ephraim Gage
Indianola Lodge No. 84 --------J.H. Baldridge

San Gabriel Lodge No. 89 --------Wm. Patterson
Waxahachie Lodge No. 90 --------R.P. Watson, Guy Stokes
Tarrant Lodge No. 91 --------W.B. White
Colorado Lodge No. 96 --------A.A. Smithwick
Wharton Lodge No. 99 --------J.H. Davis
Danville Lodge No. 101 --------T.H. Duke, C. Wilson, E.A.
Fairfield Lodge No. 103 --------C.G. Dunagan
San Jacinto Lodge No. 106 --------W.M. Reading
Jacksonville Lodge No. 108 --------G.J. Simpson
Guadalupe Lodge No. 109 --------P.M. Logan, E.A.
Greenville Lodge No. 110 --------E.H. Stevens, J.E. Wilson, F.C.
Burleson Lodge No. 111 --------A.P. Coker, N.W. Sadler
Bloomfield Lodge No. 112 --------J.R. Shellman
Mt. Hope Lodge No. 121 --------W.M. Butler
Texana Lodge No. 123 --------W. Coleman
Madison Lodge No. 126 --------R. Francis
Cushney Lodge No. 128 --------J.M. Buntin
Brazos Union Lodge No. 129 --------T.J. Fullerton
Griffin Lodge No. 132 --------T.W. Quade, J.H. Hendricks, P.C. Bishop, J.W.
Greedy
Bethel Lodge No. 134 --------Berry O'Neal
Newton Lodge No. 136 --------J.M. Robuck
Mt. Horeb Lodge No. 137 --------M.S. Skaggs
Neill Lodge No. 138 --------S.B. Owen
Keechi Lodge No. 140 --------J.O. Massey
Ochiltree Lodge No. 143 --------J.T. Simmonds
Planters Lodge No. 147 --------L.C. Warren
Marlin Lodge No. 152 --------Jas Craik
Eclectic Lodge No. 153 --------J.C. Parish
Trinity Lodge No. 157 --------Thos. Butler
McClelland Lodge No. 159 --------Abm Binkley
Athens Lodge No. 165 --------S.J. Scott
Belton Lodge No. 166 --------Herman Aiken
Monroe Lodge No. 168 --------Philip L. Crabb
Prairie Lodge No. 173 --------H.G. Quarles
Valley Lodge No. 175 --------S.A.J. Haynie
St. Paul's Lodge 177 --------Wm. Jones, Benj. F. Tarver
Post Oak Island Lodge No. 181 --------S.A. Smith, J.M. Christian
Tyrian Lodge No. 187 --------Robt. F. Green
Corpus Christi Lodge No. 189 --------M.P. Norton, Jno. Warren, E.A.
Refugio Lodge No. 190 --------A.C. Reed, J.B. Doughty
Lyons Lodge No. 195 --------M. McKinnon
Tyre Lodge No. 198 --------A.M. Anderson
Pine Lodge No. 203 --------T.J. Veasey
Frank Sexton Lodge No. 206 --------J.L. Dyer

Science Hill Lodge No. 211 --------W.A. Crawford, S.J. Scott
Farmersville Lodge No. 214 --------Moses Jones
Stanfield Lodge No. 217 --------J.J. Young
John E. Cravens Lodge No. 218 --------J.M. Morel
Bright Star Lodge No. 221 --------James Wells
Parsons Lodge No. 222 --------Silas Parsons
Bellville Lodge No. 223 --------Jasper N. Bell
Butler Lodge No. 224 --------W.W. Evans
Randolph Lodge No. 229 --------J.A. Stubblefield
Sampson Lodge No. 231 --------J.H. Welsh, W. McComb, G.L. Freeman
Lampasas Lodge No. 232 --------R.A. Dawson
Eutaw Lodge No. 233 --------A.T. Daniels, Thos. J. Clark
Sexton Lodge No. 251 --------Danl H. Davis
Cream Level Lodge U.D. --------R.H. Gibes

PROCEEDINGS OF THE M. W. GRAND LODGE OF TEXAS, AT ITS TWENTY-SIXTH ANNUAL COMMUNICATION, HELD AT THE CITY OF HOUSTON, COMMENCING ON THE SECOND MONDAY IN JUNE, A.D. 1862
DEATHS

Holland Lodge No. 1 --------W. Zimmerman, A.L. Levy, B.F. Terry
St. Johns Lodge No. 5 --------F.M. Snead, S.P. Sweeney, B.H. Kenneday
Harmony Lodge No. 6 --------Chas. Hayne, J.R. Young
Matagorda Lodge No. 7 --------D. MacFarland, J.W. McCamley, G.J. Bowie
Milam Lodge No. 11 --------T.A. Graves
Trinity Lodge No. 14 --------J.A. Howard, Z.Q. Craig
Washington Lodge No. 18 --------B. McGregor, Jas. Ringgold
Graham Lodge No. 20 --------M.C.F. Barbour, J.H. Day, Sam Lusk
Lothrop Lodge No. 21 --------R. Mathews, W.H. Kennedy, R.J. Johnson
Marshall Lodge No. 22 --------A.D. Burris, Alex Saunders, H.T. Spiby
Gonzales Lodge No. 30 --------S.H. Emerson
Leona Union Lodge No. 39 --------R.W. Chatham
Douglass Lodge No. 43 --------M.B. Banks
Euclid Lodge No. 45 --------A.L. Reed, Jas. Rhodes, J.M. Taylor, J. Donaho, Geo. Noland
Florida Lodge No. 46 --------J.A. Wilm
Warren Lodge No. 56 --------B.F. Aycock, Geo. Lewis
Woodville Lodge No. 62 --------W.F. Cotton
Hubert Lodge No. 67 --------F.H. Hubert, R.J. Swearengen
Morton Lodge No. 72 --------J.S. Leneave
Brazos Lodge No. 75 --------S. Calvert, D.A.J. Downs, S.E. Tippett
Murchison Lodge No. 80 --------J.J. Ballard
Terrell Lodge No. 83 --------Ed Harry
New Salem Lodge No. 87 --------D.W. Foreman
San Gabriel No. 89 --------Evan Williams
Goliad Lodge No. 94 --------J.B. Whitley
Sharon Lodge No. 95 --------J.E. Smith
Kickapoo Lodge No. 105 --------O.L. Wiley, R.J. Hardman
Guadalupe Lodge No. 109 --------C.L. Cox, N. Cannon
Travis Lodge No. 117 --------J. McCarty
McDonald Lodge No. 120 --------T. Irvine
Baylor Lodge No. 125 --------Thos. Hunt
Madison Lodge No. 126 --------S.F. Baker, E.A.M. Gray
Belmont Lodge No. 131 --------J.O.P. Bond
Mt. Horeb Lodge No. 132 --------J.P. Newton, A.G. Gannaway, M.S. Skaggs
Fort Worth Lodge No. 148 --------A.Y. Fowler, E.R. Mingus
Eclectic Lodge No. 153 --------W.D. Williams
Hickory Hill Lodge No. 156 --------L.A. Patillo

McClelland Lodge No. 159 --------J.R. Hill
Hopkinsville Lodge No. 183 --------W.D. Latimer, F. Pullen
Hickory Grove Lodge No. 184 --------J.H. Wallace
Refugio Lodge No. 190 --------N. Maynard
Lyons Lodge No. 195 --------W.A. Chandler
Denton Lodge No. 201 --------L.E. Hines
J.A. Baker Lodge No. 202 --------A.C. Parmer, Thos. Farris
Mt. Calm Lodge No. 204 --------J.V. Middleton
Walnut Creek Lodge No. 205 --------E.N. Clement, J.A. Prindle
Mantua Lodge No. 209 --------G.S. Fitzhugh
Farmersville Lodge No. 214 --------J.W. Daniel, W.E. Stanford, L. Glass, T. Wisdom
New Port Lodge No. 228 --------J.T. Mellard
Sampson Lodge No. 231 --------J.C. Walker
Plano Lodge No. 235 --------W.H. Robb
Brazos Lodge No. 247 --------B. McGregor
Cream Level Lodge U.D. --------R.R. Gibbs

PROCEEDINGS FOR MASONIC YEAR 1863
DEATHS

Holland Lodge No. 1 --------E.A. Palmer, Thos. S. Lubbock, W. S. Owens, H.L. Green, A.T. Paul

St. Johns Lodge No. 5 --------M.T. Patten, E. Marly

Harmony Lodge No. 6 --------C. Behling, P.L. Barziza, S.B. Hurlbut

Matagorda Lodge No. 7 --------J.W. Rudgetts, E. Schultz, J.F. Hardew

Milam Lodge No. 11 --------W.A. Dallis, A.J. Warner

Austin Lodge No. 12 --------C. Backholtz, J. Warren, B.W. Dean

Trinity Lodge No. 14 --------J.F. Sharp, J. H. Brown, Z.Q. Croiy

Friendship Lodge No. 16 -------C.Y. Cherry, Jno. Beorns, J. Robbins, J. English

Orphans Lodge No. 17 -------E. Bell, J.H. Anderson, J.W. Hutchinson, J.W. Panter

Washington Lodge No. 18 --------Thos. Price

Graham Lodge No. 20 --------H. Sherrell, L.C. Cormack

Forest Lodge No. 19 --------Ford Craner, Monks Nichols

Marshall Lodge No. 22 --------W.B. Hill

Paris Lodge No. 27 --------B.G. Hale, Thos. Dennis, J. Cuttleberry

De Witt Clinton [Lodge No. not given] --------Z.W. Eddy, A. Wood, W. N. Grant, J.S. Adams

Gonzales Lodge No. 30. --------A.D. Harris, M.L. Evans

Palestine Lodge No. 31 -------Jno. G. Gooch, R.W. Willette, A.W. Ford, D. Mott, A.L. Nicks, J.W. Gardener, S. Lemuel, H.G. Hendrix, P.C. Holmes, M.T. Sadler

LaFayette Lodge No. 34 --------H.P. Stamler, W. Wernett

Jefferson Lodge No. 38 --------Fleming Jones

Leona Union Lodge No. 39 --------S.P. Reinhard, J.A. Gilmore, G.M. Webb

Alamo Lodge No. 44 --------R.W. Campbell

Euclid Lodge No. 45 --------J.D. Hamilton, J.J.A. Parker, M. Thompson, E. Holverson, F.M. Taylor

Liberty Lodge No. 48 --------Jno. Wrigley, H.B. Johnson

Tannehill Lodge No. 52 --------W.A. Gould

St. Johns Lodge No. 53 --------H.B. Slaughter

Grand Bluff Lodge No. 54 --------Thos. D. Matthews, J.L. Beaty

Caldwell Lodge No. 56 --------W.W. Carrington, R.W. King, J. Ryan, W.W. Hill, N. Carroll, J. M. Kerby

Larissa Lodge No. 57 --------Jno. B. Harper, Jno. C. Williams

Mt. Enterprise Lodge No. 60 --------L. Morris, R.H. McCall, J. Mayfield, W.M. Young

Woodville Lodge No. 62 --------G.L. Heard, E.A. Wittlesey, W.A. Allen, W. Hanks, R.R. Neyland, M.T. Perryman

Chireno Lodge No. 66 --------W.E. Barnett, G.M. Spivey, W.C. Spivey, W.J. Wilson

Hubert Lodge No. 68 --------J.H. Robson, J.G. Legue

TEXAS MASONIC DEATHS WITH SELECTED BIOGRAPHICAL SKETCHES

Mt. Vernon Lodge No. 71 --------M. Daffrem, K.K. Smith, N.S. Harman
Morton Lodge No. 72 --------E.L. Walker, S.M. Clanton, J.C. Tomlinson
Springfield Lodge No. 74 --------Carson B. James, W.M. Lanwright
Murchison Lodge No. 80 --------J. Tate, J.J. Foster, G.W. Gurthie, C.H. Bellah, J.D. Thigpen
Rio Grande Lodge No. 81 --------F. Mabert, R.B. Scarborough, B. Lawler
Terrell Lodge No. 83 --------J. Harrison, B.F. Boyd, J.B. Blanton, R.A. Prodrill, C. Ruby, S. C. Box, J. Boyd, Jas. Gray, W.H. Stubblefield
New Salem Lodge No. 87 --------Jas. Gray
San Gabriel Lodge No. 89 --------Geo. W. Courts, J.H. Tankersly
Goliad Lodge No. 94 --------F.W. Swearington, J.C. Love
Sharon Lodge No. 95 --------P. Heath, J.M. Latta, Sam Wilson, P. Smith, J. Denson/Deunson, J.O. Rhodes
Colorado Lodge No. 96 --------R. Farchan, A.W. Miller, J.M. Smith
Canton Lodge No. 98 --------W.C. Bonner, Arthur Atchinson
Wharton Lodge No. 99 --------Thos. Thatcher, E. Pruett
Kickapoo Lodge No. 105 --------J.G. Baker ,E. Bennett, L. J. Spence
San Jacinto Lodge No. 106 --------Wiley Green
Guadalupe Lodge No. 109 --------T.H. Helleman, C. Reich
Prairie Lea Lodge No. 114 --------J.C. Cartwright
McDonald Lodge No. 120 --------W. P. Hayter, W.R. Grimes
Mt. Hope Lodge No. 121 --------R.R. Smith, J. Hammonds, J. Fotch, M.D. Maddox, G.W. Payne
Texana Lodge No. 123 --------Jno. Stevens
Baylor Lodge No. 125 --------J.H. Lewis, Thos. Hunt
Madison Lodge No. 126 --------A.C. Merriman
Brazos Union Lodge No. 129 --------J.T. Lloyd, J.T. Beroman
Belmont Lodge No. 131 --------J.J. Davidson, J. Grady
Retreat Lodge No. 133 --------Wade Allsbrook, A.C. Calloway
Newton Lodge No. 136 --------J.H. Stevenson, J.C. Mattox
Mt. Horeb Lodge No. 137 --------W.M. Chapman
Neill Lodge No. 138 --------W.B.S. Ward, D.C. Jones
Walnut Grove Lodge No. 145 --------Daniel Gilleland
Truitt Lodge No. 149 --------P.W. Harvey, W.G. Freeland, C.H. Ashton, B.H. Rowe
Cibolo Lodge No. 157 --------John H. Johnson
Eclectic Lodge No. 153 --------Jno. H. Tate, W.A. Pritchett, A.T. Brown, W.L. Farrish
Hickory Hill Lodge No. 156 --------B.M. Holloway
McClelland Lodge No. 159 --------P. Fears
Lancaster Lodge No. 160 --------W.A. Burkhead, J. Heath
Murval Lodge No. 162 --------J.A. Stevenson, C.C. Davis, B.F. Tamplin, J. Tate
Monroe Lodge No. 168 --------M. Randolph
St. Andrews Lodge No. 170 --------J. Sherrell, B. Niebours, C. G. Adams

13

Mound Prairie Lodge No. 173 --------J. Scarborough, J.R. McKain, R.C. Henderson, A.M. Horton
Post Oak Island Lodge No. 181 --------J.H. Manning
Hopkinsville Lodge No. 183 --------E.W. Christian, G. Luenvatt
Hickory Grove Lodge No. 184 --------Jno. C. Williams, A.S. Hullum
Corpus Christi Lodge No. 189 --------Jas. Baskin, L.C. Owens
Refugio Lodge No. 190 --------Dan Dunman
Leon Lodge No. 193 --------Jos. Bishop, N.S. White, W.M. Wade
Jack Titus Lodge No. 194 --------J.G. Daby
Lyons Lodge No. 195 --------J. Worrow, J.R. Perkins
Gatesville Lodge No. 197 -------P.C. Bible
Tyre Lodge No. 198 --------Jno. Vaneroy, Jr.,
J.A. Baker Lodge No. 202 --------A.Y. Farris, W.E. Harper, F.L.M. Leonard
Pine Lodge No. 203 --------S.D. Wentz
Mt. Calm Lodge No. 204 --------W.K. Middleton, C.C. Middleton, J.V. Middleton
Walnut Creek Lodge No. 205 --------T. Burrows, R.H. Thompson, C.P. Walker
W.P. Brittain Lodge No. 207 --------M.R. Morphus
Gainesville Lodge No. 210 --------Jas. A. Powers
Farmersville Lodge No. 214 --------B.R. Houton/Honton, Jno. R. Briscoe
Stanfield Lodge No. 217 --------Sam Harefield, H.C. Atchinson, E.F. Anderson,
Jno. E. Cravers Lodge No. 218 --------C.C. Turpin
Millville Lodge No. 219 --------W.T. Embry
Onion Creek Lodge No. 220 --------J.H. Stanley
Bright Star Lodge No. 221 --------J.W. Hamitt, F.L. McCorkle
Butler Lodge No. 224 --------W.L. Streety
Brahan Lodge No. 226 --------C.F. Henderson, R. Houston, B.G. Henderson
Randolph Lodge No. 229 --------W.D. Williamson, J.L. Brashear, M.L. Benson
Sampson Lodge No. 231 --------J. White, J.R. O'Neal
Lampasas Lodge No. 232 --------A.M. Tedford
Eutaw Lodge No. 233 --------J.A. McKisseck, J.W. Butrell
White Rock Lodge No. 234 --------E.M. Yager, Wm. B. Mays
Plano Lodge No. 235 --------H.H. Gossom
Lively Lodge No. 237 --------J. Ashmore
San Felipe Lodge No. 239 --------J.W. Chandler
Torbert Lodge No. 241 --------G.A. Neal, Robt. Hodges
Llano Lodge No. 242 --------E.J. Jackson, C/G Owen
Gamble Lodge No. 244 --------R.T. Jackson
Sulphur Bluff Lodge No. 246 -------J.H. Anthony, Jacob Greer, G.M. Hill, J.A. Woods
Brazos Lodge No. 247 --------W.A. Dallas
Andrew Jackson Lodge No. 249 -------R.C. Brigman, W.C. Wilson, S.J. Morgan
Sexton Lodge No. 251 --------R. Polly, R.W. Bradford
Homer Lodge No. 254 --------Sam Cole, W.H. Cleaver
Meridian Lodge No. 268 --------R.R. Gibbs
Cream Level Lodge U.D. --------R.R. Gibbs

LODGE RETURNS FOR 1866
FOR THE MASONIC YEAR A.D. 1865, A.L. 5865
DEATHS

Holland Lodge No. 1, Houston, Harris county --------George W. Capron, Philip Huffman, "EA"; A. Kendall, J.A. Phelps, A.S. Ruthven, E.H. Vasmer, John C. Hobermehl

Milam Lodge No. 2, Nacogdoches, Nacogdoches county --------J.H. Gilbert, W.B. Dameron, Thomas Rimmele, H.C. Hancock, Charles S. Taylor

Red Land Lodge No. 3, San Augustine, San Augustine county --------Jesse M. Hail, W.S. Smith, J.A. Brooks, H. Griffith, W.S. Smith, T.G. Brooks, N.J. Caraway, F.N. Horn

St. John Lodge No. 5, Columbia, Brazoria county --------S. Philips, John A. Wharton

Harmony Lodge No. 6, Galveston, Galveston county --------E.W. Moore, A.S. Ruthven, PGM

Milam Lodge No. 11, Independence, Washington county --------W.B. Roberts, an "E.A."

Austin Lodge No. 12, Austin, Travis county --------J.P. Ford, S.S. Penrod, an E.A. J.R. Jackson

Constantine Lodge No. 13, Bonham, Fannin county --------A.G. Atkins, Richard Alderson, Maxwell Martin, W. M. Stanley, W.M. Campbell, J.M. Hunt, R.A. Dethridge

Friendship Lodge No. 16, Clarksville, Red River county --------J.A.N. Murray, Moses Lype, John McCabe

Orphans Friend Lodge No. 17, Anderson, Grimes county --------T.M. Bowen, Aaron Shannon

Washington Lodge No. 18, Washington, Washington county --------E.M. Alexander, B.M. Hotfield, Theo Harper, H.E. Lockett, J.M. Naylor

Forest Lodge No. 19, Huntsville, Walker county --------John McCrary

Graham Lodge No. 20, Brenham, Washington county --------A.M. Lewis

Lothrop Lodge No. 21, Crockett, Houston county --------B.A.H. Masongale, Thomas W. Warren

Marshall Lodge No. 22, Marshall, Harrison county --------E.C. Beasley, C.L. Harnell

Clinton Lodge No. 23, Henderson, Rusk county --------M.L. McMurry, Eli Wood

Paris Lodge, No. 27, Paris, Lamar county --------R.M. Baker, B.F. Owen, W. St. Clair, H. Shelton, Daniel Williams and G.M. Eubank, F.C.

Gonzales Lodge No. 30, Gonzales, Gonzales county --------John Deer

LaFayette Lodge No. 34, Lagrange, Fayette county --------W. Hunt, W. Prim

Lavaca Lodge No. 36, Port Lavaca, Calhoun county -------- W.T. Keen

Mount Moriah Lodge No. 37, Cold Spring, Polk county --------T.H. Butler, J. McCormick

Douglass Lodge No. 43, Douglass, Nacogdoches county --------H. Filby, "an E.A."

Alamo Lodge No. 44, San Antonio, Bexar county --------Asa Mitchell

Euclid Lodge No. 45, Rusk, Cherokee county --------M.W. Henry, A.A. Cameron, J.M. Jones, P.M., W.D. Gammage

Liberty Lodge No. 48, Liberty, Liberty county --------B.F. Rodes

Tannehill Lodge No. 52, Dallas, Dallas county --------A.J. May, J. E. Jenkins, "E.A.", Jesse Cox "F.C."

Grand Bluff Lodge No. 54, Grand Bluff, Panola county --------J.P. Dixon, Wm. Langley, Sr., James M. Johns, Wm. Langley, Jr; H.C. Roguemore

Gillespie Lodge No. 55, Wheelock, Robertson county --------B. Brooks, Sheridan Cavitt, A.F. Cavitt, Robt Henry, B.J. Hines, Josiah Jordan, John H. Feeney, Francis Kellogg, John Stokes.

Warren Lodge No. 56, Caldwell, Burleson county --------J.C. Anthony, J.H. Courtney, Thos. Johnson

Mt. Enterprise Lodge No. 60, Mt. Enterprise, Rusk county --------James T. Furlow, T.C. Salmons, H.H. Scroggins, R. L. Smith

Woodville Lodge, No. 62, Woodville, Tyler county --------W.H. Bevill

Joppa Lodge No. 65, Elysian Fields, Harrison county --------Franklin Alexander, D.J. Dodson, J. F. Everett

Chireno Lodge No. 66, Chireno, Nacogdoches county --------Thos. J. Curl, C.W. Spindle, F.B. Brown, a "F.C."

Hubert Lodge No. 67, Chappell Hill, Washington county --------E.S. Buck, R. F Deggs.

Caledonia Lodge No. 68, Columbus, Colorado county --------J.J Stolls, W. J. Wright, T.W. Harris, W. Chaney, H.E. Jordt, B.F. Penrice

Boston Lodge No. 69, Boston, Bowie county --------W.H. Fore, H. Freeze, Jacob McFarland, S.H. Perkey, J. R. Smith, E.C. Turner

Mount Vernon Lodge No. 71, Mount Vernon, Titus county --------R.E. Doak

Morton Lodge No. 72, Richmond, Fort Bend county --------Constantine W. Buckley

Springfield Lodge No. 74, Springfield, Limestone county --------W.W. Oliver, M.C. Rowland

Murchison Lodge No. 80, Hallettsville, Lavaca county --------H.A. Greenwood, J.W. Rains, J.F. Spears

Terrell Lodge No. 83, Alto, Cherokee county --------Isaac Allen, D.A. Gates, D. Hullum, James W. Rainey

Waxahachie Lodge No. 90, Waxahachie, Ellis county --------John M. Hines, W.B. Richeson, T.J. Winkler, David P. Fearis, R.M. Tandy

Tarrant Lodge No. 91, Tarrant, Hopkins county --------A.H. Black, M. W. Kiger, W.H. Portwood, M. Russell, Eli Voss

Lodge No. 92, Waco, McLennan county --------John B. Ewell, B.F. Faulkner, James H. Gurley, H.B. Granbury, Frank M. Harris, Simon Matthews, John C. Newlin, Willis Summerville, M.E. Smith

Goliad Lodge No. 94, Goliad, Goliad county --------S.P. Porter

16

Colorado Lodge No. 96, Webersville, Travis county --------J.M. Costley, J.H. Hulcomb, Jacob Pevyhouse, O.M. White

Canton Lodge No. 98, Canton, Smith county --------A. Hunt, Geo. Weatherby

Unity Lodge No. 102, Moscow, Polk county --------R.T. Cannon

Fairfield Lodge No. 103, Fairfield, Freestone county --------Andrew S. Bonner, John W. Blackmon, William Clements, Z.P. Clough, G.W. Demegan, John Gregg, W.A. Huckaby, J. H. Hodges, J.A. Powell, W.F. Paxton, Edward Steele, E. Bachelor

Kickapoo Lodge No. 105, Kickapoo, Anderson county --------J.E. Smith

Jacksonville Lodge No. 108, Jacksonville, Cherokee county -------- G.M. Doherty

Burleson Lodge No. 111, Navarro, Leon county --------E. Bell, Wm. Badford, E. Chadwick, W.S. Diggs, M. Daily, C.T. Henry, M.D.S. Lang, C.G. Posey, H.R. Vinson, N. H. Wynkoop

Bloomfield Lodge No. 112, Kauffman, Kauffman county --------J.G. Lewis, W.J. Johnson, an F.C.

Magnolia Lodge No. 113, Magnolia, Anderson county --------L.W. Dumas

Prairie Lea Lodge No. 114, Prairie Lea, Caldwell county --------Ben D. Wade, Obadiah Lowry

Starr Lodge No. 118, Starrville, Rusk county --------R.J. McFarland

Flora Lodge No. 119, Quitman, Wood county --------A. Baird, William A. Crow, Silas Burleson, James M. Hustin, J.B. Christal

Texana Lodge No. 123, Texana, Jackson county --------J.M. Faught, J.B. Pearce

Coletto Lodge No. 124, Yorktown, De Witt county -------- E. Jones, J.P. York

Madison Lodge No. 126, Orange, Orange county --------Josiah Jordan

Cushney Lodge No. 128, San Marcos, Hays county --------H.R. Patton, G.F. Jones

Retreat Lodge No. 133, Courtney, Grimes county --------E.C. Davis

Bethel Lodge No. 134, Ladonia, Fannin county --------R. Harrell, John Nail

Camden Lodge No. 135, Camden, Rusk county --------Dennis Cochran

Newton Lodge No. 136, Burkville, Newton county --------W.D. Snell, W.W. Simmons, J.B. Carlton, B. Shaddock, "E.A's."

Mount Horeb Lodge No. 137, Gabriel Mills, Williamson county --------A.N. Murphy

Neill Lodge No. 138, Lexington, Burleson county --------C.C. Sanders

Herschell Lodge No. 139, Coffeeville, Upshur county --------R.A. Coombs, Joel Crawford, M.A. Chevis, W.J. Morgan, J.M. Jackson

Keechi Lodge No. 140, Centreville, Leon county --------E.F. Tubb, W.A. Pruitt, G.P. Mattison, J.W. Stegall, P.T. Young, J.Y. Pestole, W.F. Kidd, Jr.

Bethesda Lodge No. 142, Gilmer, Upshur county --------John A. Bevens, W.F. Christian, C.R. Earp, Jacob A. Derrick, Joseph Humphreys, John T. Ingram, John T. Mings, R.W. Mings, J.N. Richardson, G.T. Standford, J.C. Willingham

Winnsborough Lodge No. 146, Winnsboro, Wood county --------Thos. James, W. Moore

Planters' Lodge No. 174, [sic] Plantersville, Grimes county --------Andrew Montgomery, Aaron Shannon

Marlin Lodge No. 152, Marlin, Falls county --------J.K. Tomlinson, J.J. Coleman

Eclectic Lodge No. 153, Eclectic Grove, Fannin county --------A.D. Bourne, E.H. Inge, W. Johnson, J.E. McCoy, E. Outhouse, J.B. Potts, D.R. Patterson, L.S. Sivells, B.F. Williams, J.M. Thompson

Spring Hill Lodge No. 155, Spring Hill, Navaro county --------Henry Fullerton

Hickory Hill Lodge No. 156, Hickory Hill, Davis county --------H.G. Andrews

East Trinity Lodge No. 157, Rockwall, Kaufman county --------A.J. Ellis, Benj Dye

Wm. M. Taylor Lodge No. 158, Carmel Church, Smith county --------Hugh Neal

Murval Lodge No. 162, A. Davis', Panola county --------H. Dukes

Honey Grove Lodge No. 164, Honey Grove, Fannin county --------Wm. Merrick, E.B. Stevens, Orville Smith

Athens Lodge No. 165, Athens, Henderson county --------J.A. Clark, Gowen Hankins, G.W. Reynolds

Belton Lodge No. 166, Belton, Bell county --------R. B. Foster

Kentucky Lodge No. 167, Kentucky, Grayson county --------J.T. Clark

Monroe Lodge No. 168, Madisonville, Madison county --------E. C. Mitchell

Corsicana Lodge No. 174, Corsicana, Navarro county --------J. T. Spence

Valley Lodge No. 175, Burnet, Burnet county --------J. H. Eubank, James Hart, Lewis Martin

St Paul's Lodge No. 177, Port Sullivan, Milam county --------Elijah Bailey

Concrete Lodge No. 182, Concrete, De Witt county --------George E. More, L.S. Warren

Hopkinsville Lodge No. 183, Hopkinsville, Gonzales county --------C. Dunlop, C. T. Flint

Hickory Grove Lodge No. 184, Mount Vernon, Smith county --------S.C. George, L.P. Shackleford

Decatur Lodge No. 186, Decatur, Wise county --------Richard Boren

Tyrian Lodge No. 187, Sabine Pass, Jefferson county --------Abel Coffin, Sr.

Corpus Christi Lodge No. 189, Corpus Christi, Nueces county --------Wm Chism, John Hansaker, J.C. Macdonald, W.S. Shaw

Havana Lodge No. 191, Havana, Davis county --------John Jackson

Cusseta Lodge No. 192, Cusseta, Davis county --------James Jacobs, A. Manker, Robert Stewart, F.M. Lee

Jack Titus Lodge No. 194, Colman's Springs, Red River county --------W.N. Dilliard

Lyons Lodge No. 195, Lyons, Fayette county --------L. Coffee, W. McClure

Tyre Lodge No. 198, Tennessee Colony, Anderson county --------C.L. Rimborough, C.D. Holliman

18

Denton Lodge No. 201, Louisville, Denton county --------H.J. Gray, John Upshaw

Pine Lodge No. 203, Edom, Van Zandt county --------H. Bryant, S.D. Willingham

Mount Calm Lodge No. 204, Mount Calm, Limestone county --------W. Blackburn, Aaron Estis, W.H. Holloway, D.S. Newton, A.A. Reed, R.B. Williams

Mantua Lodge No. 209, Mantua, Collin county --------Wm. Creager

Gainesville Lodge No. 210, Gainesville, Cook county --------Thos. W. Wright

Science Hill Lodge No. 211, Science Hill, Henderson county --------T.R. Barton, G.W. Tuggle

Farmersville Lodge No. 214, Farmersville, Collin county --------G.W. Howard

Stedman Lodge No. 215, Newton, Newton county --------R. Odom

Twin Sisters Lodge No. 216, Blanco, Blanco county --------P.W. Graves, B.J. Devall

Stanfield Lodge No. 217, Denton, Denton county --------W.C. Sicer

Millville Lodge No. 219, Millville, Rusk county -------- Wesley Bonner, H. Edens, J.B. Harrell, R.S. Montgomery

Parsons Lodge No. 222, Parsons Seminary, Travis county --------P.A. Monroe, E.A. Rutledge

Miller Lodge No. 224, Tidwell Creek P.O., Hunt county --------Wm. Bates, R.F. Balthrop, Jo. Harris, M.R. Patterson

Butler Lodge No. 224a, Butler, Freestone county --------C.C. Johnson

San Saba Lodge No. 225, San Saba, San Saba county --------J.M. Hall

Sampson Lodge No. 231, Lynchburg, Harris county --------J.C. Hobermehl

Lampasas Lodge No. 232, Lampasas, Lampasas county --------J.C. Cooksey, M. Bean, Tho. B. Huling

Llano Lodge No. 242, Llano, Llano county --------H.F. Stockman

Sam Sanford Lodge No. 243, Sand Hill Church, Shelby county --------G.A. Samford

Solomon's Lodge No. 245, Union Springs Academy, Gray Rock P.O., Titus county --------Wm. Graham

Sexton Lodge No. 251, Sexton, Sabine county --------Benjamin H. Mannerlyn, David Renfro

Hondo Lodge No. 252, Hondo Valley, Medina county --------J.H. Steigler

Homer Lodge No. 254, Homer, Angelina county --------T.P. Eavans, J.W. Gaines, L. Mankin, Thos. Mouldon, A.T. Allen, J.A. Allen and J.W. Jones, "E.A."

Lake Lodge No. 255, Giles' Academy, Lamar county --------Jas. B. Barret

Waverley Lodge No. 259, Waverly, Walker county --------Ben Campbell

Ioni Lodge No. 260, Wright's Store, Anderson county --------Owen Sullivan

Milford Lodge No. 262, Milford, Ellis county --------Milton Wright

Whitesboro' Lodge No. 263, Whitesboro', Grayson county --------John M. Pickett

Grayson Lodge No. 265, Personville, Limestone county --------J.E. Pollard

Grand View Lodge No. 266, Grand View, Johnson county --------A.J. Robinson
Stevensville Lodge No. 267, Stevensville, Erath county --------Griffith Brown, W.W. Hickey, J.M. Stephen, Jackson Riley, S. Gilbert, H.C. Carr, R.B. Graves, Wm. Culver, N.M. Gillentine, W.C. Lowden
Meridian Lodge No. 268, Meridian, Bosque county --------R.S. Barnes
Phoenix Lodge No. 275, Weatherford, Parker county -------- Henry Maxwell
J.D. Giddings Lodge No. 280, Evergreen, Washington county --------C.C. Sanders
Hempstead Lodge No. 281, Hempstead, Austin county --------Christian Ahrenbeck

RETURNS OF LODGES FOR THE MASONIC YEAR
A.D. 1867, A. L. 5867
DEATHS

Holland Lodge No. 1, Houston, Harris county --------Minor Bawsell, Andrew Crawford, A.J. Chevanne, Thomas Johns, B.E. Jamison, Wm. H. King, Henry Fleishman, Larkin Martin, Robert O Rielley, I. C. Spence, J. M. M. Swan,-- Eleven Master Masons. H.W. Benchly, A.P. Pruitt, and Sam Tuttle--Three Fellow Crafts. J.W. Stump and Hu T. Scott--Two Entered Apprentices.

Milam Lodge No. 2, Nacogodoches, Nacogdoches county --------W.T. Collins, W. Voight

Red Land Lodge No. 3, San Augustine, San Augustine county --------J. M. McAuley, 1866, and Entered Apprentice B.F. Price

St. Johns Lodge No. 5, Columbia, Brazoria county --------S.L. Johnson, R.G Salmon, S.C. West

Harmony Lodge No. 6, Galveston, Galveston county --------B.F. Clark, Alex Edmondstone, J.S. Gillaspie, Robt Hughes, James E. Haviland, Jas. Hyde, Edward Ing, Lorin Kent, Alvin Reed, Alvin Mack, J.A. Steele, James A. Nerts, Jaques Weiss--Total 13

Milam Lodge No. 11, Independence, Washington county --------John L. Young

Austin Lodge No. 12, Austin, Travis county --------B.P. Hollingsworth, H. Wilke

Constantine Lodge No. 13, Bonham, Fannin county --------Allen Alterberry, John T. Hart

Trinity Lodge No. 14, Livingstone, Polk county --------J.H. Brown, Z.Q. Craig, A.P. Garner, F.M. Harrell, J.A. Howard, J.H. Jones, W.T. Lewis, D.D. Moore, W.F. Matthews, M.T. Nettles, J.N. Oliphant, J.F. Sharp

Friendship Lodge No. 16, Clarksville, Red River county --------L.L. Bailey, John H. Darnell, Edward L. Dew, A.K. Ellett, Amos McCollock

Orphans Friend Lodge No. 17, Anderson, Grimes county --------Uriah F. Case, Henry Fanthorp, and T. Taliaferro, an EA

Washington Lodge No. 18, Washington, Washington county -------- Titus Holliday

Forest Lodge No. 19, Hunstville, Walker county --------A.M. Branch, W.M. Barrett, Wm Birdwell, Thos. Carothers, Charles H. Chandler, R.J. Heftin, J.C.P. Kenneymore, James F. Logan, J.C. Outlaw, J.F. Rhodes, Benton Sweeney, J. T. Sims, S.S. Sheppard

Graham Lodge No. 20, Brenham, Washington county --------Josiah Barnett, A. Campbell, Noah Hill, W.F. Jarrell, John McFarland, N.B. Roff, Charles Stevenson, W.H. Terrell, John L. Watkins, and H.N. Sternes, F.C.

Lothrop Lodge No. 21, Crockett, Houston county --------J.H. Legan, John Wortham

Marshall Lodge No. 22, Marshall, Harrison county --------Wm. Allen, T.F. Craig, R. Fitzpatrick, G.G. Gregg, J.C. Harris, Jas McClennon, E. Murrell, Charles Tally, T. Twitty

Montgomery Lodge No. 25, Montgomery, Montgomery county --------M.E. Frabick, J.M. McRae

Paris Lodge No. 27, Paris, Lamar county --------John T. Harmon, J. W. Lynn

De Witt Clinton Lodge No. 29, Jasper, Jasper county --------W.J. Ganard, M.P. Goode, Wm. Smith

Gonzales Lodge No. 30, Gonzales, Gonzales county --------Master Masons, W.A. Hall, I.G. Jones and J.C.L. Nyegaard--------Total 3. Fellow Craft W.B. Thomas and Entered Apprentice W.B. Thompson

Palestine Lodge No. 31, Palestine, Anderson county --------J.C. Burdett, W.B. Frazier, J. Steelcup, O.C. Terrill, M.D. Vaughn

LaFayette Lodge No. 34, Lagrange, Fayette county --------M.O. Dimon, G.A. Echol, Z.M. French, C.R. Markman, Jas. Nicholson, J.S. Potter, G.C. Ragin, Vol Korn, F.P. Hood, B. Shropshire, C.P. Smith, N.F. Turnage, J.H. Ujffy

Lavaca Lodge No. 36, Port Lavaca, Calhoun county --------James W. Snodgrass

Jefferson Lodge No. 38, Jefferson, Marion county --------G. Rucker

Leona Union Lodge No. 39, Leona, Leon county --------Wm. Evans

Alamo Lodge No. 44, San Antonio, Bexar county --------R.W. Black, John A. Wheeler

Euclid Lodge No. 45, Rusk, Cherokee county --------Stock Ewin, Frank H. Daniels, Robert Green, Thomas T. Graves, Pat Henry

Florida Lodge No. 46, Round Top, Fayette county --------S.R. Lewis, F.E. Miller, C.P. Rankin

Liberty Lodge No. 48, Liberty, Liberty county --------William Berthier, Henry B. Duncan, William Meyer, S.H. Marbut and Phillip K. Smith, F.C.M.

St. Johns Lodge No. 51, McKinney, Collin county --------D.M. Crutchfield, T.B. Morgan

Tannehill Lodge No. 52, Dallas, Dallas county --------John B. Buchman, J.L. Smith, Stephen Schaeffer, David B. Thomas, H.K. Valentine, Wm B. Patillo--Total 6

St. Johns Lodge No. 53, Tyler, Smith county --------A.H. Ramsour, Ben Scott, B.T. Selman

Grand Bluff Lodge No. 54, Grand Bluff, Panola county -------- Simeon Buford, W.C. Hamous

Warren Lodge No. 56, Caldwell, Burleson county --------J.M. Bell, L.J. Carroll, E.H. Green, A. Moseley, W.B. Sullivan

Larissa Lodge No. 57, Larrissa, [sic] Cherokee county --------John T. Smith

Woodville Lodge No. 62, Woodville, Tyler county --------D.C. Enloe, John Work

Rocky Mount Lodge No. 63, Bunker Hill, Rusk county, post office London --------S. Crestie

Joppa Lodge No. 65, Elysian Fields, Harrison county --------Joseph Boirsean

Hubert Lodge No. 67, Chappell Hill, Washington county --------John Conner, W.R.D. Crockett, D.H. Colman, J.E. Crockett, J.A. Haynie, T.J. Jackson,

James W. McDade, J.R. Moore, E.W. Rogers, James Allen, Thomas Wooldridge. Total 11

Caledonia Lodge No. 68, Columbus, Colorado county --------W.G. Degraffenried, G.W. Engle, G.W. Thatcher, W. Tonage, W.B. Yates, an E.A. --Total 5

Boston Lodge No. 69, Boston, Bowie county --------C.C. Hawkins, J.W. Leigh, J.J. McClosky

Temple Lodge No. 70, Mount Pleasant, Titus county --------G.B. Clifton, W.S. Stephens

Mount Vernon Lodge No. 71, Mount Vernon, Titus county. Lone Star Post Office --------A.J. Dabbs

Morton Lodge No. 72, Richmond, Fort Bend county --------J. Dillaird, J.C. Eason, H. Kiggins, F.M. McCaven, D.C. Norwood, Theophilus Sumenton

Springfield Lodge No. 74, Springfield, Limestone county --------D.F. Davis

Concord Lodge No. 77, Concord Church, Harrison county. Jonesville Post Office --------Thomas Poag

Oasis Lodge No. 79, Dangerfield, Titus county --------J.N. Hammill

Murchison Lodge No. 80, Halletsville, Lavaca county --------M. Pendergrass

Rio Grande Lodge No. 81, Brownsville, Cameron county --------Sanford Kidder, H.U. Thorbune and Entered Apprentices J.C. Beeseman, and J. Strodtman

Indianola Lodge No. 84, Indianola, Calhoun county --------Sam McBride

Tusculum Lodge No. 86, Pine Tree Church, Upshur county, Earpville Post Office --------Augustus Mosely

Andrew Jackson Lodge No. 88, Linden, Davis county. F.M. Henry Post Office. --------N. Gupton, J.C. Moore

San Gabriel Lodge No. 89, Georgetown, Williamson county --------Joseph Ruberth, and J.S. Ming, EA.

Waxahachie Lodge No. 90, Waxahachie, Ellis county --------W.C. Sweete, James M. Shepherd

Tarrant Lodge No. 91, Tarrant, Hopkins county --------Eli Lindley

Waco Lodge No. 92, Waco, McLennan county --------W.D. Bedwell, Jno. H. Farmer, H.M. Hood, R.M. Hargrove, E.M. Young, R.H. Leonard, FC

Augusta Lodge No. 93, Augusta, Houston county --------G. Gresham, D.S. Kirkpatrick

Goliad Lodge No. 94, Goliad, Goliad county --------J.B. Borroum, A.N. Smith, Jacob Rupley, an EA.

Sharon Lodge No. 95, Pine Hill, Rusk county --------James A. Long

Colorado Lodge No. 96, Webberville, Travis county --------G.W. Bacon, W.J. Flaniken, J. Owings, J.G. Scruggs, J.T. Ricks, J. Pearce, an Entered Apprentice

Canton Lodge No. 98, Canton, Smith county. Troupe Post Office --------R.L. Bradford

Danville Lodge No. 101, New Danville, Rusk county --------J.D. Dickson, R. Taylor

Fairfield Lodge No. 103, Fairfield, Freestone county --------E. Bacheller

Kickapoo Lodge No. 105, Kickapoo, Anderson county --------T.B. Henderson
Jacksonville Lodge No. 108, Jacksonville, Cherokee county --------W.C. Dennison, G.W. Hutchison, Wade Jarrett, J.T. Teters
Guadalupe Lodge No. 109, Seguin, Guadalupe county --------J.S. Calvert
Burleson Lodge No. 111, Navarro, Leon county, Navarro post office via Centreville, Leon county --------John B. White
Bloomfield Lodge No. 112, Kauffman, Kauffman county --------S.P. Andrews, G.W. Brach, R.B. Baird, W.H. Ragsdale, Wm Turney and C. J. Hardin, an E.A.
Prairie Lea Lodge No. 114, Prairie Lea, Caldwell county --------Wm. M. Burns
Red River Lodge No. 116, Pine Creek, Red River county. Riomatia Post Office --------Fellow Craft C. N. Wright
Travis Lodge No. 117, Sherman, Grayson county --------S. T. Hunter, E. M. Jones, R. H. Moore, N. B. Reed
Starr Lodge No. 118, Starrville, Smith county --------Wyley Bradwell, Joseph Ogburn, G. A. Steuard
McDonald Lodge No. 120, Linn Flat, Nacogdoches county --------A.Q. Mayier
Mount Hope Lodge No. 121, Mount Hope, Tyler county. Peach Tree Village Post Office --------Henry Cliburn, Amos Mahaffey
Quitman Lodge No. 122, Chatfield, Navarro county --------R. N. Baird
Texana Lodge No. 123, Texana, Jackson county --------D. R. Coleman, J. A. Woolfold
Colletto Lodge No. 124, Yorktown, De Witt county -------- E. M. Edwards
Madison Lodge No. 126, Orange, Orange county --------S. H. Coyle, J.H. Hannah, John Kutcher
Cushney Lodge No. 128, San Marcos, Hays county --------C. Kyle
Brazos Union Lodge No. 129, Bryan, Brazos county --------Ben Hubert, B.S Whitaker
Belmont Lodge No. 131, Belmont, Gonzales county --------J.S. Rogers and Entered Apprentice G. F. Shrum
Retreat Lodge No. 133, Courtney, Grimes county --------R. J. Inge, H. McEacham, and Entered Apprentice T. C. Ashford
Bethel Lodge No. 134, Ladonia, Fannin county --------R. Cobb
Camden Lodge No. 135, Camden, Rusk county. Walling's Ferry Post Office --------W. D. Young
Newton Lodge No. 136, Burkville, Newton county --------Wm. Brailsford
Mount Horeb Lodge No. 137, Gabriel Mills, Williamson county. Mahomet Post Office, Burnett county --------A. Smith
Neill Lodge No. 138, Lexington, Burleson county --------O.H.P. Garrett, D.M. Palmer
Herschell Lodge No. 139, Coffeeville, Upshur county --------Jesse Seale, E. D. Wyatt, a F.C.
Castillian Lodge No. 141, Canton, Van Zandt county --------H.F. Blackwell, H. F. Chalk, R. K. Gibbs, J.R.C. Henderson, W.F. Palmer, A.G. Parker, F. Simpson, Wm. Tate and Hy H. Burns, EA.

24

Bethesda Lodge No. 142, Gilmer, Upshur county --------L. Crain, E. A.
Ochiltree Lodge No. 143, Melrose, Nacogdoches county --------T. S. Blakey
Pierce Lodge No. 144, Sterling, Robertson county. Owensville Post Office --------Foster Brigance, Robert Calvert, William Calvert, J. T. Love, J. D. Love, G.W.T. Mitchell, Joseph Owen, W. Strange, B. A. Woodward, J.C.C. Brittell, William Wharton. Total 11.
Walnut Grove Lodge No. 145, San Anders, Milam county. Cameron Post Office --------John Oliver
Fort Worth Lodge No. 148, Fort Worth, Tarrant county --------Francis Knaar
Truitt Lodge No. 149, Truitt's Store, Shelby county. Center Post Office --------J.C. Tatum, A.J.G. Tatum
Marlin Lodge No. 152, Marlin, Falls county --------J.B. Barton, J.C. Brown, W.E. Hunnicutt, J.H. Pierson, J.M. Stallworth, also Entered Apprentice A.L. Sowders
Eclectic Lodge No. 153, Eclectic Grove, Fannin county. Warren Post Ofice --------H. H. Davis
Spring Hill Lodge No. 155, Spring Hill; Navarro county --------R. A. Younger
Hickory Hill Lodge No. 156, Hickory Hill, Davis county --------W.B. Ochiltree, P.G.M; I.V. Browning, W.D. Everette, J. T. Harris, H. H Little. Total 5.
East Trinity Lodge No. 157, Rockwall, Kauffman county --------F. P. Deguire
Wm. M. Taylor Lodge No. 158, Concord Church, Smith county. Tyler Post Office --------Jordon Brown
Athens Lodge No. 165, Athens, Henderson county --------R.H. Royall
Belton Lodge No. 166, Belton, Bell county --------Nicholas Spurgin
Kentucky Lodge No. 167, Kentucky Town, Grayson county --------C.J. Scott, M. Pitman
Monroe Lodge No. 168, Madisonville, Madison county --------Job S. Collard
San Anders Lodge No. 170, Cameron, Milam county --------S. W. M. Lewis
Mound Prairie Lodge No. 173, Mound Prairie, Anderson county, post office Plentitude --------J. H. Derden
Corsicana Lodge No. 174, Corsicana, Navarro county --------J .G. Bishop
Valley Lodge No. 175, Burnett, Burnett county --------James H. Smith
St Paul's Lodge No. 177, Port Sullivan, Milam county --------Samuel L. Berry, D. R. Cole, Jeremiah Collins, B. M. Lauderdale, John T. Perkins. Total 5.
Post Oak Island Lodge No. 181, Post Oak Island, Williamson county, Sand-fly post office, Bastrop county --------M. F. Jordan
Hopkinsville Lodge No. 183, Hopkinsville, Gonzales county --------Rev. Henry Long
Hickory Grove Lodge No. 184, Mount Vernon, Smith county, post office Etna --------M. Bayliss
Decatur Lodge No. 186, Decatur, Wise county --------Chs I. Browdie, J.B. Mullhollon
Tyrian Lodge No. 187, Sabine Pass, Jefferson county --------T.A. Hamilton
Corpus Christi Lodge No. 189, Corpus Christi, Nueces county --------J. Love, J.N. Morgan, J.W. Scott, and G. Robertson, E.A.

Refugio Lodge No. 190, Refugio, Refugio county --------Daniel C. Doughty

Havana Lodge No. 191, Douglassville, Davis county --------E.C. Collier, W.G. Green, H. Waddell

Jack Titus Lodge No. 194, Coleman's Springs, Red River county. Savannah Post Office --------John Maggard

Aquilla Lodge No. 196, Hillsboro, Hill county --------James R. Cherry, Thomas Johns

Tyre Lodge No. 198, Tennessee Colony, Anderson county --------Wiley Caldwell, S.H. Garrett

Alamita Lodge No. 200, Helena, Karnes county --------J.M. Sprouse, J.R. Trimble

James A. Baker Lodge No. 202, Ebenezer Baptist Church, Walker county. Huntsville Post Office --------D.H. Kerr

Pine Lodge No. 203, Edom, Van Zandt county -------- J. W. Davison

Mount Calm Lodge No. 204, Mount Calm, Limestone county --------J. L. Coulter

Mantua Lodge No. 209, Mantua, Collin county. Hiland Post Office --------H.N. Walcott

Gainesville Lodge No. 210, Gainesville, Cooke county --------J.J. Diamond, J.A. Smith

Science Hill Lodge No. 211, Science Hill, Henderson county --------W. C. Walker

Steadman Lodge No. 215, Steadman, Newton county --------Thomas Holmes, Sr., F.P. Price, J. R. Rogers, and H.C. Fancher, a Fellow Craft Mason

John E. Cravens Lodge No. 218, Dresden, Navarro county --------A.S. Ainsworth

Millville Lodge No. 219, Millville, Rusk county --------G. H. Wright

Onion Creek Lodge No. 220, Onion Creek, Travis county. Austin Post Office --------C.C. McKinney

Bright Star Lodge No. 221, Sulphur Springs, Hopkins county, Bright Star post office --------G.B. Carter, D. W. McNabb

Parsons Lodge No. 222, Parsons Seminary, Travis county. Webberville Post Office --------F. Tweedle

Bellville Lodge No. 223, Bellville, Austin county --------J. T. Bell, B.E. Roach

San Saba Lodge No. 225, San Saba, San Saba county --------James Ketchum, F.C.

Brahan Lodge No. 226, Concrete School House, Wilson county. La Vernia Post office --------J. W. Thompson, John Wheeler

Newport Lodge No. 228, Newport, Walker county --------J.C. Rawls, J.T. Williamson

Sampson Lodge No. 231, San Jacinto, Harris county, Lynchburg post office --------W. D. Hucherson

Eutaw Lodge No. 233, Eutaw, Limestone county --------W.T. Pearsons, T.S. Jones, H.H. Logan, J.B. Rogers

Relief Lodge No. 236, Rush Ceek, Navarro county --------J. Gallamore

Lively Lodge No. 237, Fosset & Davis' Store, Denton county. Little Elm Post Office --------L.W. Jones
Fayetteville Lodge No. 240, Fayetteville, Fayette county --------John O. Allen
Torbert Lodge No. 241, Turner's Point, Kauffman county --------John Campbell, John Wilson
LLano Lodge No. 242, Town of Llano, Llano county --------Thos. B. Ives, A.J. Jackson, H.F. Stockman
Sam Sanford Lodge No. 243, Sand Hill, Shelby county, Center Post Office --------J.W. Thomas, in 1866, A. Tuberville
Gamble Lodge No. 244, Bastrop, Bastrop county --------A.B. Tanner
Adah Zillah Lodge No. 247, Millican, Brazos county --------J.C. Holliday, W.W. Simmons, Frank Tompson, J. W. Weaver, B. S. Whitaker
Sexton Lodge No. 251, Sexton, Sabine county --------Wm. Nethery
Homer Lodge No. 254, Homer, Angelina county --------W. H. Fairchilds
Beeville Lodge No. 261, Beeville, Bee county --------A.J. Cook
Milford Lodge No. 262, Milford, Ellis county --------J. M. Caruthers, G.M. Davis
Whitesboro' Lodge No. 263, Whitesboro', Grayson county --------L. Witt
Grayson Lodge No. 265, Personville, Limestone county --------T. Foley
Grand View Lodge No. 266, Grand View, Johnson county --------D.T. Lawrence
Stephenville Lodge No. 267, Stephenville, Erath county --------S. M. Yancy
Pilot Point Lodge No. 270, Pilot Point, Denton county --------E. Emberson
Prairie Point Lodge No. 271, Prairie Point, Wise county, post office Decatur --------F. M. Robinson
Phoenix Lodge No. 275, Weatherford, Parker county --------Oliver Loving, Jno. H. Taylor
Mountain Lodge No. 277, Burleson Spring, Williamson county. Liberty Hill Post Office --------H. J. Bledsoe
Brownwood Lodge No. 279, Brownwood, Brown county -------- Alfred Tate
Hempstead Lodge No. 281, Hempstead, Austin county --------John Kane, W.A. McDade, J. W. McDade, D. Winters
Winchester Lodge No. 282, Winchester, Fayette county --------Wm. H. Parr
Pleasanton Lodge No. 283, Pleasanton, Atascosa county --------Benjamin E. Fuller, Joel M. Walker
Eastern Star Lodge No. 284, Nogarlis Prairie, Trinity county. Penington Post Office --------A.J. Womack, P. P. Ainsworth
Acton Lodge No. 285, Acton, Hood county --------J.P. Tolbert
Beaumont Lodge No. 286, Beaumont, Jefferson county --------A.J. Ward, and E. Stephenson, E.A.
Tyler Prairie Lodge No. 290, Pennington, Trinity county --------B.B. Ellis, J. R. Spence
Kimball Lodge No. 292, Kimball, Bosque county --------T. B. Hatcher
Tucker Lodge No. 297, Galveston, Galveston county --------A. B. Thompson
Navasota Lodge No. 299, Navasota, Grimes county --------M. Blackburn, J.T. Eppinger, W. H. McWaters, P.H. Smith, J. E. Williams. Total 5.

Cedar Creek Lodge No. 300, Tryon's Church, Brazos county. Bryan Post Office --------Joshua Seal

Blackwell Lodge No. 302, Charleston, Hopkins county --------J. W. Conelit

Littleton Fowler Lodge No. 305, Hemphill, Sabine county --------R. H. Smith

Shiloh Lodge No. 307, Hall, Hunt county --------Jas. Cowen

Hull's Store Lodge No. 309, Panola county. Woods Post Office --------Jno. M. Parker

Bryan Station Lodge No. 311, Bryan's Station, Milam county, Post Office Cameron --------L. Robinson, Feb 29, 1868

PROCEEDINGS GRAND LODGE
OF TEXAS 1869
RETURNS OF LODGES FOR THE MASONIC YEAR
A.D. 1868, A.L. 5868
DEATHS

Holland Lodge No. 1, Houston, Harris county --------Thad. M. Hooper, Geo. Morgan, G.E. Sandcliff. Total 3.

Red Land Lodge No. 3, San Angustine, San Angustine County --------Thos. M. Smith

St. Johns Lodge No. 5, Columbia, Brazoria County --------P.P. McRae

Harmony Lodge No. 6, Galveston, Galveston county --------Chas. H. Hughs, J.L. Watkins; D.H. Grove, a Fellow Craft, J.H. Davidson, Le Baron Drury, Jr., Louis G. Lear, Entered Apprentices.

Milam Lodge No. 11, Independence, Washington county --------W.D. Williams and T.M. Cox, F.C.

Austin Lodge No. 12, Austin, Travis county --------S.J. Wood, F.C. and G.W. Glascock

Constantine Lodge No. 13, Bonham, Fannin county --------A.E. Pace

Friendship Lodge No. 16, Clarksville, Red River county --------John Woolridge, an E.A.

Orphans Friend No. 17, Anderson, Grimes county --------Gavin B. Black

Washington Lodge No. 18, Washington, Washington county --------H.R. Cartmell.

Forest Lodge No. 19, Huntsville, Walker county --------A.J. Edwards

Graham Lodge No. 20, Brenham, Washington county --------Peter Donly, N.T. Edney, Ben Stones.

Lothrop Lodge No. 21, Crockett, Houston county --------B.L. Goodman, John Millican.

Marshall Lodge No. 22, Marshall, Harrison county --------Jno. D. Evans, Jno. L. Wall, S.W. Webb.

De Witt Clinton Lodge No. 29, Jasper, Jasper county --------W. Allen, Simom Weiss [Wiess]

Gonzales Lodge No. 30, Gonzales, Gonzales county --------N. Chevalier, A.J. McKean, Charles Spath, E.M. Walker. Total 4.

LaFayette Lodge No. 34, LaGrange, Fayette county --------H.M. Eisinmere, Sam Gans.

Lavaca Lodge No. 36, Port Lavaca, Calhoun county --------J.A. Deen.

Mount Moriah Lodge No. 37, Cold Springs, Polk county --------A.J. Love.

Jefferson Lodge No. 38, Jefferson, Marion county --------D.N. Alley, Joseph Jeffers.

Leona Union Lodge No. 39, Leona, Leon county --------F.M. Oden.

Douglass Lodge No. 43, Douglass, Nacogdoches County --------Marion Russell.

Alamo Lodge No. 44, San Antonio, Bexar county --------F.G. Fawcett.

TEXAS MASONIC DEATHS WITH SELECTED BIOGRAPHICAL SKETCHES

Euclid Lodge No. 45, Rusk, Cherokee county --------A.C. Gibson, W.A. Hicks, W.H. Mullins, Wm. Roberts, A.H. Shanks. Total 5.

Liberty Lodge No. 48, Liberty, Liberty county --------F.H. Marbut

St. Johns Lodge No. 51, McKinney. Collin county --------M.R. Parish

Grand Bluff Lodge No. 54, Grand Bluff, Panola county --------Wm. Fields

Warren Lodge No. 56, Caldwell, Burleson county --------E.J. Chance, J.S. Jarrett, Wm. Oldham.

Larissa Lodge No. 57, Larissa, Cherokee county --------John Kellough, Jno. M. Taylor.

Mt. Enterprise Lodge No. 60, Mt. Enterprise, Rusk county --------R.L. Hill.

Woodville Lodge No. 62, Woodville, Tyler county --------H.H. Hudson, W.B. Holt.

Chireno Lodge No. 66, Chireno, Nacogdoches county --------James L. Ewing and John D. Windham.

Hubert Lodge No. 67, Chappell Hill, Washington county --------Jacob Vinland.

Boston Lodge No. 69, Boston, Bowie county --------G.W. Morrow.

Temple Lodge No. 70, Mount Pleasant,Titus county --------M.A. Harris, and D.W. Jones, F.C.

Morton Lodge No. 72, Richmond, Fort Bend county --------J.H. Wright, F.C. and M.M."s A.H. Foster, Ed Parker, J.S. Vandegraff.

Springfield Lodge No. 74, Springfield, Limestone county --------James A. Billington, W.E. Hewett. Total 2.

Cameron Lodge No. 76, Clinton, De Witt county --------Thornton Chrisholm.

Concord Lodge No. 77, Concord Church, Harrison county --------Wm. Patterson, D.M. Jones.

Oasis Lodge No. 79, Dangerfield, Titus county --------E.D. Hood, J.O. Parr, R.H. Turner.

Murchison Lodge No. 80, Halletsville, Lavaca county --------G.W. Brown.

Rio Grande Lodge No. 81, Brownsville, Cameron county --------Justinian A.H. Kuttner.

Indianola Lodge No. 84, Indianola, Calhoun county --------W.W. Diviney.

New Salem Lodge No. 87, New Salem, Rusk county --------J.H. Hogan, Wm. Howerton, J.A. Medford, J.L. Browden.

Tarrant Lodge No. 91, Tarrant, Hopkins county --------Entered Apprentices Gilbert Smith and John Simms.

Augusta Lodge No. 93, Augusta, Houston county --------L.W. White, W.W. Williams, R.B. Lewis.

Goliad Lodge No. 94, Goliad, Goliad county --------E. Luter.

Sharon Lodge No. 95, Pine Hill, Rusk county --------E. Allred, John Morris

Colorado Lodge No. 96, Webberville, Travis county --------J.N.B Williams

Newburn Lodge No. 97, Buena Vista, Shelby county --------R. Yarborough.

Danville Lodge No. 101, New Danville, Rusk county --------James Farnbrough, F.C.; T.J. Powell, E.A.

Fairfield Lodge No. 103, Fairfield, Freestone county --------W.L. Cooley, W.B. Moores.

Kickapoo Lodge No. 105, Kickapoo, Anderson county --------W.C. Early.
Burleson Lodge No. 111, Navarro, Leon county --------T.W. Herring, T.W. Dailey.
Bloomfield Lodge No. 112, Kaufman, Kaufman county --------J.C. Burge, L.T. Nash.
Travis Lodge No. 117, Sherman, Grayson county --------W.W. Boyd, John H. Wilson.
Mount Hope Lodge No. 121, Mount Hope, Tyler county --------G.W. Sanford.
Quitman Lodge No. 122, Chatfield, Navarro county --------W.D. Frame, J.A. Farmer, J.O. Jones, T.C. Williams.
Colletto Lodge No. 124, Yorktown, De Witt county --------J.A. Miller, A.M. Summers.
Belmont Lodge No. 131, Belmont, Gonzales county --------T.E. Green, J.P. King, J.M. Smith.
Retreat Lodge No. 133, Courtney, Grimes county --------S. Barrett, J.M. Cosgrove, J.L. Cox.
Bethel Lodge No. 134, Ladonia, Fannin county --------J.L. Dillingham, S. Kinman.
Camden Lodge 135, Camden, Rusk county --------Entered Apprentices W.T. Alston and G. Lumkins; J. Etheredge, M.M.
Newton Lodge No. 136, Burkville, Newton county --------S.S. Swearington.
Lexington Lodge No. 138, Lexington, Burleson county --------J.W. Harrison.
Herschell Lodge No. 139, Coffeeville, Upshur county --------W.W. Robertson.
Keechi Lodge No. 140, Centreville, Leon county --------Jacob W. Stegall.
Ochiltree Lodge No. 143, Melrose, Nacogdoches county --------William Wilson
Pierce Lodge No. 144, Sterling, Robertson county -------James P. Wood, E.A. Mason.
Walnut Grove Lodge No. 145, San Anders, Milam county --------A.B. Parrott, L. Robinson, R.S. Wiley.
Winnsborough Lodge No. 146, Winnsborough, Wood county --------A.J. Odom.
Planters Lodge No. 147, Plantersville, Grimes county -------Benjamin K. Butts.
Fort Worth Lodge No. 148, Fort Worth, Tarrant county --------Thos. Loyd, R. Troax.
Truitt Lodge No. 149, Truitt's Store, Shelby County --------Willam Oliver, James Rowe.
Marlin Lodge No. 152, Marlin, Falls county --------J.E. Franks.
Eclectic Lodge No. 153, Eclectic Grove, Fannin county --------S. Colbert, H.H. Lansford.
Cotton Gin Lodge No. 154, Cotton Gin, Freestone county --------G.W. Ross.
Spring Hill Lodge No. 155, Spring Hill, Navarro county --------Wm. Fullerton, Wm. H. Garner.
McClellan Lodge No. 159, Union Hill, Washington Couinty --------Jno. B. Kent.
Lancaster Lodge No. 160, Lancaster, Dallas county --------Robert Brotherton, A.A. James, T.J. Weatherford.
Honey Grove Lodge No. 164, Lodge Hall, Fannin county --------Jacob Leeman

31

Athens Lodge No. 165, Athens, Henderson county --------A.J. McDonald

Belton Lodge No. 166, Belton, Bell county --------Warren Pruett, and J.T. Darwin, F.C.

San Anders Lodge No. 170, Cameron, Milam county --------N.T. Riggin, L.M. Miner. Total 2.

Mound Prairie Lodge No. 173, Mound Prairie, Anderson county --------J.D. Billips, A.K.W. Jones

St. Paul's Lodge No. 177, Port Sullivan, Milam county --------T.W. Cunningham, L. Chatham, John S. Livingston, B.W. Maddox

Hardeman Lodge No. 179, Plum Creek, Caldwell county --------L.L.A. Lamkin and W.J. Brown, F.C.

Post Oak Island Lodge No. 181, Post Oak Island, Williamson county --------Jeremiah Lee, an E.A.

Hopkinsville Lodge No. 183, Hopkinsville, Gonzales county --------L.L. Fowler, J.M. Moore, D.C. Powers

Hickory Grove Lodge No. 184, Etna, Smith county --------Saml Henderson, John Meador

White Oak Lodge No. 185, White Oak, Hopkins county --------W.R. Craft, J. Huggins, J.H. Allen, John S. Hill

Tyrian Lodge No. 187, Sabine Pass, Jefferson County --------J.F. Truitt

Corpus Christi Lodge No. 189, Corpus Christi, Nueces county --------M.G. Turner

Havana Lodge No. 191, Douglassville, Davis County -------- R. Perryman

Cusseta Lodge No. 192, Cusseta, Davis county --------J. Bobo, C.R. Forsyth, J. Lewis, R. Perryman and W.A. Moore, F.C. Returns of 1867. Returns of 1868 wanted.

Leon Lodge No. 193, Lodge Room, Bell county --------Alonzo Beeman and Entered Apprentice Miles Wallers

Jack Titus Lodge No. 194, Coleman's Springs, Red River county --------O.B. Wodge

Aquilla Lodge No. 196, Hillsborough, Hill County --------Ezkiel Green, Martin Smith

Gatesville Lodge No. 197, Gatesville, Coryell county --------T.S. Alford

Tyre Lodge No. 198, Tennessee Colony, Anderson county --------Wm. East, Thomas Hudson

Alamita Lodge No. 200, Helena, Karnes county --------John Littleton

Denton Lodge No. 201, Louisville, Denton county --------L.A. Sanders; Fellow Craft, D.K. Tanahill; Entered Apprentances, W. Bowson and A.B. Danks/Banks

Jas. A. Walker Lodge No. 202, Ebenezar Baptist Church, Walker county --------J.A. Oliphint

Mount Calm Lodge No. 204, Mount Calm, Limestone county --------L. Holman

Frank Sexton Lodge No. 206, Pittsburg, Upshur County --------J.C. Birdsong, A. T. Rodgers and A.M. Pistol, E.A.

Mantua Lodge No. 209, Mantua, Collin county --------Wm. Davenport, J.W. Hayhurst

32

Gainesville Lodge No. 210, Gainesville, Cook County --------Wm. Bean, Wm. Cloud, J.A. Gound, J.C. St.John, J.A. Moore. Total 4. and Benjamin McFarland, an E.A.

Farmersville Lodge No. 214, Farmersville, Collin county --------H. R. Lyday

Twin Sisters Lodge No. 216, Blanco, Blanco county --------Thos. Carson, Thos. S. Speer.

J.E. Cravens Lodge No. 218, Dresden, Navarro county --------J.R. Boydston, Hugh Forgey, M.B. Jones

Parsons Lodge No. 222, Parsons Seminary, Travis county --------Ed Harrington

Bellville Lodge No. 223, Bellville, Austin county --------Clinton Fort

Miller Lodge No. 224, White Rock, Hunt county --------S.G. Culver

San Saba Lodge No. 225, Lodge Room, San Saba county --------G.B. Ketcham, J.B. Hext, W.W. Mabry

Newport Lodge No. 228, Newport, Walker county --------Geo. H. Milliken

Sampson Lodge No. 231, San Jacinto, Harris county --------O. Hare

Lampasas Lodge No. 232, Lampasas, Lampasas County --------S. Howell

Lively Lodge No. 237, Little Elm, Denton county --------J.Y. Stewart

Fayetteville Lodge No. 240, Fayetteville, Fayette county --------W.L. Walker

Llano Lodge No. 242, Llano, Llano county --------O.C. J. Phillips

Sam Sanford Lodge No. 243, Sand Hill, Shelby county --------Wm. M. Bell

Sulphur Bluff Lodge No. 246, Sulphur Bluff, Hopkins county --------John W. Conditt, W.N. Dawson

Sexton Lodge No. 251, Sexton, Sabine county --------Wm. Ligram

J.A. Lawrence Lodge No. 257, Antioch Church, Smith County --------J.F. Boswell

Whitesborough Lodge No. 263, Whitesborough, Grayson County --------G.L. Hatfield, an E.A.

Carthage Lodge No. 264, Carthage, Panola county --------Joshua Cherry, W.C. Trabue, W.H. Watson

Grayson Lodge No. 265, Personville, Limestone county --------E. Bottom, an E.A.

Grand View Lodge No. 266, Grand View, Johnson County --------J.S. Wheeler

Meridian Lodge No. 268, Meridian, Bosque county --------M.W. Fuller

Pilot Point Lodge No. 270, Pilot Point, Denton county --------W.T. Skinner

Dixie Lodge No. 272, Knoxville, Cherokee county --------James Childress

J.D. Giddings Lodge No. 280, Evergreen, Washington county --------J.W. Harrison

Hempstead Lodge No. 281, Hempstead, Austin county --------Wm. B. Young

Pleasanton Lodge No. 283, Pleasanton, Atascosa county --------F.G. Faucett

Eastern Star Lodge No. 284, Nogarlus Prairie, Trinity county --------J.D Dunkin

Beaumont Lodge No. 286, Beaumont, Jefferson county --------J. G. Westcoat

Stonewall Lodge No. 287, Stonewall, Nacogdoches --------L.H. Caver, L.M. Button

John Armstrong Lodge No. 291, Lodge Room, Bosque county --------P. Paulson

Kimball Lodge No. 292, Kimball, Bosque county --------Jacob DeCordova

Mars Hill Lodge No. 293, Springville, Wood county --------Levi McGee
Nathan Corley Lodge No. 294, Magonlia Springs, Jasper county --------Richard Williams
Scyene Lodge No. 295, Scyene, Dallas county --------G.W. Guess
Salado Lodge No. 296, Salado, Bell county --------J.C. Kitchen
Tucker Lodge No. 297, Galveston, Galveston county --------Robert Hardie, J.H. Westcott
Moulton Lodge No. 298, Moulton, Lavaca County --------J. Castleman
Navasota Lodge No. 299, Navasota, Grimes county --------J.Cross Jones
Cedar Grove Lodge No. 308, Cedar Grove, Kaufman county --------M. Johnson, L.C.
Hull's Store Lodge No. 309, Woods Post Office, Panola county --------James Rowe, G.H. Wilson

PROCEEDINGS OF THE GRAND LODGE
OF TEXAS 1870
RETURNS OF LODGES FOR THE MASONIC YEAR
A.D. 1869, A.L. 5869
DEATHS

Holland Lodge No. 1, Houston, Harris county--------Chas J. Grainger, T.B.J. Hadley

St. Johns Lodge No. 5, Columbia, Brazoria county --------Lewis M. Strobel

Lodge No. 6, Galveston, Galveston county --------L.M. Hitchcock, Orrin Brown, J.R. Burch, F.G. Casey, Matt Gengler, Jno. S. Sydnor, P.T. Williams

Austin Lodge No. 12, Austin, Travis county --------S. Crosby, S.T. Smith, John Horan

Constantine Lodge No. 13, Bonham, Fannin county --------James M. Cook, G.M. Stanfield, Thompson Stansel

Friendship Lodge No. 16, Clarksville, Red River county --------Wm. P. Dickson, Richard H. Jackson

Washington Lodge No. 18, Washington, Washington county --------G.W. Crawford, John Watson

Forest Lodge No. 19, Huntsville, Walker county --------D.W. Mock

Lothrop Lodge No. 21, Crockett, Houston county --------Jacob Allbright, John Collins, Wm. P. Leaverton

Clinton Lodge No. 23, Henderson, Rusk county --------Ben Smither, T.M. Yates

Montgomery Lodge No. 25, Montgomery, Montgomery county --------W.S. Taylor

De Witt Lodge No. 29, Jasper, Jasper county --------W.M. Neyland, John Frazier

Gonzales Lodge No. 30, Gonzales, Gonzales county --------Jno. S. Baldridge, J.K. Davis

LaFayette Lodge No. 34, Lagrange, Fayette county --------C. Leisemann, J.L.D. Blackburn

Mount Moriah Lodge No. 37, Cold Springs, Polk county --------Rob Smith

Jefferson Lodge No. 38, Jefferson, Marion county --------Alex McKimmins, T.W. Britton, Julian S. Foscue

Leona Union Lodge No. 39, Leona, Leon county --------H.H. Logan, Jno. H. Potts

Douglass Lodge No. 43, Douglass, Nacogdoches county --------J.C. Birdwell

Alamo Lodge No. 44, San Antonio, Bexar county --------David H. Brown, F.C.; Ewen Cameron

Euclid Lodge No. 45, Rusk, Cherokee county -------- W.J. Gregory

Florida Lodge No. 46, Round Top, Fayette county --------O.A. Daniel

Liberty Lodge No. 48, Liberty, Liberty County --------W.W. Duvall, A.H. Mayer

St. Johns Lodge No. 51, McKinney, Collin county --------David Wylie

Tannehill Lodge No. 52, Dallas, Dallas county --------Walter Knott, A.D. Rice

Grand Bluff Lodge 54, Grand Bluff, Panola county --------Elijah Sentell, an E.A.

Warren Lodge No. 56, Caldwell, Burleson county --------R.S. Farrell, Spencer Rice

Larissa Lodge No. 57, Larissa, Cherokee county --------Reuben Robertson

Woodville Lodge No. 62, Woodville, Tyler county --------B.F. Ross

Rocky Mount Lodge No. 63, Bunker Hill, Rusk county, post office London --------J.L. Nelson, Wm. Harlan

Joppa Lodge No. 65, Elysian Fields, Harrison county --------Richard P. Haynes

Hubert Lodge No. 67, Chappell Hill, Washington county--------James Glass, E.R. Moore, G.W. Routt, an E.A.

Caledonia Lodge No. 68, Columbus, Colorado county --------Wm. Alley, R.E. Davis, Wm. B. Roever, George Henry, an E.A., D.E. Putney, an E.A.

Boston Lodge No. 69, Boston, Bowie county--------G.H. Bobo, W.A. Nunneley

Temple Lodge No. 70, Mount Pleasant, Titus county --------Alfred Lewellen, Benjamin Talbert, H. Dillahunty, T.L. Simpson, and J.E. England, E.A.'s

Mount Vernon Lodge No. 71, Mount Vernon, Titus county --------J.D. Caudle, N.J. Gurley

Springfield Lodge No. 74, Springfield, Limestone county --------G.W. Johnson, Jno. T. Anglin, N.J. Alford

Oasis Lodge No. 79, Dangerfield, Titus county --------E.R. Truett

Rio Grande Lodge No. 81, Brownsville, Cameron county --------Luke S. Bust, Chas Russell

Terrell Lodge No. 83, Alto, Cherokee county --------S.M. McGaughey, H.B. Stephens

Indianola Lodge No. 84, Indianola, Calhoun county --------S. A. White, Adam Murdock

New Salem Lodge No. 87, Lodge Room, Rusk county, post office New Salem --------M.L. Deaton, Joseph Shepherd, W.E. Hartless, an E.A.

Waxahachie Lodge No. 90, Waxahachie, Ellis county --------Joseph Picket, S.P. Lewis, D.D. Leech

Tarrant Lodge No. 91, Tarrant, Hopkins county --------James F. Fuller, W.E. Ewing, an E.A.

Sharon Lodge No. 95, Pine Hill, Rusk county --------J.H. Roquemore, J.H. Chapman, J.W. Little, C.B. Furlow

Canton Lodge No. 98, Canton, Smith county, post office Troup --------James T. Allen, A.M. Elkins

Guadalupe Lodge No. 109, Seguin, Guadalupe county --------John P. Campbell

Prairie Lea Lodge No. 114, Prairie Lea, Caldwell county --------Hugh Houston, F. A. McKinny, an E.A.

Travis Lodge No. 117, Sherman, Grayson county --------C.C. Quillin

Starr Lodge No. 118, Starrville, Smith county --------James Allen

Flora Lodge No. 119, Quitman, Wood county --------J.F. Warren, W.H. Burford

Colletto Lodge No. 124, Yorktown, De Witt county --------H.G. Woods

Madison Lodge No. 126, Orange, Orange county --------A.W. Hannah, H.J. Adams, J.E. Brinson, G. Erixson, G.C. Gilmore, L.R. Thomas

Brazos Union Lodge No. 129, Bryan, Brazos county --------G.B. Brown, J.T. Conway, John Hudson, J.M. Price, William Smith, W.C. Moseley

El Paso Lodge No. 130, El Paso, El Paso county --------Jarvis Hubble

Belmont Lodge No. 131, Belmont, Gonzales county --------P.B. Littlefield, W.V. Ramsey, D.R. Stribling, A.N. Wood

Retreat Lodge No. 133, Courtney, Grimes county --------Alfred Tate

Lexington Lodge No. 138, Lexington, Burleson county --------D.C. Jones

Herschell Lodge No. 139, Coffeeville, Upshur county --------H.D. Palmer, Wm. Hambright, an E.A.

Keechi Lodge No. 140, Centreville, Leon county --------Abram Edins, John H. Potts

Bethesda Lodge No. 142, Gilmer, Upshur county --------R.F. Ford

Pierce Lodge No. 144, Calvert, Robertson county --------Wm. Anderson, W.P. Love, Jas H. Thweatt, an E.A., Jas P. Wood, an E.A.

Winnsborough Lodge No. 146, Winnsborough, Wood county --------Thos. Linley, A.J. Nance

Planters Lodge No. 147, Plantersville, Grimes county --------James Lawrence

Fort Worth Lodge No. 148, Fort Worth Masonic Hall, Tarrant county--------Thomas Lloyd

Marlin Lodge No. 152, Marlin, Falls county --------J.E. Harrison, an F.C.

Eclectic Lodge No. 153, Eclectic Grove, Fannin county, post office New Warren --------E.J. Holland

Cotton Gin Lodge No. 154, Cotton Gin, Freestone county --------R.A. Lasiter

Hickory Hill Lodge No. 156, Hickory Hill, Davis county --------W.D. Drewitt

Murval Lodge No. 162, Murval, Panola county, post office Pine Hill, Rusk county --------W.H. Taylor

Athens Lodge No. 165, Athens, Henderson county --------Jas Adams, Jas A. Goodgame

Belton Lodge No. 166, Belton, Bell county --------J.D. Scott, J.A. Ewing

Kentucky Lodge No. 167, Kentucky Town, Grayson county --------Wm. W. West

Monroe Lodge No. 168, Madisonville, Madison county -------- Jno. Longbotham, W.P. Taylor

Mound Prairie Lodge No. 173, Mound Prairie, Anderson county --------J.F. Corder, T.L. Pinson, A.O. McKorkle

St. Paul's Lodge No. 177, Port Sullivan, Milam county --------Joel T. Perkins, Samp P. Ferguson, Wm. Pendavis

Concrete Lodge No. 182, Concrete, De Witt county --------W.H. Hollan, M. Louis, an E.A.

Hopkinsville Lodge No. 183, Hopkinsville, Gonzales county --------J.K. Zumwalt, A.J. Denson

Hickory Grove Lodge No. 184, Mount Vernon, Smith county --------Isaac Byers, N.P. Deshong, Allen Rushing

White Oak Lodge No. 185, White Oak, Hopkins county --------W.G. Past

Decatur Lodge No. 186, Decatur, Wise county --------J.B. Earhart

Tyrian Lodge No. 187, Sabine Pass, Jefferson county --------H.C.L. Keith

Corpus Christi Lodge No. 189, Corpus Christi, Nueces county --------John Riggs

Refugio Lodge No. 190, Refugio, Refugio county --------John Choate

Leon Lodge No. 193, Lodge Room, Bell county, post office Aiken --------N. Mitt Smith

Jack Titus Lodge No. 194, Coleman's Springs, Red River county, post office Clarksville --------Manley Scroggins

Aquilla Lodge No. 196, Hillsboro', Hill county --------John C. Snead, Joseph O. Wade

Tyre Lodge No. 198, Tennessee Colony, Anderson county --------E.E. Lowder

Denton Lodge No. 201, Lewisville, Denton county --------J.H. Allen

Pine Lodge No. 203, Edom, Van Zandt county --------J.J. O'Quinn

Mantua Lodge No. 209, Mantua, Collin county, post office Highland --------S.M. Dysart, J. Stanbeaugh [Stinebaugh?]

Dresden Lodge No. 218, Dresden, Navarro county--------B.F. Carroll, sr, PM; Isaac Taylor, G.W. Clary

Parsons Lodge No. 222, Parsons Seminary, Travis county, post office Austin --------S.M. Cain

Bellville Lodge No. 223, Bellville, Austin county --------E.T. Bonney, Henry Kastrop

San Saba Lodge No. 225, San Saba, San Saba county --------W.H.H. Harrell, H.T. Vittiloe

Round Rock Lodge No. 227, Round Rock, Williamson county --------N.S. Tisdale, J.C. McMordie, an F.C.

New Port Lodge No. 228, New Port, Walker county --------T.B. Spivey

Sampson Lodge No. 231, San Jacinto, Harris county, post office Lynchburg --------John Grozer

Lampasas Lodge No. 232, Lampasas, Lampasas county --------James Gibson, James Fudge, Calvin Scott, an E.A.

Eutaw Lodge No. 233, Eutaw, Limestone county --------J.Y. Stevenson

White Rock Lodge No. 234, Walnut Grove, Dallas county, post office Trinity Mills --------Henry Parish

Relief Lodge No. 236, Rush Creek, Navarro county --------D.W. Sherrell

Lively Lodge No. 237, Masonic Hall, Denton county, post office Little Elm --------H.F. Wear, Geo Wear

San Felipe Lodge No. 239, San Felipe, Austin county --------J.O. Gray

Torbert Lodge No. 241, Turner's Point, Kaufman county --------Robert Dunken, G.J. Good

Llano Lodge No. 242, Llano, Llano county --------P.M. Chas Haynes, John Martin

Gamble Lodge No. 244, Bastrop, Bastrop county --------J.W. Watson

A. Jackson Lodge No. 249, Pine Town, Cherokee county --------J.L. Brown

Sexton Lodge No. 251, Sexton, Sabine county, post office San Augustine --------Jas M. Smith

Hondo Lodge No. 252, Medina Valley, Medina county, post office New Fountain --------B. F[?] Cockerell, B.F. Brice, an E.A.

J.A. Lawrence Lodge No. 257, Antioch Church, Smith county, post office Mount Carmel --------Lazarns Hitt

Oakland Lodge No. 258, Oakland, Colorado county --------M. Vester

Beeville Lodge No. 261, Beeville, Bee county --------C.C. Cook

Whitesboro' Lodge No. 263, Whitesboro', Grayson county --------C.C. Quillian, S.H. Livingston, Jas Livingston

Carthage Lodge No. 264, Carthage, Panola county --------W.H. Cooper, J.B. Reese, W.P. Anderson, Thomas Lacy, S.H. Likens

Grayson Lodge No. 265, Personville, Limestone county --------J. Betts, I.C. Kennedy

Stephensville Lodge No. 267, Stephensville, Erath county --------James McCarty, an F.C.

Meridian Lodge No. 268, Meridian, Bosque county --------Charles Logan, Jno. C. McGee, R.A. Hester, a F.C.

Pleasant Hill Lodge No. 269, Pleasant Hill Church, Upshur county, post office Simpsonville --------G.W. Petty, an E.A.

Phoenix Lodge No. 275, Weatherford, Parker county --------E.A. Cox

Harmony Hill Lodge No. 289, Harmony Hill, Rusk county --------N.A. Vinson

Tyler Prairie Lodge No. 290, Pennington, Trinity county --------J.A. Thomas, J.B. Anderson, P.V. Green

Kimball Lodge No. 292, Kimball, Bosque county --------A.J. Puckett

Mars Hill Lodge No. 293, Springville, Wood county --------R. Magee

Salado Lodge No. 296, Salado, Bell county --------A. Tinnon

Navasota Lodge No. 299, Navasota, Grimes county --------E.J. Hearne, J.F. Perry

G.W. Foster Lodge No. 306, Nelsonville, Austin county, post office Travis--------- Enos Sullivan

Shiloh Lodge No. 307, Masonic Hall, Hunt county, post office Greenville --------J.T. Cox, an E.A.

Red Rock Lodge No. 310, Red Rock, Bastrop county --------J.T. Faulkner

Bryant Station Lodge No. 311, Bryant Station, Milam county --------Jas P. Cook

Alvarado Lodge No. 314, Alvardo, Johnson county --------Wm. O. Wright

Cleburne Lodge No. 315, Cleburne, Johnson county --------J.C. Holland

Rockport Lodge No. 323, Rockport, Refugio county --------H.C. Ives

Perryville Lodge No. 328, Perryville, Bastrop county, post office Young's Settlement --------E.R. Gentry

RETURNS OF LODGES FOR THE MASONIC YEAR
A.D. 1870, A.L. 5870
DEATHS

Holland Lodge No. 1, Houston, Harris county --------D.W.C. Farmer, G. Gerson, L.B. Michaud, J. Lewis Talman

Red Land Lodge No. 3, San Augustine, San Augustine county --------Solomon Miller, M. Cartwright

Constantine Lodge No. 13, Bonham, Fannin county --------James Baker, M.P. Johnson, E.M. Ward

Trinity Lodge No. 14, Livingston, Polk county --------Wiley Peebles, S.J. Weathington, C.R. Dunnam

Friendship Lodge No. 16, Clarksville, Red River county --------J.T. Griffin, D.C. Russell, Geo. W. Scoggins

Orphans Friend No. 17, Anderson, Grimes county --------James C. Stevenson

Forest Lodge No. 19, Huntsville, Walker county --------Chas. G. Keenan

Graham Lodge No. 20, Brenham, Washington county --------W.W. Wheeler, E.A.

Lothrop Lodge No. 21, Crockett, Houston county --------D.R. Hazelett, J.M. White, an EA

Marshall Lodge No. 22, Marshall, Harrison county --------W.F. Baldwin, C.A. Frazer

Clinton Lodge No. 23, Henderson, Rusk county --------James R. Armstrong

Paris Lodge No. 27, Paris, Lamar county --------J.J. Poindexter, John R. Patton, Samuel R. Mebane

Gonzales Lodge No. 30, Gonzales, Gonzales county --------W.A. Kendell, M. McKnight

Palestine Lodge No. 31, Palestine, Anderson county --------Alex E. McClure, J.J. Bordeaux, W.B. Key, e.a.

LaFayette Lodge No. 34, LaGrange, Fayette county --------R.S. Sheppard, John Trousdale

Lavaca Lodge No. 36, Lavaca, Calhoun county --------Sylvester Burley

Mt. Moriah Lodge No. 37, Cold Springs, San Jacinto county --------J.J.J. Simmons

Jefferson Lodge No. 38, Jefferson, Marion county --------L.T. Craver, J.C. Todd, Fred White

Leona Union Lodge No. 39, Leona, Leon county --------Thos. N. Vestol

Alamo Lodge No. 44, San Antonio, Bexar county --------M.B. Jones, S. Sampson

Euclid Lodge No. 45, Rusk, Cherokee county --------Daniel McCaskill

Florida Lodge No. 46, Round Top, Fayette county --------John Barber

Warren Lodge No. 56, Caldwell, Burleson county --------E.W. Courtney

Mt. Enterprise Lodge No. 60, Mt. Enterprise, Rusk county --------F.M. Hudeman, e.a.

Woodville Lodge No. 62, Woodville, Tyler county --------R.S. Holland, O.L. Wooten

Joppa Lodge No. 65, Elysian Fields, Harrison county --------T.G. Deavenport, B.R. Harris

Hubert Lodge No. 67, Chappell Hill, Washington county --------W.H. Sherman, W.E. Stokes

Caledonia Lodge No. 68, Columbus, Colorado county --------Alexander Lookup, W.B. Perry, John Trussell, R.B. Johnson, an E.A.

Boston Lodge No. 69, Boston, Bowie county --------S.T. Mote, W.J. Wyse, N.B. Brooks, P. Creed, an E.A.

Morton Lodge No. 72, Richmond, Fort Bend county --------Felix G. Secrest, H.M. Daughtry, e.a.

Springfield Lodge No. 74, Springfield, Limestone county --------S.L. Lampkin

Cameron Lodge No. 76, Clinton, De Witt county --------Oliver H. Stapp

Concord Lodge No. 77, Concord Church, Harrison county, post office Jonesville --------A.B. Wright

Oasis Lodge No. 79, Dangerfield, Titus county --------M.G. Harris

Murchison Lodge No. 80, Hallettsville, Lavaca county --------A.K. Foster

Rio Grande Lodge No. 81, Brownsville, Cameron county --------A.H. Kuttner, E.F. Leichardt, W.J.B. Stenson, H.B. Twitty

Terrell Lodge No. 83, Alto, Cherokee county --------B.M. Dowdell

Indianola Lodge No. 84, Indianola, Calhoun county --------C.R. Geyer

Pine Bluff Lodge No. 85, Rock Springs, Freestone county --------B.T. Hammett

Waxahachie Lodge No. 90, Waxahachie, Ellis county --------W.C. Sanders

Waco Lodge No. 92, Waco, McLennan county --------John Shaw, A.M. Clingman, John A. Winn

Augusta Lodge No. 93, Augusta, Houston county --------B.F. Watts, G.W. Wilson

Goliad Lodge No. 94, Goliad, Goliad county --------Joseph Warren

Colorado Lodge No. 96, Webberville, Travis county --------B.M. Hamilton, John M. McDuff, D.J. Anderson, an f.c.

Newburn Lodge No. 97, Buena Vista, Shelby county --------W.P. Smith

Canton Lodge No. 98, Canton, Smith county. Post office, Troup --------J.E. Rucker

Fairfield Lodge No. 103, Fairfield, Freestone county --------D.L. Carter

Kickapoo Lodge No. 105, Kickapoo, Anderson county --------J.C. Oldham, R.H. Watkins

Jacksonville Lodge No. 108, Jacksonville, Cherokee county --------S.D. Morse

Guadalupe Lodge No. 109, Seguin, Guadalupe county --------A. Babel

Bloomfield Lodge No. 112, Kaufman, Kaufman county --------Henry Moore, J.L. Leath

Magnolia Lodge No. 113, Magnolia, Anderson county --------W.H. Farrish, W.H. Lang

Prairie Lea Lodge No. 114, Prairie Lea, Caldwell county --------John Vaughn, John McClane

Red River Lodge No. 116, Pine Creek Church, Red River county --------James T. Flemming

Travis Lodge No. 117, Sherman, Grayson county --------E. Wood, J.W. Wood, e. a.

Flora Lodge No. 119, Quitman, Wood county --------Green Coleman, e. a. Jacob R. Lacy, J.H. Minton, Peter Thompson, T.H. Benton, A.K. Webster

Quitman Lodge No. 122, Chatfield, Navarro county --------J.K. Cooksey, L.B. Thomas

Texana Lodge No. 123, Texana, Jackson county --------F.W. Armstrong

Baylor Lodge No. 125, Gay Hill, Washington county --------L.L. Lincecum

Madison Lodge No. 126, Orange, Orange county --------John Meriman

Brazos Union Lodge No. 129, Bryan, Brazos county --------J.B. Bouchelle, J.J. Gainer, W.H.A. Cyrus

El Paso Lodge No. 130, El Paso, El Paso county --------Gaylord J. Clark

Belmont Lodge No. 131, Belmont, Gonzales county --------L.C. McGinnis, W.C. Pickins, Jas. T. Foster

Lexington Lodge No. 138, Lexington, Burleson county --------A.J. Marley

Herschell Lodge No. 139, Coffeeville, Upshur county --------R.J. Shipp, Saml Hanley, S.D. Phillips, an E A.

Keechi Lodge No. 140, Centreville, Leon county --------Mack Curry, J.T. Gresham, Jos. Lamberth

Castillian Lodge No. 141, Canton, Van Zandt county --------T.W. Clark, Levi Moore

Bethesda Lodge No. 142, Gilmer, Upshur county --------Austin Walker

Ochiltree Lodge No. 143, Melrose, Nacogdoches county --------William Wilson

Pierce Lodge No. 144, Calvert, Robertson county --------Wm. S. Colburn, W.H. Garrett, David Hoskins, John R. Beeson, Jas. H. Logan

Winnsborough Lodge No. 146, Winnsboro, Wood county --------W.A. Coglin

Fort Worth Lodge No. 148, Fort Worth, Tarrant county --------L.B. Conwell, J.T. Turner

Sam Sanford Lodge No. 149, Center, Shelby county --------Jesse Amason, William Scott, James Truit

Marlin Lodge No. 152, Marlin, Falls county --------F.M. Oaks, e. a.

Eclectic Lodge No. 153, Eclectic Grove, Fannin county --------J.H. Scruggs, John M. Bourland, A.P. Eastman, T.P. Eubanks, R. Allred

Cotton Gin Lodge No. 154, Cotton Gin, Freestone county --------Lewis Deming

Spring Hill Lodge No. 155, Spring Hill, Navarro county --------Cyrus Spence

Lancaster Lodge No. 160, Lancaster, Dallas county --------J.H. Gibson

Honey Grove Lodge No. 164, Honey Grove, Fannin county --------Geo. W. Moore

Athens Lodge No. 165, Athens, Henderson county --------Jas. Barnett, an e.a.

Monroe Lodge No. 168, Madisonville, Madison county --------F.W. Harms, J.S. Collard, Henry Walters, Fellow Crafts

Jas. F. Taylor Lodge No. 169, Fort Crawford, Harrison county. Post office, Hallville --------E.P. Wells, A.J. Williams

San Anders Lodge No. 170, Cameron, Milam county --------G.A. Batte, Sen, Lu Batte, F. Meyer, W.P. Norman, John Story

Mound Prairie Lodge No. 173, Mound Prairie, Anderson county. Post office Plenitude --------J.E. McCain

Corsicana Lodge No. 174, Corsicana, Navarro county --------Jesse L. Cunningham

Valley Lodge No. 175, Burnet, Burnet county --------R.R. Kelly, J.L. Gibbs, an e.a.

St. Paul's Lodge No. 177, Port Sullivan, Milam county --------Reuben A. Smith, James Hardcastle, G.W. Sarter

Hardeman Lodge No. 179, Johnson's Store, Caldwell county, post office Plum Creek --------John E. Evans, James McAlister, Thomas Ellison, James O. Jackson

Post Oak Island Lodge No. 181, Post Oak Island, Williamson county. Post office Sandfly, Bastrop county --------A.W. Fort, David Scott

Hopkinsville Lodge No. 183, Hopkinsville, Gonzales county --------J.B. West, N.C. Kent

Hickory Grove Lodge No. 184, Etna, Smith county --------F. Deshong

White Oak Lodge No. 185, White Oak, Hopkins county --------J.A. Smith, W.M. Payn

Decatur Lodge No. 186, Decatur, Wise county --------Jno. W. Knight, C.C. Gose

Corpus Christi Lodge No. 189, Corpus Christi, Nueces county --------Somers Kinney, E. A.

Cusseta Lodge No. 192, Cussetta, Davis county --------W.J. Stanton

Aquilla Lodge No. 196, Hillsboro, Hill county --------James T. Turner

Gatesville Lodge No. 197, Gatesville, Coryell county --------T.D. Cooper, David Cox, J.A. Haynes, J.G. Jacob

Tyre Lodge No. 198, Tennessee Colony, Anderson county --------J.R. Scarbrough, D.M. Mynatt, a Fellow Craft

Alamita Lodge No. 200, Helena, Karnes county --------R.A. Butler, Jas. Callahan

James A. Baker Lodge No. 202, Ebenzer Baptist Church, Walker county, Post office, Huntsville --A.J. McGown, S.B. Randall

Pine Lodge No. 203, Edom, Van Zandt county --------W.A. Enos, A. Gibson, a Fellow Craft

Mount Calm Lodge No. 204, Mount Calm, Limestone county --------Haughton Hughes

Frank Sexton Lodge No. 206, Pittsburg, Upshur county --------T.L. Garret, E.A.

McMahon Lodge No. 208, Lockhart, Caldwell county --------Wm. Jordan, H.C. Wright, J. McCurley, e.a.

Mantua Lodge No. 209, Mantua, Collin county --------J. Tate, an E.A.

Gainesville Lodge No. 210, Gainesville, Cook county --------M.A. Elliott

Science Hill Lodge No. 211, Science Hill, Henderson county --------W.C. Pickering

43

Bright Star Lodge No. 221, Sulphur Springs, Hopkins county --------Isaac Ardis
Bellville Lodge No. 223, Bellville, Austin county --------J.W. Perrine
Miller Lodge No. 224, White Rock, Hunt county --------Green Boyd
Butler Lodge No. 224a, Butler, Freestone county --------J.T. Boykin
San Saba Lodge No. 225, San Saba, San Saba county --------John T. Davis
Newport Lodge No. 228, Newport, Walker county --------John W. Spivey, Thos. P. McMillian
Randolph Lodge No. 229, Pleasant Grove, Houston county. Post office, Crockett --------Jas. English
Sampson Lodge No. 231, San Jacinto, Harris county. Post office Lynchburg --------J.P. Harrel
Eutaw Lodge No. 233, Old Town of Eutaw, Limestone county. Post office, Kosse --------J.M. Springfield, W.H. Mitchell
Relief Lodge No. 236, Rush Creek, Navarro county --------R.S. Jemison, Beverly M. Berry
San Felipe Lodge No. 239, San Felipe, Austin county --------Jefferson Holden, e.a.
Gamble Lodge No. 244, Bastrop, Bastrop county --------F. Culp
Adah Zillah Lodge No. 247, Millican, Brazos county --------J.M. Price, Wright Dixon, H.H. Sanger, James Fagan, W.M. Brazier, an F.C.
A. Jackson Lodge No. 249, Pine Town, Cherokee county --------W.F. Marlow, L.M. Allen
Sexton Lodge No. 251, Sexton, Sabine county. Post office, San Augustine --------Daniel Henderson, e.a., Thompson Allen
J. A. Lawrence Lodge No. 257, Antioch Church, Smith county. Post office Mount Carmel --------Tarlton Bond, W.K. Glen
Whitesboro' Lodge No. 263, Whitesboro', Grayson county --------White M. Richards, e. a.
Carthage Lodge No. 264, Carthage, Panola county --------S.W. Goram
Grayson Lodge No. 265, Personville, Limestone county --------B.W. Aycoff
Dixie Lodge No. 272, Knoxville, Cherokee county --------W.G. Engledow, C.M. Hicks
Phoenix Lodge No. 275, Weatherford, Parker county --------H.D. Bingham
Stonewall Lodge No. 287, Stonewall, Nacogdoches county. Post office, Douglass --------W.H. Thompson
Grapevine Lodge No. 288, Grapevine, Tarrant county --------Isaac Newton, Daniel Starr, Chas. Baker
Salado Lodge No. 296, Salado, Bell county --------J.T. Mabry, B.H. Elliot
Tucker Lodge No. 297, Galveston, Galveston county --------Jas. Carville, J.R. Romaine, M.W. Baker, A. Cohen, Henry Blum
Cedar Creek Lodge No. 300, Tryon Church, Brazos county, post office Bryan City --------John Hudson, J.H. Thomas
Starksville Lodge No. 303, Starksville, Lamar county --------Wm. M. Parks
Live Oak Lodge No. 304, Live Oak Academy, Hays county. Post office Mountain City --------J.A. White

44

Shiloh Lodge No. 307, Shiloh Hall, Hunt county. Post office Lone Oak --------S.W. Weaver, A.J. Harden

Bryant Station Lodge No. 311, Bryant Station, Milam county. Post office, Cameron --------G.J. Hendrix, J.M. Burns, M. Cooly

William Foster Lodge No. 312, Fosterville, Anderson county --------R.H. Watkins

Zion Lodge No. 313, Stonewall Jackson Institute, Grimes couny. Post office Anderson --------F.W. Hams

David Lodge No. 318, David's Mill, Freestone county. Post office, Fairfield --------W.B. Acuff

Fort Richardson Lodge No. 320, Jacksboro, Jack county --------W.M. Harper, an e. a.

Rockport Lodge No. 323, Rockport, Refugio county --------C.J. Kher

RETURNS OF LODGES UNDER THE JURISDICTION OF THE
GRAND LODGE OF TEXAS FOR THE MASONIC YEAR
A.D. 1871, A.L. 5871
DEATHS

Holland Lodge No. 1, Houston, Harris county --------W.D. Robinson, W.L. Withers

Milam Lodge No. 2, Nacogdoches, Nacogdoches county --------J.S. Roberts

Red Land Lodge No. 3, San Augustine, San Augustine county --------James Ellison, Jno. G. Berry

St. Johns Lodge No. 5, Columbia, Brazoria county --------A.G. Alesworth, E.A.; A. McCloy, E.A.

Harmony Lodge No. 6, Galveston, Galveston --------John Bone, C.B.F. Eisensmidt, D. Richardson, E.J. Sherman, A.B. Trowell, J.D. Waters

Milam Lodge No. 11, Independence, Washington county --------A.W. Wood

Austin Lodge No. 12, Austin, Travis county --------I.B. Collins, F.K. House

Constantine Lodge No. 13, Bonham, Fannin county --------Ed. Reid, Jno. M. Wells

Friendship Lodge No. 16, Clarksville, Red river county --------M.R. Bowles, J.E. Barry, John Scaff, T.R. Wilson, W.N. Woodfin, E.A.

Orphans Friend No. 17, Anderson, Grimes county --------Mathew J. Duke, Robert C. Neblett

Forest Lodge No. 19, Huntsville, Walker county --------George V. Perrie, J.C. Rome

Graham Lodge No. 20, Brenham, Washington county --------George Hellman, William Smith, Thos. Hood

Lothrop Lodge No. 21, Crockett, Houston county --------Wm. M. Taylor, PGM; F.C. Wise

Marshall Lodge No. 22, Marshall, Harrison county --------M.J. Hall, Sr.; Wils Curlin, W.H. Bristow, John T. Mills

Clinton Lodge No. 23, Henderson, Rusk county --------J.M. Dodson, J.H. Parsons, C.W. Cole

Montgomery Lodge No. 25, Montgomery, Montgomery county --------Charles Jones

Paris Lodge No. 27, Paris, Lamar county --------W.H.H. Long, L.R. Clay, J.W. Hancock

De Witt Clinton Lodge No. 29, Jasper, Jasper county --------John J. Jones, Hanibal Good

Gonzales Lodge No. 30, Gonzales, Gonzales county -------- L.R. Bratton, R.R. Kitchen

Palestine Lodge No. 31, Palestine, Anderson county --------R.M. Montgomery

Layette Lodge No. 34, LaGrange, Fayette county --------R.H. Lewis, J.W. Veazey

Jefferson Lodge No. 38, Jefferson, Marion county --------A.D. McCutcheon, J.C. Murphy, Sr., H. Switzer, A. Vaughn

46

Leona Union Lodge No. 39, Leona, Leon county --------Robert Rogers, A.J. Thomas

Alamo Lodge No. 44, San Antonio, Bexar --------John Bolger, J.D. Thein, F.J. Clark, a F.C.

Euclid Lodge No. 45, Rusk, Cherokee --------Josiah Middleton, W.W. McDougald, A. Jones, E.A.'s

Florida Lodge No. 46, Round Top, Fayette county --------R.A. Williams

St. Johns Lodge No. 51, McKinney, Collin county --------Oliver Hedgeoxe

Tannehill Lodge No. 52, Dallas, Dallas county --------Jno. G. Pipkin, J.H. Hodges, W. Milwee, J.A. Freeman

St. Johns Lodge No. 53, Tyler, Smith county --------J.B. Bates

Grand Bluff Lodge No. 54, Grand Bluff, Panola county --------John Miller, an E.A.

Larissa Lodge No. 57, Larissa, Cherokee county --------A.O. Alexander

Mt. Enterprise Lodge No. 60, Mt. Enterprise, Rusk county --------John T. Furlow

Woodville Lodge No. 62, Woodville, Tyler county --------R.K. Ratcliffe

Rocky Mount Lodge No. 63, Bunker Hill, Rusk county, post office London --------R.E. Wynne

Chireno Lodge No. 66, Chireno, Nacogdoches county --------Jesse Crisp, J.J. Jackson

Hubert Lodge No. 67, Chappell Hill, Washington county --------T.R. Owens, an E.A.

Caledonia Lodge No. 68, Columbus, Colorado county --------Williamson Daniels, J.J. Loomis

Boston Lodge No. 69, Boston, Bowie county --------S.D. Poer, J.D. Battle

Morton Lodge No. 72, Richmond, Fort Bend county --------Jno. H. Hand, M.M. and C.O. Kelly, an E.A.

Springfield Lodge No. 74, Springfield, Limestone county --------James Anglin

Cameron Lodge No. 76, Clinton, De Witt county --------James W. Meador

Murchison Lodge No. 80, Hallettsville, Lavaca county --------Frank C. Kelly, W.J. Holman, an E.A.

Terrell Lodge No. 83, Alto, Cherokee county --------Allen Jones

Tusculum Lodge No. 86, Pine Tree Church, Upshur county --------J.G. Lummus, an E.A.

Andrew Jackson Lodge No. 88, Linden, Cass county -------- L.E. Watson

San Gabriel Lodge No. 89, Georgetown, Williamson county --------J.A. Clark, W.J. Peace, G.M.D. Mason

Waxahachie Lodge No. 90, Waxahachie, Ellis county -------W.T. Briggs, T.W. Cosby, C.C. Overstreet, J.F. Tittle, E.A.

Tarrant Lodge No. 91, Tarrant, Hopkins county -------James Hooten

Waco Lodge No. 92, Waco, McLennan county --------M.J. Lindsey, B.T. Richey, W.J. Saunders

Augusta Lodge No. 93, Augusta, Houston county --------Robert Jarratt

Goliad Lodge No. 94, Goliiad, Goliad county --------J.C. Hall, W.C. Cartright, Jno. N. Smith, an E.A.

Sharon Lodge No. 95, Pine Hill, Rusk county --------John Wherry
Newburn Lodge No. 97, Buena Vista, Shelby county --------J.L. King
Unity Lodge No. 102, Moscow, Polk county --------Joe Turner
Fairfield Lodge No. 103, Fairfield, Freestone county --------Jesse Sheffield
Kickapoo Lodge No. 105, Kickapoo, Anderson county --------A.A. Gillian
San Jacinto Lodge No. 106, Danville, Montgomery county --------Zill McCaleb
Jacksonville Lodge No. 108, Jacksonville, Cherokee county --------R.R. Jowell, D.G. Templeton
Bloomfield Lodge No. 112, Kaufman, Kaufman county --------C.W. Crouch
Magnolia Lodge No. 113, Magnolia, Anderson county --------A.J. Morgan
Red River Lodge 116, Pine Creek Church, Red River county --------J.N. Boman
Travis Lodge No. 117, Sherman, Grayson county -------- John Wilson, an E.A.
Starr Lodge No. 118, Starrville, Smith county --------Joshua Ginn
Flora Lodge No. 119, Quitman, Wood county --------Giles N. Harris, L.A. Rinehart
McDonald Lodge No. 120, Linn Flat, Nacogdoches county -------- John Prather
Texana Lodge Mo. 123, Texana, Jackson county --------R.L. Snodgrass
Baylor Lodge No. 125, Gay Hill, Washington county, post office Long Point --------C.W. Adams
El Paso Lodge No. 130, El Paso, El Paso county --------John Y. Bryant
Belmont Lodge No. 131, Belmont, Gonzales county --------A. Ellis; M.H. Beaty, F.C.
Retreat Lodge 133, Courtney, Grimes county --------C. Bennett
Bethel Lodge No. 134, Ladonia, Fannin county --------J.M. Rigney, W.P. Petty
Mount Horeb Lodge No. 137, Gabriel Mills, Williamson county, post office Mahomet, Burnet county --------B. Simpson
Lexington Lodge No. 138, Lexington, Burleson county --------W.A. Kendrick, J.H. Hardcastle
Herschell Lodge No. 139, Coffeeville, Upshur county --------J.M. Parker, E. Gaskin, F.C.
Keechi Lodge No. 140, Centreville, Leon county --------Adam Lagrone, M.M.; J.H. Mays, E.A.
Castillian Lodge No. 141, Canton, Van Zandt county --------W.H. Haley, J.W. Wood, M. Thompson
Bethesda Lodge No. 142, Gilmer, Upshur county --------Gilbert Buel, S.H. Moon, F.C.
Pierce Lodge No. 144, Calvert, Robertson county --------C.W. Garrett, J.M. Garrett, J.J. Hodge, W.S. Hicks
Winnsborough Lodge No. 146, Winnsboro, Wood county --------John A. Thompson
Planters' Lodge N0. 147, Plantersville, Grimes county --------J.W. Laurance, an E.A.; A.Z. Hill, a F.C. ; B.Z. Hill
Fort Worth Lodge No. 148, Fort Worth, Tarrant county --------J.H. George
Sam Sanford Lodge No. 149, Center, Shelby county --------J.H. Clardy
Marlin Lodge No. 152, Marlin, Falls county --------D.G. Barton, an E.A.

Eclectic Lodge No. 153, Eclectic Grove, Fannin county, post office Warren --------C. Carter, J.D. Lankford, F.G. McLish

Cotton Gin Lodge No. 154, Cotton Gin, Freestone county --------J.B. Lennard, A.A. Lewis

Hickory Hill Lodge No. 156, Hickory Hill, Cass county --------T.E. Nesbett

Honey Grove Lodge No. 164, Honey Grove, Fannin county --------Wm. Cross, P.E. Pulliam, Entered Apprentices

Kentucky Lodge No. 167, Kentucky Town, Grayson county --------R.L. Anderson

Monroe Lodge No. 168, Madisonville, Madison county --------D.N. Cammack, O.E. Sheeler, G.N. Sandell, O.S. Mason, W. Robuck

James F. Taylor Lodge No. 169, Hallville, Harrison county --------J.E. Crain

Mound Prairie Lodge No. 173, Mound Prairie, Anderson county --------W.P. Jacobs, T.C. Hooker, W.H. Lawrence

Corsicana Lodge No. 174, Corsicana, Navarro county --------J.W. Garner, C.A. Hill

St. Paul's Lodge No. 177, Port Sullivan, Milam county --------Thos. J.H. Anderson, G.M.; A.P. Cunningham, Leopold Elkes

Post Oak Island Lodge No. 181, Post Oak Island, Williamson county, post office Young's Settlement, Bastrop county --------G.N. Williams

Concrete Lodge No. 182, Concrete, De Witt county --------Lewis Peebles, R.H. Stoll, L.B. Bachelor

Hickory Grove Lodge No. 184, Etna, Smith county --------Edward Prince

White Oak Lodge No. 185, Saratoga, Hopkins county, post office White Oak --------W.R. Heart

Corpus Christi Lodge No. 189, Corpus Christi, Nueces county --------Alden McLaughlin

Jack Titus Lodge No. 194, Coleman's Springs, Red River county, post office Clarksville --------W.H. Flemming, H.N. Gains

Lyons Lodge No. 195, High Hill, Fayette county --------James C. Callison

Tyre Lodge No. 198, Tennessee Colony, Anderson county --------J.A. Woolverton, G.D. Kimbrough

Alameta Lodge No. 200, Helena, Karens county --------T.J. Reagan

Pine Lodge No. 203, Edom, Van Zandt county --------E. McCrarie

Mount Calm Lodge No. 204, Mount Calm, Limestone county --------Boyd Wellington

McMahan Lodge No. 208, Lockhart, Caldwell county --------J.F. Powers, O. Bishop, J. Langley

Mantua Lodge No. 209, Mantua, Collin county --------Thaddeus Parris, Samuel Porter Brown

Gainesville Lodge No. 210, Gainesville, Cook county --------Maupin Milton

Science Hill Lodge No. 211, science Hill, Henderson county, post office Athens --------I. Martin, M. Thompson

Dresden Lodge No. 218, Dresden, Navarro county -------- Wm. Conger

Onion Creek Lodge No. 220, Lodge Room, Travis county, post office Austin --------Mark Thomas, A.B. Crosthwait, F.C.

49

Bright Star Lodge No. 221, Sulphur Springs, Hopkins county --------H.J. Bass, W.E. Posey, J.T. Turner
Brahan Lodge No. 226, Lavernia, Wilson county --------T.J. Vivian
Round Rock Lodge No. 227, Round Rock, Williamson county --------Wm. Armstrong, W.F. Bailey
New Port Lodge No. 228, New Port, Walker county --------Leroy Thomas, W.H. Palmer
Sampson Lodge No. 231, San Jacinto, Harris county, post office Lynchburg --------C.T. Frost
Eutaw Lodge No. 233, Old Town of Eutaw, Limestone county, post office Kosse --------J.R. Green, S.E. Lightsey, A.H. McDaniel
White Rock Lodge No. 234, Walnut Grove, Dallas county, post office Trinity Mills --------J.M. Allen
Relief Lodge No. 236, Rush Creek, Navarro county --------A.J. Morgan, W.W. Taylor
Lively Lodge No. 237, Masonic Hall, Denton county --------J.B. Rodgers, Sr.
San Felipe Lodge No. 239, San Felipe, Austin county --------Wm. E. Munger
Fayetteville Lodge No. 240, Fayetteville, Fayette county --------Green Andrews, F.M. Johnson
Gamble Lodge No. 244, Bastrop, Bastrop county --------E.C. Blakey, J.H. Wilbarger, an E.A.
Sulphur Bluff Lodge No. 246, Sulphur Bluff, Hopkins county --------W.R. Hart
Hondo Lodge No. 252, Hondo Valley, Medina county, post office New Fountain --------H.G. Boycus
Homer Lodge No. 254, Homer, Angelina county --------A.L. Hudiburgh, S.M. Baird
J.A. Lawrence Lodge No. 257, Antioch Church, Smith county, post office Tyler --------J.H. Wood
Oakland Lodge No. 258, Oakland, Colorado county --------Jas. English, an E.A.
Beeville Lodge No. 261, Beeville, Bee county --------Patterson Clark
Whitesboro' Lodge No. 263, Whitesboro', Grayson county --------J.H. Williams
Stephenville Lodge No. 267, Stephenville, Erath county --------H.W. Clark, J.M. Phillips, L.G. Howard, an E.A.
Meridian Lodge No. 268, Meridian, Bosque county --------J.J. Jacobs
Pilot Point Lodge No. 270, Pilot Point, Denton county --------A. Gounah, A.B. Harwell
Dixie Lodge No. 272, Knoxville, Cherokee county --------A.J. Griffin
Phoenix Lodge No. 275, Weatherford, Parker county --------A.S. Caperton, A.E. Toler, D.A. Norton
Brownwood Lodge No. 279, Brownwood, Brown county --------George W. Pugh
Pleasanton Lodge No. 283, Pleasanton, Atascosa county --------J.W. Cooper, J.R. Hoy, C.S. Turner
Eastern Star Lodge No. 284, Nogarlis Prairie, Trinity county --------W.J. Wheelington, T.H. Kinley

Acton Lodge No. 285, Acton, Hood county --------W.L. Rippetoe, P.M., M.L. Halford

Beaumont Lodge 286, Beaumont, Jefferson county --------Geo. A. Pattillo

Stonewall Lodge No. 287, Stonewall, Nacogdoches county, post office Douglass --------J.A.C. Milton

Kimball Lodge No. 292, Kimball, Bosque county --------B.M. Willingham

Mars Hill Lodge No. 293, Emory, Rains county --------A. Danley

Nathan Corley Lodge No. 294, Magnolia Springs, Jasper county --------Nathan Corley

Scyene Lodge No. 295, Scyene, Dallas county --------F.M. Brisendine

Tucker Lodge No. 297, Galveston, Galveston county --------J.J. Labatt

Moulton Lodge No. 298, Moulton, Lavaca county --------S.H. Walker

Starksville Lodge No. 303, Starksville, Lamar county --------John Harmon, J.R. Robbins

Littleton Fowler Lodge No. 305, Hemphill, Sabine county --------J.M. Drawhorn

Shiloh Lodge No. 307, Shiloh Hall, Hunt county, post office Lone Oak --------J.A. Schenck, W.E. Laroque

Hull's Store, Lodge No. 309, Woods, Panola county --------I.S. Henson, E.A.

Zion Lodge No. 313, Stonewall Jackson Institute, Grimes county, post office, Iola --------J.W. Lee

Alvarado Lodge No. 314, Alvarado, Johnson county --------A.C. Hoyle, D.S. Purdom

Comanche Lodge No. 316, Comanche, Comanche county --------Benj. James

Prairieville Lodge No. 322, Prairieville, Kaufman county, post office Kemp --------Satcher Wood

Carolina Lodge No. 330, Lodge Hall, Falls county, post office Carolina --------James Loftin

Leesburg Lodge No. 334, Leesburg, Gonzalas county, post office Belmont --------A.M. Self

J.H. Gurley Lodge No. 337, Waco, McLennan county --------J.W. Hines, F.C.

Bowling Lodge No. 343, Bowling, Leon county --------J.C.B. Payne

Fish Creek Lodge No. 344, Marysville, Cooke county, post office Gainesville --------M.H. Loveless

White Rock Lodge No. 347, White Rock Church, McLennan county, post office Waco --------W.M. Austin

Tulip Lodge No. 348, Tulip, Fannin county, post office Bonham --------R.D. Patterson

Etam Lodge No. 353, Hempstead, Austin county --------Z.M.P. Motley

Tehuacana Lodge No. 358, Tehuacana, Limestone county --------A.A. Lewis

Patrick Lodge No. 359, Owensville, Robertson county --------J.W. Sandifer, S.R. Lightsey, W.S. Hicks

RETURNS OF LODGES
UNDER THE JURISDICTION OF THE
GRAND LODGE OF TEXAS FOR THE MASONIC YEAR
A.D. 1872, A.L. 5872
DEATHS

Holland Lodge No. 1, Houston, Harris county --------W.D. Andrews, Philip B. George, Erastus S. Perkins, Benjamin Wolf, J. Wesley Johnson, James Middleton

Milam Lodge No. 2, Nacogdoches, Nacogdoches county --------W.R.T. Christopher, G.W. Hill, James A. Fulghim

Harmony Lodge No. 6, Galveston, Galveston county --------E.B. Nichols, P.G.M.; William B. Slade, Joseph W. Taylor, H.G. Wickworth

Milam Lodge No. 11, Independence, Washington county --------N.A. Clampit, J.T. Hill

Austin Lodge No. 12, Austin, Travis county --------M.H. Bowers, W.W. Evans, J.B. Bacon, E.M. Earnest, J.A. Mercer, an E.A.

Trinity Lodge No. 14, Livingston, Polk county --------Demetrius Willis, S. Turner, an E.A.

Friendship Lodge No. 16, Clarksville, Red River county --------M.C. Gilliam, an E.A.; J.F. Warren, a F.C.

Washington Lodge No. 18, Washington, Washington county --------B.F. Wilson, D.F. Adair, G.N. Stewart, an E.A.

Lothrop Lodge No. 21, Crockett, Houston county --------J.S. Kyle, J.D. Richardson, Wm. M. Beavers, G.A. Kyle, R.R. Russell, an E.A.

Marshall Lodge No. 22, Marshall, Harrison county --------T.A. Pattillo, E.A. Watson, A. Kullmann, Lee Sanders, J.E. Lias, an E.A.

Gonzales Lodge No. 30, Gonzales, Gonzales county --------Jacob Levy, W.D. Goff

Palestine Lodge No. 31, Palestine, Anderson county --------Shelby Crawford, J. Quisenberry, J.T. Tally

LaFayette Lodge No. 34, LaGrange, Fayette county --------Walker C. Turnage

Lavaca Lodge No. 36, Lavaca, Calhoun county --------John D. Brower, Henry Earle, A.W. Norris, J.W. Randall, an E.A.

Jefferson Lodge No. 38, Jefferson, Marion county --------L.L. Bloomingdale, T.J. Cornelius, Jacob Sterne, W.P. Williams; and J.W. Cook, J.M. Hobay, J.T. Penn, Entered Apprentices

Leona Union Lodge No. 39, Leona, Leon county --------Alex Patrick

Alamo Lodge No. 44, San Antonio, Bexar county --------Gustav Persch, W.G. Jett

Euclid Lodge No. 45, Rusk, Cherokee county --------G.W. Hardaway, John T. Aycock, Jefferson Shook, J.A. Miller, a F.C.

St. Johns Lodge No. 51, McKinney, Collin county --------J.D. Bellew, Uriah Smith

Tannehill Lodge No. 52, Dallas, Dallas county --------J.K.P. Record, W.M.; Chas. G. Newton, M.J. Moore, C.H. Kelsoe

Warren Lodge No. 56, Caldwell, Burleson county --------T.J. Haddox, Wm. Ryan, D. Moseley, a F.C.; J.D. Teaff, an E.A.

Mt. Enterprise Lodge No. 60, Mt. Enterprise, Rusk county --------W.M. Ross

Chireno Lodge No. 66, Chireno, Nacogdoches county --------R.E. Mettauer

Caledonia Lodge No. 68, Columbus, Colorado county --------L.J.B. Shaw, R. Schwerien, both E.A. Masons

Springfield Lodge No. 74, Springfield, Limestone county --------Robert Montgomery, A.A. Lewis

Cameron Lodge No. 76, Clinton, De Witt county --------Frank White

Concord Lodge No. 77, Concord Church, Harrison county, post office Jonesville --------H.F. Witherspoon

Rio Grande Lodge No. 81, Brownsville, Cameron --------J.B. Burris, John Murphy

Indianola Lodge No. 84, Indianola, Calhoun county --------Isaac Brower

Pine Bluff Lodge No. 85, Rock Springs, Freestone county, post office Fairfield --------John H. Towles

Tusculum Lodge No. 86, Pine Tree Church, Upshur county, post office Longview --------E.A. Dozier

New Salem Lodge No. 87, New Salem, Rusk county --------O. Higginbotham, John Cooper, John Kennedy, John Dunlap

Andrew Jackson Lodge No. 88, Linden, Cass county --------J.W. Humphrey

San Gabriel Lodge No.89, Georgetown, Williamson county --------D.B. McDaniel, J.C. Damron

Waco Lodge No. 92, Waco, McLellan county --------Wm. Yeates, Isam Brown

Augusta Lodge No. 93, Augusta, Houston county --------W.J. Penick

Sharon Lodge No. 95, Pine Hill, Rusk county --------W.O. Hoyle, J.J. Rockman

Colarado Lodge No. 96, Webberville, Travis county --------D.J. Anderson, a F.C.

Newburn Lodge No. 97, Buena Vista, Shelby county --------Nathan Timns

Canton Lodge No. 98, Canton, Smith county, post office Troup --------Wm. Ellison, T.J. Stamps, W.A. Bradford, R. Pinson

Danville Lodge No. 101, New Danville, Rusk county --------J.T. Beal, A.J. Griffin, an E.A., H.H. Hickey

Fairfield Lodge No. 103, Fairfield, Freestone county --------James B. Rogers, John T. Murray, W.F. Daniel

Kickapoo Lodge No. 105, Kickapoo, Anderson county --------J.B. Miller, John A. Wasson

Guadalupe Lodge No. 109, Seguin, Guadalupe county --------J.E. Park, Nat Benton, an E.A., A.W. Lay, an E.A.

Magnolia Lodge No. 113, Magnolia, Anderson county, post office Prairie Point --------W.B. Rose, Jno. F. Talley

Prairie Lea Lodge No. 114, Prairie Lea, Caldwell county --------Joseph A. McCord

Travis Lodge No. 117, Sherman, Grayson county --------M. Walsh, R. Jackson, J.C.D. Blackburn, H.M. Carroll, an E.A.

Starr Lodge No. 118, Starrville, Smith county --------J.M. Wherton

Flora Lodge No. 119, Quitman, Wood county --------James K. Ronsavill

Mount Hope Lodge No. 121, Mount Hope, Tyler county --------Archibald Laird

Quitman Lodge No. 122, Chatfield, Navarro county --------W.P. Wood

Texana Lodge No. 123, Texana, Jackson county --------Z. Bankhead

Madison Lodge No.126, Orange, Orange county --------A.T. Chenault, J.H. Baughn, A.G. Swain

Brazos Union Lodge No.129, Bryan, Brazos county --------J.B. Nabors, Batte Peterson

Belmont Lodge No. 131, Belmont, Gonzales county --------J.B. Roberts

Retreat Lodge No. 133, Courtney, Grimes county --------Ivey Daniel

Bethel Lodge No. 134, Ladonia, Fannin county --------T.B. Elliot, D.C. Partlow, a F.C.

Camden Lodge No. 135, Camden, Rusk county, post office Brown's Bluff --------Andrew Watt

Lexington Lodge No. 138, Lexington, Burleson county --------H.C. McDaniel

Herschell Lodge No. 139, Coffeeville, Upshur county --------J.C. Waller, a F.C.

Castillian Lodge No. 141, Canton, Van Zandt county --------A.M. James, T.J. Acker

Bethesda Lodge No. 142, Gilmer, Upshur county --------S.W. Beasley, G.T. Henry

Ochiltree Lodge No. 143, Melrose, Nacogdoches county --------B.R. Shadden

Pierce Lodge No. 144, Calvert, Robertson county --------H. Haynes

Winnsborough Lodge No. 146, Winnsboro, Wood county --------John A. Goldsmith

Planters Lodge No. 147, Plantersville, Grimes county --------Isaac Baker

Fort Worth Lodge No. 148, Fort Worth, Tarrant county --------G.W. McClusky

Sam Sanford Lodge No. 149, Center, Shelby county --------W.L. McCary, W.E. Hailey

Marlin Lodge No. 152, Marlin, Falls county --------W.M. McGauhey, Joe Coody

Eclectic Lodge No. 153, Eclectic Grove, Fannin county --------T.E. Garnett, H. Colbert, L. Wnitefield, J.M. Patton

Cotton Gin Lodge No. 154, Cotton Gin, Freestone county --------Jos Lynn

Spring Hill Lodge No. 155, Spring Hill, Navarro county --------John T. Fullerton, H.J. Wright

East Trinity Lodge No. 157, Rockwall, Kaufman county --------Burrel Parker

Wm. M. Taylor Lodge No. 158, Garden Valley, Smith county --------John Ellison

McClellan Lodge No. 159, Union Hill, Washington county, post office Burton --------G.P.H. Gambill, James G. Carter

Murval Lodge No. 162, Clayton, Panola county --------J.C. Strange

Athens Lodge No. 165, Athens, Henderson county --------R.P. Stewart, J.M. Forrester

Belton Lodge No. 166, Belton, Bell county --------R.B. Kavanaugh, W.T. McFarland, J.N. Dameron

Monroe Lodge No. 168, Madisonville, Madison county --------Newton Randolph

James F. Taylor Lodge No. 169, Hallville, Harrison county --------Charles Slater

San Anders Lodge No. 170, Cameron, Milam county --------J.H. Hodges

Mound Prairie Lodge No. 173, Mound Prairie, Anderson county, post office Plenitude --------W.A. Harding, W.A. Sheffield

Valley Lodge No. 175, Burnet, Burnet county --------T.J. Johnson

St. Paul's Lodge No. 177, Port Sullivan, Milam county --------John M. Kemp, W.H. White

Hopkins Lodge No. 180, Blackjack Grove, Hopkins county --------J.F. Ladd, J.W. Alexander

Post Oak Island Lodge No. 181, Post Oak Island, Williamson county, post office Elgin, Bastrop county --------James R. Price

Hopkinsville Lodge No. 183, Hopkinsville, Gonzales county --------E.B. Laird

Hickory Grove Lodge No. 184, Etna, Smith county --------John Gilliland, W.B. Thompson, James H. Moore

Tyrian Lodge No. 187, Sabine Pass, Jefferson county --------James McCall, C.H. Alexander, John Hampshire, Benj Johnson, Sr.

Cusseta Lodge No. 192, Cusseta, Cass county --------R.H. Griffin

Leon Lodge No. 193, Lodge Room, on Leon river, Bell county, post office Moffattown --------John Nichols, an E.A.

Jack Titus Lodge No. 194, Coleman Springs, Red River county, post office Clarksville --------W.F. Bearden

Lyons Lodge No. 1195, High Hill, Fayette county --------W.H.S. Lee, a F.C.

Aquilla Lodge No. 196, Hillsboro, Hill county --------Thomas Ball, W.H. Goodwin, L.M. Bateman

Gatesville Lodge No. 197, Gatesville, Coryell county --------F.A. Hamburg, an E.A.

Tyre Lodge No. 198, Tennessee Colony, Anderson county --------J.N. Green, J.N. Woolverton

Mount Calm Lodge No. 204, Mount Calm, Limestone county --------Leathers Kincheon

Frank Sexton Lodge No. 206, Pittsburg, Upshur county --------J.M. Taylor, G.W.T. Stamps, an E.A.

McMahan Lodge No. 208, Lockhart, Caldwell county --------L.B. Wright, Sr.

Mantua Lodge No. 209, Mantua, Collin county -------Larkin Anderson

Gainesville Lodge No. 210, Gainesville, Cooke county --------Beriah Frazier, Thomas F. Whalley

Science Hill Lodge No. 211, Science Hill, Henderson county, post office Athens --------B.H. Woodward

Farmersville Lodge No. 214, Farmersville, Collin county --------J.P. Mayers

Stanfield Lodge No. 217, Denton, Denton county --------T.J. McDowell

Dresden Lodge No. 218, Dresden, Navarro county -------John Pinckston, A.T. Lancaster

Bright Star Lodge No. 221, Sulphur Springs, Hopkins county --------J.J. Coulter, J.S. Mitchell, an E.A.

Parsons Lodge No. 222, Parsons Seminary, Travis county, post office Manor --------W.T. Alford, W.W. Atwood

Butler Lodge No. 224a, Butler, Freestone county --------M.G. Johnson, W.B. Rose

Round Rock Lodge No. 227, Round Rock, Williamson county --------B.T. Bowmer

Newport Lodge No. 228, Newport, Walker county --------Joseph Werner, W.L. Evans

Sampson Lodge No. 231, Lynchburg, Harris county --------F.W. Miller, A.H. White

Lampasas Lodge No. 232, Lampasas, Lampasas county --------S.W. Sparks, M.J. Scott

Eutaw Lodge No. 233, Kosse, Limestone county --------J.R. Reid, O.C. Goodson

White Rock Lodge No. 234, Walnut Grove, Collin county, post office Trinity Mills --------J.C. Huffime, an E.A.; Redman Stanley, an E.A.; B.H. Williams, an E.A.

Plano Lodge No. 235, Plano, Collin county --------J.W. Russell, Jesse Wharton, Isham Pittman

Relief Lodge No. 236, Wadeville, Navarro county --------Thos. H. Stringer

Llano Lodge No. 242, Llano, Llano county --------J.M. Young

Gamble Lodge No. 244, Bastrop, Bastrop county --------O.W. Shipp, John L. Foster

Sulphur Bluff Lodge No. 246, Sulphur Bluff, Hopkins county --------W.N. Whiteside, John M. Bentley

Adah Zillah Lodge No. 247, Millican, Brazos county --------J.E. Millican

A. Jackson Lodge No. 249, Pine Town, Cherokee county --------James Odom, Wiley Thomason

Black Point Lodge No. 250, St. Mary's, Refugio county, --------A.M. Gary

Sexton Lodge No. 251, Sexton, Sabine county, post office San Augustine --------John D. Reynolds

Hondo Lodge No. 252, New Fountain, Medina county --------Frank Shultee

Milford Lodge No. 262, Milford, Ellis county --------W.A. Jennings

Whitesboro' Lodge No. 263, Whitesboro', Grayson county --------H.S.D. Steel, Asa Davis, D.C. Rogers

Carthage Lodge No. 264, Carthage, Panola county --------Wade Harley

Grayson Lodge No. 265, Lost Prairie, Limestone county, post office Personville --------Thos. B. Gilbert

Stephenville Lodge No. 267, Stephenville, Erath county --------S.V. Edwards, F.M. Ross

Pleasant Hill Lodge No. 269, Simpsonville, Upshur county --------James Hogan

Dixie Lodge No. 272, Knoxville, Cherokee county --------Stephen Morris

Brownwood Lodge No. 279, Brownwood, Brown county --------J.W. Mullin, an E.A.
Winchester Lodge No. 282, Winchester, Fayette county --------W.D. Young, Jas Spaulding, an E.A.
Pleasanton Lodge No. 283, Pleasanton, Atascosa county --------J.K.P. Childress
Acton Lodge No. 285, Acton, Hood county --------J.D. Young
Beaumont Lodge No. 287, Beaumont, Jefferson county --------N. Wiess
Grapevine Lodge No. 288, Grapevine, Tarrant county --------Mathew Green, G.B. Gideon
Mars Hill Lodge No. 293, Emory, Rains county --------Thos. C. Bain, J.F. Shook
Salado Lodge No. 296, Salado, Bell county --------W.K. Karns
Tucker Lodge No. 297, Galveston, Galveston county --------Isaiah Burton, J.C. Wallis
Navasota Lodge No. 299, Navasota, Grimes county --------R.H. Geisel, E.C. Ackerman
Cedar Creek Lodge No. 300, Tryon Church, Brazos county, post office Bryan City --------John McMurry, J.A. Head, Thos. Piles, an E.A., E. Adams, an E.A.
Osage Lodge No. 301, Osage, Colorado county --------S.D. McLeary, W.L. Adkins
Starksville Lodge No. 303, Starksville, Lamar county --------L. Whitfield, A.J. Bolinger, an E.A.
Live Oak Lodge No. 304, Live Oak Academy, Hays county --------J.M. Hamilton
Littleton Fowler Lodge 305, Hemphill, Sabine county --------J.M. Watson
Cedar Grove Lodge No. 308, Cedar Grove, Kaufman county --------A.D. Miller
William Foster Lodge No. 312, Fosterville, Anderson county --------R.B. Wardroup, Thos. Price
Alvarado Lodge No. 314, Alvardo, Johnson county --------Samuel Snodgrass
Cleburne Lodge No. 315, Cleburne, Johnson county --------J.B. Hudgins
Palo Pinto Lodge No. 319, Palo Pinto, Palo Pinto county --------C.S. Dobbs
Fort Richardson Lodge No. 320, Jacksboro, Jack county --------E.P. Tuman, Alexander McIntyre
Cedar Bayou Lodge No. 321, Cedar Bayou, Chambers county, post office Cedar Bayou, Harris county --------Wm. H. Kelly
Prairieville Lodge No. 322, Prairieville, Kaufman county --------L.D. Staver, J.H. Harrison, W. Bailey Moore
Bandera Lodge No. 321, Bandera, Bandera county --------M. Weston
Evergreen Lodge No. 325, Oakville, Live Oak county --------Samuel Beckman
Perryville Lodge No. 328, Perryville, Bastrop county, post office Elgin --------C.G. Brinson
Gray Lodge No. 329, Houston, Harris county --------E.L. Massie
Cream Level Lodge No. 332, Cream Level, Van Zandt county, post office Canton --------D.M. Wilson
Birdston Lodge No. 333, Birdston, Navarro county --------James T. Neal, J.V. Keel

Leesburg Lodge No. 334, Leesburg, Gonzales county, post office Belmont --------B.S. Fields

E.M. Wilder Lodge No. 339, Power's Chapel, Falls county --------James M. Golston, M.M. Knight

Sunshine Lodge No. 341, Sunshine, Bell county, post office Volo --------C.H. Mathews

Bowling Lodge No. 343, Bowling, Leon county, post office Marquez --------W.P. Hayman

Fish Creek Lodge No. 344, Marysville, Cook county --------J.F. Blood

Tom Anderson Lodge No. 346, Fraimville, Burleson county --------E. Oswalt, James Hill

Tulip Lodge No. 348, Tulip, Fannin county, post office Bonham --------J.C. Wyatt

Wm. C. Young Lodge No. 349, Elizabethtown, Denton county --------J.L. Lamkins

Bremond Lodge No. 350, Bremond, Robertson county --------W. Keigwin, A. Moses, an E.A.

Pottersville Lodge No. 351, Pottersville, Limestone county --------L.J. Irwin

Etam Lodge No. 353, Hempstead, Austin county --------Z.M.P. Motley, John H. Glass, Sr., John Tuffly

Clifton Lodge No. 360, Clifton, Bosque county --------O.J. Regness

Golden Rule Lodge No. 361, Hearne, Robertson county --------P.L. Mathews

Dexter Lodge No. 372, Shiloh Church, Cook county, post office Whitesboro' --------W.R. Nall

Northern Star Lodge No. 377, Nashe's Mill, Lamar county, post office Paris --------N. Britton

Iredell Lodge, U.D., Iredell, Bosque county --------M.D. Blue

RETURNS OF LODGES
FOR THE MASONIC YEAR
A.D. 1873, A.L. 5873
DEATHS

Holland Lodge No. 1, Houston, Harris county --------Isaac Colman, Christian F. Duer, Manheim Jacobs, Henry Telge, an F.C.
Red Land Lodge No. 3, San Augustine, San Augustine county --------A.P. Cartwright, W.H. Slaughter, J.W. Gayle, W.W. Holman
St John's Lodge No. 5, Columbia, Brazoria county --------James Hays
Harmony Lodge No. 6, Galveston, Galveston county --------Otto Artz, J.J. Price, Wm. R. Smith, Wm. J. Smith, P.J. Willis
Milam Lodge No. 11, Independence, Washington county --------J.E. Lipscomb, N. Boyt, an E.A.
Austin Lodge No. 12, Austin, Travis county --------Thomas Baker, R.J. Rambo, Marcus L. Ford, W.F. Ford
Constantine Lodge No. 13, Bonham, Fannin county --------Mathew Davidson
Trinity Lodge No. 14, Livingston, Polk county --------C.J. Etheridge
Orphans Friend Lodge No. 17, Anderson, Grimes county --------Hiram Barney
Washington Lodge No. 18, Washington, Washington county --------J.L. Farquahar
Forest Lodge No. 19, Huntsville, Walker county --------J.H. Murray
Graham Lodge No. 20, Brenham, Washington county --------F. Gehrmann
Lothrop Lodge No. 21, Crockett, Houston county --------B.T. Ellis, Wm. Wortham
Marshall Lodge No. 22, Marshall, Harrison county --------T.B. Wilson, A. Hartranft, A. Wasmouth, F.C.; T.A. Harris, W.T. Brooks, E.A.'s
Montgomery Lodge No. 25, Montgomery, Montgomery county --------A.S. Lipscomb
Paris Lodge No. 27, Paris, Lamar county --------J.B. Denton, C.C. Waters
De Witt Clinton Lodge No. 29, Jasper, Jasper county --------F.M. Stewart, W.A. Ferguson, S.R. Goode
Gonzales Lodge No. 30, Gonzales, Gonzales county --------G.W. Franklin
Palestine Lodge No. 31, Palestine, Anderson county --------W.B. Husty, John Rodgers, John G. Scott, J.S. Weatherspoon
LaFayette Lodge No. 34, La Grange, Fayette county -------William Young, A.H. Cross, J.S. Powell, John Drisdale
Jefferson Lodge No. 38, Jefferson, Marion county --------S.W. Bayliss, F.H. Durr, Warren Hecox, Rufus Muse, J.H. Smith and A.B. Bayliss, an E.A.
Leona Union Lodge No. 39, Leona, Leona county --------Thos. B. Keese, T.G. Well
Alamo Lodge No. 44, San Antonio, Bexar county --------Thos. H. Stribling, Thomas Whitehead, P.M.; G.A. Gibson, a F.C.
Euclid Lodge No. 45, Rusk, Cherokee county --------James Carson, H.B. Turner, a F.C.

Florida Lodge No. 46, Round Top, Fayette county --------W.B.B. Ligon

Liberty Lodge No. 48, Liberty, Liberty county --------Pryor Bryan, P.L. Palmer

St. Johns Lodge No. 51, McKinney, Collin county --------H.H. Tucker, N.C. Harris

Tannehill Lodge No. 52, Dallas, Dallas county --------Allen Beard, J.R. Lassater, J.E. Hawkins, W.W. Burton, an E.A.

St. Johns Lodge No. 53, Tyler, Smith county --------J.M. Whitaker, J.T. Raspberry, D.M. Buie, Thomas Meadows

Grand Bluff Lodge No. 54, Grand Bluff, Panola county --------Wm. L. McCain

Larissa Lodge No. 57, Larissa, Cherokee county --------Thos. N. Adkins

Rocky Mount Lodge No. 63, Overton, Rusk county --------Saml. Gautt, N.J. Howell, Wm. Wood

Joppa Lodge No. 65, Elysian Fields, Harrison county --------Henry Hensley

Hubert Lodge No. 67, Chappell Hill, Washington county --------W.C. Deggs, B.C. Meredith

Caledonia Lodge No. 68, Columbus, Colorado county --------Julius Goelzsch, Charles E. Bateman, Vincenzo Battaglia, J.J. Smith, Noah Bonds, Geo. Billert, N.T.S. Compton, Leopold Steiner

Boston Lodge No. 69, Boston, Bowie county --------M.V. Johnson, S.B. McDonald, G.W. Robinson

Mount Vernon Lodge No. 71, Mount Vernon, Titus county, post office Lone Star --------T.F. Briarly

Morton Lodge No. 72, Richmond, Fort Bend county --------Henry Dunlavy, P.L. West, N.C. Davis, an E.A.

Springfield Lodge No. 74, Mexia, Limestone county --------L.T.M. Plummer

Cameron Lodge No. 76, Clinton, De Witt county --------Pitkin B. Taylor

Concord Lodge No. 77, Concord Church, Harrison county, post office Jonesville --------D. Ashton and Ed Bussey, E.A.'s

Oasis Lodge No. 79, Daingerfield, Titus county --------T.W. McDaniel

Murchison Lodge No. 80, Hallettsville, Lavaca county --------N.H. Cox, Paul Malick, C.S. Davis

Rio Grande Lodge No. 81, Brownsville, Cameron county --------A.M. Sanders

Terrell Lodge No. 83, Alto, Cherokee county --------J.H. Agnew, John Henderson, W.C. Lowery, A.M. McCollough, F.V. Young

Indianola Lodge No. 84, Indianola, Calhoun county --------Wm. Bornefeldt, Peter Wilson

Pine Bluff Lodge No. 85, Rock Springs, Freestone county, post office Fairfield --------Henry S. Hill, Richard Eskridge, an E.A.

Tusculum Lodge No. 86, Pine Tree Church, Gregg county, post office Longview --------R.E. Calloway

Andrew Jackson Lodge No. 88, Linden, Cass county --------J.P. Wood, W.H. Riggs, an F.C.

Waxahachie Lodge No. 90, Waxahachie, Ellis county --------James Hyde, B.W. Watson, Samuel Farrar, A.A. Foster

Waco Lodge No. 92, Waco, McLennan county --------James T. Miller

Augusta Lodge No. 93, Augusta, Houston county --------W.T. Miller

Sharon Lodge No. 95, Pine Hill, Rusk county --------J.F. Finley, J.W. Williams, Wm. Walton, H. Leslie, an E.A.

Newbern Lodge No. 97, Buena Vista, Shelby county --------George Bogam, John Conway, J.L. Moon

Canton Lodge No. 98, Canton, Smith county, post office Troupe --------Thos. H. Weatherby

Danville Lodge No. 101, Kilgore, Rusk county --------R.W. Baxter

San Jacinto Lodge No. 106, Willis, Montgomery county --------Saml. Little

Jacksonville Lodge No. 108, Jacksonville, Cherokee county --------W.P. Dobson, F.M. George

Prairie Lea Lodge No. 114, Prairie Lea, Caldwell county --------Marshall Tuttle

Travis Lodge No. 117, Sherman, Grayson county --------Joseph Hall, Wm. D. Fitch, J.N. Ferret, John C. Conner

Starr Lodge No. 118, Starrville, Smith county --------E.P. Moore, W.A. Jackson, J.Z. Browning, Joshua Starr

Flora Lodge No. 119, Quitman, Wood county --------Joseph Rainwater, John P. Baldwin

Quitman Lodge No. 122, Chatfield, Navarro county --------Henry Pannill, an E.A., J.A. Clayton, an E.A., J.K. Humphries, an F.C.

Texana Lodge No. 123, Texana, Jackson county --------S.P. Ferrell

Madison Lodge No. 126, Orange, Orange county --------C.W. Jackson, Jas. Linford, an E.A.

Brazos Union Lodge No. 129, Bryan, Brazos county --------J.M. Roberts

El Paso Lodge No 130, El Paso, El Paso county --------D.C. Marsh

Retreat Lodge No. 133, Courtney, Grimes county --------W.S. Draper, S. Forsythe, E.A.'s

Bethel Lodge No. 134, Ladonia, Fannin county --------O.P. Richardson

Camden Lodge No. 135, Camden, Rusk county, post office Harmony Hill --------W.J. Reedy

Newton Lodge No. 136, Burkeville, Newton county --------Wm. Norvell, S.W. Snell, Lewis Conner, who was among the suspended for non-payment of dues.

Lexington Lodge No. 138, Lexington, Burleson county --------O.W. Jones

Herschell Lodge No. 139, Coffeeville, Upshur county --------W.D. Clarke

Keechi Lodge No. 140, Centreville, Leon county --------S.L. Jeeter

Castillian Lodge No. 141, Canton, Van Zandt county --------James Hubbard, W.F. Palmer

Ochiltree Lodge No. 143, Melrose, Nacogdoches county --------T.A.B. Hardy

Pierce Lodge No. 144, Calvert, Robertson county --------G.W. Gooch, M.C. Riggs, H. Wynn, Thos. Gerrard, J.A. Watson, W.A. Baker, G.F. Randolph, Spencer Lahue, R.A. Crawford, W.C. Gibson, an E.A., H.L. Wickey, an E.A.

Winnsborough Lodge No. 146, Winnsboro, Wood county --------E.W. Dodgin, W.F. Beall

Fort Worth Lodge No. 148, Fort Worth, Tarrant county --------Tyra A. Thomas, Wm. M. King, Benj. B. Hayney, Charles Turner

Marlin Lodge No. 152, Marlin, Falls county --------W.L. Davenport

Eclectic Lodge No. 153, Eclectic Grove, Fannin county --------J.K. Degraftenried, Thos. Hill

Cotton Gin Lodge No. 154, Cotton Gin, Freestone county --------J.A. Rawls

Spring Hill Lodge No. 155, Spring Hill, Navarro county --------B.J.C. Hill

Hickory Hill Lodge No. 156, Hickory Hill, Cass county --------J.M. Blanton

McClellan Lodge No. 159, Union Hill, Washington county, post office Burton --------Sam H. Summers, J.A. Green

Lancaster Lodge No. 160, Lancaster, Dallas county --------Robert Downey, H.L. Roy, William Spencer

Murval Lodge No. 162, Clayton, Panola county, post office Carthage --------Wm. Walton, Wm. H. Wootan

Honey Grove Lodge No. 164, Honey Grove, Fannin county --------E. Hogue, Jno. Hobbs

Belton Lodge No. 166, Belton, Bell county --------D.P.H. Mallony

Kentucky Lodge No. 167, Kentucky Town, Grayson county --------G.T. Perrin, W.P. Head

Monroe Lodge No. 168, Madisonville, Madison county --------J.W. Park, James Oliver

James F. Taylor Lodge No. 169, Hallville, Harrison county --------G.E. Teat, R.T. Hatley, D. McKenney, an E.A., John Estus, an E.A.

San Anders Lodge No. 170, Cameron, Milam county --------E.J. Lumpkin, W.M. Williams

Mound Prairie Lodge No. 173, Mound Prairie, Anderson county --------J.G. Caldwell, an E.A.

St. Paul's Lodge No. 177, Port Sullivan, Milam county --------S.H. Nunelly, Wm. Tubeville

Hardeman Lodge No. 179, Plum Creek, Caldwell county --------J.G. Hind, J.M. Hysan

Post Oak Island Lodge No. 181, Post Oak Island, Williamson county --------R C. Smith

Hopkinsville Lodge No. 183, Hopkinsville, Gonzales county --------H.N. McKellar

Hickory Grove Lodge No. 184, Etna, Smith county --------H.H. Kirkland

White Oak Lodge No. 185, Pine Forest, Hopkins county, post office White Oak --------J.A. Richmond

Leon Lodge No. 193, Lodge Room, Bell county, post office Moffattown --------James B. Allen

Lyons Lodge No. 195, High Hill, Fayette county --------D.G. Mayes, John Peeler

Aquilla Lodge No. 196, Hillsboro, Hill county --------Richard Mattinly, B.F. Clampet

Gatesville Lodge No. 197, Gatesville, Coryell county --------J.M. Longmire

Tyre Lodge No. 198, Tennessee Colony, Anderson county --------J.A. Fulton

Alamita Lodge No. 200, Helena, Karnes county --------R.F. Haskins

Denton Lodge No. 201, Lewisville, Denton county --------I.M. Wade

James A. Baker Lodge No. 202,   Ebenzer Baptist Church, Walker county, post office Huntsville --------S.M. Jenkins, E. Wilson

Mount Calm Lodge No. 204, Mount Calm, Limestone county --------A.A. Waddell, G.W. Crist

Frank Sexton Lodge No. 206, Pittsburg, Upshur county --------T.T. Carlock, G.R. Adar, S.M. Proctor, an F.C., D.R. Lindsey, an E.A., Wm. H. Proctor, an E.A.

Mantua Lodge No. 209, Mantua, Collin county, post office Vanalstyne --------Andrew Hayherse, an E.A.

Gainesville Lodge No. 210, Gainesville, Cooke county --------Chester B. Gould, W.D. Ellis

Farmersville Lodge No. 214, Farmersville, Collin county --------J.A. Ball, J.S. Duff, James Thompson

Blanco Lodge No. 216, Blanco, Blanco county --------B.A. Brown, Hiram Bryant

Stanfield Lodge No. 217, Denton, Denton county --------J.W. Wilks, L.M. Fry

Dresden Lodge No. 218, Dresden, Navarro county --------Ethan Melton, A.T. Gunter, an E.A,

Onion Creek Lodge No. 220, Lodge Room, Travis county, post office Austin --------R.H.L. Crosthwait, Hugh McBride

Bright Star Lodge No. 221, Sulphur Springs, Hopkins county --------M.C. Mahaffey

Parsons Lodge No. 222, Parsons Seminary, Travis county, post office Manor --------Ed Larne, John Robb

Bellville Lodge No. 223, Bellville, Austin county --------Thomas Chapman

Miller Lodge No. 224, near White Rock, Hunt county --------J.N. Simmons, J.T. Moore, C.O. Evans

Butler Lodge No. 224a, Butler, Freestone county --------W.M. McDaniel, W.H. Adkins

Lampasas Lodge No. 232, Lampasas, Lampasas county --------W.B. Pace, J.E. Chalk, D.W. Taylor, Joshua S. Brown, an E.A.

Eutaw Lodge No. 233, Kosse, Limestone county --------N.M. Crenshaw, L.J. Erwin, J.H. Herbison

Plano Lodge No. 235, Plano, Collin county --------T. Blackburn, Thos. J. Malone

Relief Lodge No. 236, Wadeville, Navarro county --------W.L. Brice

Fayetteville Lodge No. 240, Fayetteville, Fayette county --------Clement Allen

Torbert Lodge No. 241, Turner's Point, Kaufman county --------J.R. Fulgium

Gamble Lodge No. 244, Bastrop, Bastrop county --------Wm. Thompson, Chauncey Johnson

Gray Rock Lodge No. 245, Gray Rock, Titus county --------D. Griffin, a F.C.

Sulphur Bluff Lodge No. 246, Sulphur Bluff, Hopkins county --------I.M. Chapman, C.H. Sims

Adah Zillah Lodge No. 247, Millican, Brazos county --------B.H. Knox, Peter Burns, H.B. Rector

A. Jackson Lodge No. 249, Pine Town, Cherokee county, post office Rusk --------Benjamin Morris, J.W. Armstrong, J.P. Guttry

Black Point Lodge No. 250, St. Mary's , Refugio county --------Cyrus W. Ezery

Sexton Lodge No. 251, Milam, Sabine county --------R.H. Davis, Silas Carpenter

Hondo Lodge No. 252, New Fountain, Medina county --------George Redins

Homer Lodge No. 254, Homer, Angelina county --------B.F. Hill

J.A. Lawrence Lodge No. 257, Antioch Church, Smith county, post office Tyler --------Jesse Morris

Milford Lodge No. 262, Milford, Ellis county --------Champe Carter, Sr.

Whitesboro' Lodge No. 263, Whitesboro', Grayson county --------Sevier Shannon, J.H. Harrison, R.P. Henry, H.R. Hodges, A. Estel, an E.A. W.M. Richards, an E.A.

Carthage Lodge No. 264, Carthage, Panola county --------Payton W. Clements, an E.A.

Grand View Lodge No. 266, Grand View, Johnson county --------J.T. Mabry, John J. Harrell

Meridian Lodge No. 268, Meridian, Bosque county --------King Harvick, J.W. Smith, I.W. Harrall

Pilot Point Lodge No. 270, Pilot Point, Denton county --------Benj McAdams, R.B. Vermillion

Phoenix Lodge No. 275, Weatherford, Parker county --------Abram Fain

Mountain Lodge No. 277, Burleson Springs, Williamson county, post office Liberty Hill --------B.L. Renick, Marshall Vaught

Brownwood Lodge No. 279, Brownwood, Brown county --------Z.T. McKinnis

Winchester Lodge No. 282, Winchester, Fayette county --------A.T. Jenkins, J.M. Walker

Pleasanton Lodge No. 283, Pleasanton, Atascosa county --------Pleas Childress

Eastern Star Lodge No. 284, Centralia, Trinity county, post office Pennington --------Isaac Moore, T.C. Craig

Beaumont Lodge No. 286, Beaumont, Jefferson county --------James M. Long

Stonewall Lodge No. 287, Stonewall, Nacogdoches county --------J.G. Blackburn

Tyler Prairie Lodge No. 290, Pennington, Trinity county --------William Earl

Kimball Lodge No. 292, Kimball, Bosque county --------L.P. Strang

Mars Hill Lodge No. 293, Emory, Rains county --------John A. Allred, W.G. McGee, J.D. McKey, a F.C.; T.J. Kerr, an E.A.

Nathan Corley Lodge No. 294, Magnolia Springs, Jasper county --------W.N. Smith

Scyene Lodge No. 295, Scyene, Dallas county --------Thomas E. Corcoran

Salado Lodge No. 296, Salado, Bell county --------W.H. Garrette

Tucker Lodge No. 297, Galveston, Galveston county --------J.L. Hill; M.T. English, an E.A.

Navasota Lodge No. 299, Navasota, Grimes county --------W.J. Peterson, E.D. Johnson, J.Y. Matthews (Worshipful Master elect)

Live Oak Lodge No. 304, Live Oak Academy, Hays county, post office Mountain City --------T.D. Robertson

Littleton Fowler Lodge No. 305, Hemphill, Sabine county --------N. Hayden, an E.A.
G.W. Foster Lodge No. 306, Nelsonville, Austin county --------J.D. Dixon, W.D. King, an E.A., D.F. Ward, an E.A.
Shiloh Lodge No. 307, Shiloh Hall, Hunt county, post office Lone Oak --------H.C, Stilwell, H.W. Boggs
Hull's Store Lodge No. 309, Woods, Panola county --------A. Knight
Red Rock Lodge No. 310, Red Rock, Bastrop county --------J.S. Sorrell, W.F. Waterson
Zion Lodge No. 313, Stonewall Jackson Institute, Grimes county, post office Iola --------John E. Horton, Richard Trant, a F.C.
Alvarado Lodge No. 314, Alvarado, Johnson county --------Samuel Jack, Leroy Richardson, H.M. Tarrence
Cleburne Lodge No. 315, Cleburne, Johnson county, post office Noland's River --------T.L. Bennett, Moses Ashbrooks
Palo Pinto Lodge No. 319, Palo Pinto, Palo Pinto county --------J.B. Veale
Fort Richardson Lodge No. 320, Jacksboro, Jack county --------J.B. Edwards
Prairieville Lodge No. 322, Prairieville, Kaufman county --------J.M. Adams
Victoria Lodge No. 326, Victoria, Victoria county --------E.H. Gaylord
Gray Lodge No. 329, Houston, Harris county --------Wm. C. Wilson
Carolina Lodge No. 330, Lodge Hall, Falls county, post office West Falls --------O.C. Gardner, an E.A.
Mansfield Lodge No. 331, Mansfield, Tarrant county --------Mordecai F. Holland, Calvin Wyatt
Greenville Lodge No. 335, Greenville, Hunt county --------T.T. McDonald
Florence Lodge No. 338, Florence, Williamson county --------Nathan Vaughan
Fish Creek Lodge No. 344, Marysville, Cook county --------J.S. McGarity, M.L. Marshall
Jim Truitt Lodge No. 345, Willow Grove, Shelby county --------John May
Bremond Lodge No. 350, Bremond, Robertson county --------W.C. Boone
Etam Lodge No. 353, Hempstead, Waller county --------D.S. Allen, John Brook, Jr., M.L. Fulton
Groesbeck Lodge No. 354, Groesbeck, Limestone county --------E.E. Jennings, G.W. Seawright
Clinton Lodge No. 360, Clifton, Bosque county --------H. Tellison, R. Frazier
Sand Spring Lodge No. 365, Sand Spring, Wood county, post office Hawkins --------J.B. Haney, R.P. McCorkerel
Salem Lodge No. 368, Thigpen's Gin, Washington county, post office Ledbetter, Fayette county --------L. Robinson, J.H. Phillips, a F.C.
Ennis Lodge No. 369, Ennis, Ellis county --------G.W. Derden
Ovilla Lodge No. 370, Ovilla, Ellis county --------H.H. Ware
Eureka Lodge No. 371, Veal's Station, Parker county --------J. Pell Matlock
Fannin Lodge No. 374, Ransom Butler's, Fannin county, post office Orangeville --------W.P. Moore

Station Creek Lodge No. 376, Station Creek, Coryell county, post office Comanche Springs, McLennan county --------W.H. Perry, W. Davis
Bald Prairie Lodge No. 387, Bald Prairie, Robertson county, post office Englewood --------Z.H. Farmer
LaFayette Lodge No. 388, LaFayette, Upshur county --------B.R. Bennett
Beckville Lodge No. 389, Beckville, Panola county --------Thomas Farrow
Middletown Lodge No. 391, Christian Church, Goliad county, post office Weesatche --------J.N. Lee
Reevesville Lodge No. 396, Reevesville, Grayson county --------C.W. Thomas
Elk Horn Lodge No. 402, Stiles' Schoolhouse, Red River county, post office Annona --------W.J. Dinwiddle
Lone Star Lodge No. 403, Denison, Grayson county --------John S. Day
Jewett Lodge U.D., Jewett, Leon county --------J.L. Jeter

TEXAS MASONIC DEATHS WITH SELECTED BIOGRAPHICAL SKETCHES

RETURNS OF LODGES FOR THE MASONIC YEAR
A.D. 1875, A.L. 5875
DEATHS

Holland Lodge No.1, Houston, Harris county --------Peter W. Gray, H. Burleth, an E.A.
Milam Lodge No. 2, Nacogdoches, Nacogdoches county --------H. Muckleroy
St. Johns Lodge No. 5, Columbia, Brazoria county --------F. Vogel
Harmony Lodge No. 6, Galveston, Galveston county --------Wm. T. Austin, Wm. Brown, Wm. H. Hays, John C. Walter, A.H. Edey, M.T. Olde, E.A.'s
Austin Lodge No. 12, Austin, Travis county --------S.B. Brush
Constantine Lodge No. 13, Bonham, Fannin county --------J.S. Williams, Wm. Watkins, C.L. Luper, E.A.'s
Trinity Lodge No. 14, Livington, Polk county --------Nathaniel Bailey, Jas B. Williams
Friendship Lodge No. 16, Clarksville, Red River county --------A.E. Thompson, T.J. Tucker, F.C.
Orphans' Friend Lodge No. 17, Anderson, Grimes county --------James E. Tidwell
Forrest Lodge No. 19, Hunstville, Walker county --------H.B. Baldwin, J.H. Banton
Graham Lodge No. 20, Brenham, Washington county --------August Seelhorst
Lothrop Lodge No. 21, Crockett, Houston county --------Riley J. Blair, Walters Beeson, an E.A.
Marshall Lodge No. 22, Marshall, Harrison county --------S. Mamlok, W.W. Nesbitt
Clinton Lodge No. 23, Henderson, Rusk county --------F.M. Buckalew, Mayer Leperman, an E.A.
Montgomery Lodge No. 25, Montgomery, Montgomery county --------F.H. Womack
Paris Lodge No. 27, Paris, Lamar county --------A. Travelstead, Jas. J. Walker
Gonzales Lodge No. 30, Gonzales, Gonzales county --------J.W. Stell. J.J. Conner, F.A. Kellman, J.W. Carroll, John Fuller, G. Hubert, W.P. Matthews, E.A.'s
Palestine Lodge No. 31, Palestine, Anderson county --------John Montgomery
LaFayette Lodge No. 34, LaGrange, Fayette county --------H. Renick, T.W. Yates
Lavaca Lodge No. 36, Lavaca, Calhoun county --------James Graham
Mount Moriah Lodge No. 37, Cold Springs, San Jacinto county --------J.S. Cleveland, R.D. Haden
Jefferson Lodge No. 38, Jefferson, Marion county --------W.R. Bradley, J.A. Crump, A. Bradshaw, an E.A.
Leona Union Lodge No. 39, Leona, Leon county --------J.J. Pope
Alamo Lodge No. 44, San Antonio, Bexar county --------J.B. Hall, S.G. Newton, G.B. Torrey

67

Eucid Lodge No. 45, Rusk, Cherokee county --------S.J. Lewis, J.D. Martin, A.J. Dulaney, A.J. Copeland

St. Johns Lodge No. 51, McKinney, Collin county --------Robert A. Baaird, T.L. Rudolph

Tannehill Lodge No. 52, Dallas, Dallas county --------Jno. T. Ault, E. Horton, Geo. W. Stevenson

St. Johns Lodge No. 53, Tyler, Smith county --------N.P. Moore

Grand Bluff Lodge No. 54, Grand Bluff, Panola county --------Thomas Farrow, M.W. Beck

Warren Lodge No. 56, Caldwell, Burleson county --------Henry J. Nix, William J. Hill, J.M. Haddox

Rocky Mount Lodge No. 63, Overton, Rusk county --------T.B. Mayfield

Joppa Lodge No. 65, Elysian Fields, Harrison county --------W.W. Westmoreland, John Rudd, A.W. Tucker

Hubert Lodge No. 67, Chappell Hill, Washington county --------L.H. Ogbourn, an E.A.

Caledonia Lodge No. 68, Columbus, Colorado county --------W.S. Good, E.A.; Harmon Merseberger, E.A.

Temple Lodge No. 70, Mount Pleasant, Titus county --------Josh Stephens

Mt. Vernon Lodge No. 71, Mt. Vernon, Titus county, post office Lone Star--------E.A. Arnold, G.L. Rutherford

Springfield Lodge No. 74, Mexia, Limestone county --------Silas K. Anglin, J.B. Vannandingham, Jno. S. Row, David Bates, an E.A.

Cameron Lodge No. 76, Clinton, De Witt county --------Johnson Henrys

Oasis Lodge No. 79, Dangerfield, Titus county --------J.T. Turntine, William Williams, B.M. Irvin

Murchison Lodge No. 80, Hallettsville, Lavaca county --------J. Douling, H.R. McLean, T.H. Streich, M. Lattim, F.C.

Rio Grande Lodge No. 81, Brownsville, Cameron county --------R.B. Foster, A. Mauk

New Salem Lodge No. 87, New Salem, Rusk county --------B.F. Walker, Samuel Barron

San Gabriel Lodge No. 89, Georgetown, Williamson county --------W.M. McBeth, F.C., Samuel Wilson, E.A., J.C. Damron, E.A.

Waxahachie Lodge No. 90, Waxahachie, Ellis county --------H.D. Marchbanks, J.H. McWhirter, E.W. Rogers

Waco Lodge No. 92, Waco, McLennan county --------F.J. Trusty

Augusta Lodge No. 93, Augusta, Houston county --------Asa Thompson

Goliad Lodge No. 94, Goliad, Goliad county --------E.T. Smith

Colorado Lodge No. 96, Webberville, Travis county --------J.B. Banks

Newburn Lodge No. 97, Buena Vista, Shelby county --------R.E. Jones

Danville Lodge No. 101, Kilgore, Gregg county --------T.M. Leach, W.W. Thompson, an E.A.

Unity Lodge No. 102, Moscow, Polk county --------J.D. Wilson

Fairfield Lodge No. 103, Fairfield, Freestone county --------T.L. Wylie, J.B. Johnson, L.R. Wortham

Guadalupe Lodge No. 109, Seguin, Guadalupe county --------Jeptha Lay

Bloomfield Lodge No. 112, Kauffman, Kauffman county --------J.D. Belew, T.M. Ward

Prairie Lee Lodge No. 114, Prairie Lea, Caldwell county --------Geo. F. Raymer, Thos. Mooney

Travis Lodge No. 117, Sherman, Grayson county --------David Lambert

Starr Lodge No. 118, Starrville, Smith county --------S.B. Haney

Texana Lodge No. 123, Texana, Jackson county --------B.B. Pearce, R.R. Berryhill, an F.C.; J.T. Pearce, an E.A.; R. Spinks, an E.A.; J.M. Stanton

Baylor Lodge No. 125, Gay Hill, Washington county --------R.E.B. Baylor

Madison Lodge No. 126, Orange, Orange county --------Wm. Smith

Brazos Union Lodge No. 129, City of Bryan, Brazos county --------Z.P. Pearson, Peter M. Brown, J.T. Cyrus, James Walker, Wm. McIntosh, J.K. Smith, an E.A.

El Paso Lodge No. 130, El Paso, El Paso county --------Simeon Hart

Keechi Lodge No. 140, Centreville, Leon county --------Harmon St.John

Castillian Lodge No. 141, Canton, Van Zandt county --------D.C. Tyler

Bethesda Lodge No. 142, Gilmer, Upshur county --------M.T. Sanford

Ochiltree Lodge No. 143, Melrose, Nacogdoches county --------B.F. Rector, L.V. Price

Fort Worth Lodge No. 148, Fort Worth, Tarrant county --------J.C. Gambrell, T.A. Hamby

Marlin Lodge No. 152, Marlin, Falls county --------A.G. Perry, L.G. Scogin

Eclectic Lodge No. 153, their Hall, near Warren, Fannin county --------W.R. Chaffin, John Girard

Cotton Gin Lodge No. 154, Cotton Gin, Freestone county -------R.R. Echols, W.G. McInnis

Hickory Hill Lodge No. 156, Hickory Hill, Cass county -------- W.W. Morris

East Trinity Lodge No. 157, Rockwall, Rockwall county --------G.L. Tucker

Wm. M. Taylor Lodge No. 158, Garden Valley, Smith county --------J.P. Arthur

McClellan Lodge No. 159, Union Hill, Washington county --------W.L. Murray, F.W. McGuire

Athens Lodge No. 165, Athens, Henderson county --------P.T. Tannehill, B.F. Iley, an E.A.

Belton Lodge No. 166, Belton, Bell county --------A.J. Powers

Kentucky Lodge No. 167, Kentucky Town, Grayson county --------Jno. W. Chenoweth, T.E. Montgomery, Jas. T. Lackey

Monroe Lodge No. 168, Madisonville, Madison county --------T.W. Mitchell

San Anders Lodge No. 170, Cameron, Milam county --------John Joseph Thomma, Erino Westbrook

Corsicana Lodge No. 174, Corsicana, Navarro county --------J.L. Halbert, Joseph White, L.H. Newburgh

St. Paul's Lodge No. 177, Port Sullivan, Milam county --------Blanton Streetman, W.H. Varner

Hardaman Lodge No. 179, Plum Creek, Caldwell county --------B.P. Crenshaw

Hopkins Lodge No. 180, Blackjack Grove, Hopkins county --------O.C. Mitchell

Post Oak Island Lodge No. 181, Post Oak Island, Williamson county --------J.L. Armstrong

White Oak Lodge No. 185, Pine Forest, Hopkins county --------F.R. Turner

Tyrian Lodge No. 187, Sabine Pass, Jefferson county --------John Gibney, J.G.D. Murray

Refugio Lodge No. 190, Refugio, Refugio county --------D.J. Holland

Cusseta Lodge No. 192, Cusseta, Cass county --------John M. Fleming

Leon Lodge No. 193, Lodge Room, Bell county, post office Moffettown --------S.P. Kirk

Aquilla Lodge No. 196, Hillsboro, Hill county --------J.B. Williams

Gatesville Lodge No. 197, Gatesville, Coryelle county --------D. McCarty

Tyre Lodge No. 198, Tennessee Colony, Anderson county --------J.R. Brown

Denton Lodge No. 201, Lewisville, Denton county --------Joseph Knight, D.J. McCombs, Cas. Hall

James A. Baker Lodge No. 202, Ebenzer Baptist church, Walker county --------Jack Valentine

Pine Lodge No. 203, Edom, Van Zandt county --------J.H. Ross, J.N. White

Frank Sexton Lodge No. 206, Pittsburg, Camp county --------C.W. Crawford

McMahon Lodge No. 208, Lockhart, Caldwell county --------P.B. Chiles, G.W. Shoaf, C.D. Crenshaw

Gainesville Lodge No. 210, Gainesville, Cook county --------Dudley Horn

Farmersville Lodge No. 214, Farmersville, Collin county --------Allen Hall, G.B. Robinson

Blanco Lodge No. 216, Blanco, Blanco county -------Bennett Bass

Stanfield Lodge No. 217, Denton, Denton county --------C.T. Welse

Dresden Lodge No. 218, Dresden, Navarro county --------N.F. Jones, J.T. Spann

Bright Star Lodge No. 221, Sulphur Springs, Hopkins county --------Wm. M. Ewing, T.D. Cullors

Bellville Lodge No. 223, Bellville, Austin county --------G. Hillbolt, an E.A.

San Saba Lodge No. 225, San Saba, San Saba county --------S.A. Houston, Saml Epley

Round Rock Lodge No. 227, Round Rouck, Williamson county --------A.G. Collyer

Newport Lodge No. 228, Newport, Walker county --------E. Wilkerson, Nathaniel West, R.E. Harris, an E.A.

Lampasas Lodge No. 232, Lampasas, Lampasas county --------J.M. Hill

Eutaw Lodge No. 233, Kosse, Limestone county --------J.R. Pringle

Relief Lodge No. 236, Wadeville, Navarro county --------A.M. Kelso, R.H. Ware, D.F. Ramsey

Gamble Lodge No. 244, Bastrop, Bastrop county --------Abner Jones, W.J. Cain, J.B. Wiggins

Sulphur Bluff Lodge No. 246, Sulphur Bluff, Hopkins county --------John Stanley

Adah Ziliah Lodge No. 247, Millican, Brazos county --------N.R. Goin, S.F. Garner

Sexton Lodge No. 251, Milam, Sabine county --------Harris Vickers

Hondo Lodge No. 252, New Fountain, Medina county --------W.A. Patterson, an E.A.

Beeville Lodge No. 261, Beeville, Bee county --------William Miller, G.W. McClanahan, T.J. Smith, J.L. Smith

Milford Lodge No. 262, Milford, Ellis county --------M. Dickson, J.A. Allen

Whitesboro' Lodge No. 263, Whitesboro', Grayson county --------Wm. McClain, Thos. Newton, Wm. Roberts

Carthage Lodge No. 264, Carthage, Panola county --------Jos. J. Wilson

Grayson Lodge No. 265, Lost Prairie, Limestone county --------J.H. Woodward

Grand View Lodge No. 266, Grand View, Johnson county --------J.M. Boyd, Jos. Grahm, T.D. Savage

Stephenville Lodge No. 267, Stephenville, Erath county --------J.T. Dooley, James McCarrty, an F.C.

Dixie Lodge No. 272, Zavala or Troupe Station, Smith county --------C.E. Childers, J.D. Eidom

Phoenix Lodge No. 275, Weatherford, Parker county --------J.M. Cole, A.H. Green

Brownwood Lodge No. 279, Brownwood, Brown county --------C.M. Webb

J.D. Giddings Lodge No. 280, Giddings, Lee county --------Eli Jones

Pleasanton Lodge No. 283, Pleasanton, Atascosa county --------E.B. Harrison, A.H. Kean, J.A. Cocke, Isaac S. Wright

Eastern Star Lodge No. 284, Centralia, Trinity county, --------R.R. Taylor, J.D. Turner, Isham Stanley

Beaumont Lodge No. 286, Beaumont, Jefferson county --------W.T. Simmons

Stonewall Lodge No. 287, Stonewall, Nacogdoches county --------D.H. Hughes, Jas. E. Wallace

Grapevine Lodge No. 288, Grapevine, Tarrant county --------W.L. Jones, Davis Stennt, an E.A.

Harmony Hill Lodge No. 289, Harmony Hill, Rusk county --------J.M. Chamness, Tatum Menifee

Mars Hill Lodge No. 293, Emory, Rains county --------Geo. McCravey

Scyene Lodge No. 295, Scyene, Dallas county --------H.C. Caldwell, an E.A.

Salado Lodge No. 296, Salado, Bell county --------W.T. Etheridge

Tucker Lodge No. 297, Galveston, Galveston county --------W.W. Davidson, Wm. Brown, W.S. White, W.C. Estelle, an E.A

Navasota Lodge No. 299, Navasota, Grimes county --------P.B. Perry

Cedar Creek Lodge No. 300, Tryon Church, Brazos county --------L. Lockridge, H. Bowden, Wm. King, an F.C.

Blackwell Lodge No. 302, Charleston, Delta county --------Joel Blackwell

Shiloh Lodge No. 307, Shiloh, Hunt county --------Jo. Babb, an E.A.

Cedar Grove Lodge No. 308, Cedar Grove, Kaufman county --------Casper McBride, Jesse Kerkendall, W. Sullivan, an F.C.

Red Rock Lodge No. 310, Red Rock, Bastrop county --------Wm. Awalt
Bryant Station Lodge No. 311, Bryant Station, Milam county --------G.W. Chatten, John H. Cook
Wm. Foster Lodge No. 312, Fosterville, Anderson county --------J.C. Gerdner, E.A.; J.M. Williams, W.T. Brown, S.P. Lewis, J.R. Goddley
Alvarado Lodge No. 314, Alvarado, Johnson county --------Wm. Rogers
Cleburne Lodge No. 315, Cleburne, Johnson county --------T.H. Riser, G.J. Reeves
Comanche Lodge No. 316, Comanche, Comanche county --------A.L. Stone, Jo. G. Hardin
David Lodge No. 318, David's Mill, Freestone county --------L.A. Gilliland, M.R.D. Richards
Palo Pinto Lodge No. 319, Palo Pinto, Palo Pinto county --------G.N. Lasater, F.C.
Cedar Bayou Lodge No. 321, Cedar Bayou, Chambers county --------L.R. Sherman, R. Weedin
Prairieville Lodge No. 322, Prairieville, Kaufman county --------J.T. Allen
Rockport Lodge No. 323, Rockport, Aransas county --------M. Abrams, Leon Lehman, an F.C.
Victoria Lodge No. 326, Victoria, Victoria county --------Alfred Farrer, An E.A.
Brazoria Lodge No. 327, Brazoria, Brazoria county --------S.S. Perry, Alanson Taylor
Mansfield Lodge No. 331, Mansfield, Tarrant county --------D.G. Hodges, Isaiah Gardiner, D.S. Bloodworth
Cream Level Lodge No. 332, Cream Level, Van Zandt county --------E.W. Gebbs
Birdston Lodge No. 333, Birdston, Navarro county --------H.W. Pickering
Greenville Lodge No. 335, Greenville, Hunt county --------H.C. Hale
J.R. Gurley Lodge No. 337, Waco, McLennan county --------C.M. Harvey
Davilla Lodge No. 340, Davilla, Milam county --------A.J. Whitefield
Fish Creek Lodge No. 344, Marysville, Cooke county --------J.M. Allen
Wm. C. Young Lodge No. 349, Elizabeth, Denton county --------Harvy Cox
Bremond Lodge No. 350, Bremond, Robertson county --------Wm. Bingham, an F.C.
Pottersville Lodge No. 351, Pottersville, Limestone county --------W.S. Woods
Groesbeck Lodge No. 354, Groesbeck, Limestone county --------J.J. Stewart, W.F. McCrory, J.H. Seawright
Prairie Lodge No. 355, Prairie Valley, Hill county --------J.D. Fitzgerrold
Tehuacana Lodge No. 358, Tehuacana, Limestone county --------Doak Lowry
Patrick Lodge No. 359, Owensville, Robertson county --------Z.H. Farmer
Oenaville Lodge No. 363, Oenaville, Bell county --------R.S. Spencer
Eagle Lodge No. 369, Eagle Lake, Colorado county --------Isaac J. Frazar
Brushy Lodge No. 367, Brushy Hall, Panola county --------Abijah D. Davis
Ennis Lodge No. 369, Ennis, Ellis county --------Isaiah King
Eureka Lodge No. 371, Veal's Station, Parker county --------W.P. Gregg

Dexter Lodge No. 372, Dexter City, Cooke county --------J.G. Crabtree
Northern Lodge No. 377, Nash's Mill, Lamar county --------J.F. Boyet
Morales Lodge No. 378, Morales, Jackson county --------C.C. Moore
Halesboro Lodge No. 381, Halesboro, Red River county --------John Ashley
Bald Prairie Lodge No. 387, Bald Prairie, Robertson county --------P.G. Milstead, Z.H. Founer
Paloxy Lodge No. 393, Lodge Room, Hood county --------Jn. Byram
Reevesville Lodge No. 396, Reevesville, Grayson county --------J.M. Walker
Elk Horn Lodge No. 402, Stiles' School House, Red River county --------D.D. Hocott
Rockdale Lodge No. 414, Rockdale, Milam county --------E. Westbrooks
Bolivar Lodge No. 418, Bolivar, Denton county --------E.W. Bentley
Coltharp Lodge No. 419, Coltharp, Houston county --------G.G. Oliver
Rambo Lodge No. 426, Lodge Room, Travis county, post office Onion Creek --------W.A. Townsley
Golden Lodge No. 437, Golden Drain Bayou, Rusk county --------John Boardman, S.R. Higgs
Coryell Lodge No. 442, Jonesboro, Coryell county --------Daniel McCarley
DeKalb Lodge U.D., DeKalb, Bowie county --------E.T. Birdwell

RETURNS OF LODGES
FOR THE MASONIC YEAR A.D. 1876, A.L. 5876
DEATHS

Holland Lodge No. 1, City of Houston, Harris county --------Wm. P. Massey, John Henry Ivey.

St. Johns Lodge No. 5, Columbia, Brazoria county --------W.R. Shuford

Harmony Lodge No. 6, Galveston, Galveston county --------The following Entered Apprentices have been dropped, their whereabouts unknown; supposed to be dead: Miguel Arxe, Henry Bartlett, C.W. Caldwell, Thomas Carrington, Thos. B. Cook, R.H. Dugan, J.M. Keys, A. King, J.W. Kirby, John Lawne, C.L. Martin, Asa Robbins, J.G. Simmons, George Smith, W.B. Steppie, W.E. Torbert

Austin Lodge No. 12, Austin, Travis county --------J.P. Cope

Constantine Lodge No. 13, Bonham, Fannin county --------S.J. Spotts, J.A. Edwards

Friendship Lodge No. 16, Clarksville, Red River county --------W.C. Cheatham

Forest Lodge No. 19, Huntsville, Walker county --------George Fearhake

Lothrop Lodge No. 21, Crockett, Houston county --------John Blair

Jefferson Lodge No. 38, Jefferson, Marion county --------H.A. Cutrer

Leona Union Lodge No. 39, Leona, Leon county --------A.J. Ross

Alamo Lodge No. 44, San Antonio, Bexar county --------A.J. Kern, Jas. N. Fisk

Euclid Lodge No. 45, Rusk, Cherokee county --------Wright Cossey, Jesse M. Carter

St. Johns Lodge No. 51, McKinney, Collin county --------Z.T. Chandler, R.B. Higgins

St. Johns Lodge No. 53, Tyler, Smith county --------Joseph Valentine

Grand Bluff Lodge No. 54, Grand Bluff, Panola county --------J.D. Lyon, W.S. Bunyard

Joppa Lodge No. 65, Elysian Fields, Harrison county --------W. Tiller

Hubert Lodge No. 67, Chappell Hill, Washington county --------R.W. Chappell

Springfield Lodge No. 74, Mexia, Limestone county --------Alfred Hicks

Concord Lodge No. 77, Concord Church, Harrison county, post office Jonesville --------J.L. Bedell

Terrell Lodge No. 83, Alto, Cherokee county --------George W. Knox

Indianola Lodge No. 84, Indianola, Calhoun county --------Charles B. Burbank

Tusculum Lodge No. 86, Pine Tree Church, Gregg county, post office Longview --------A.T. Castleberry

New Salem Lodge No. 87, New Salem, Rusk county --------Nathan Wallace

Waxahachie Lodge No. 90, Waxahachie, Ellis county --------William Kerr

Colorado Lodge No. 96, Webberville, Travis county --------S.B. Harris, an E.A.

Fairfield Lodge No. 103, Fairfield, Freestone county --------H.C. Jennings

San Jacinto Lodge No. 106, Willis, Montgomery county --------J.C. Herring, Richard Williams, Sr.

Jacksonville Lodge No. 108, Jacksonville, Cherokee county --------F.M. Inge

TEXAS MASONIC DEATHS WITH SELECTED BIOGRAPHICAL SKETCHES

Travis Lodge No. 117, Sherman, Grayson county --------James A. Maupin
Starr Lodge No. 118, Starrville, Smith county --------John Wilson
Brazos Union Lodge No. 129, Bryan, Brazos county --------J.A. Semones
Retreat Lodge No. 133, Courtney, Grimes county --------J.M. Cabeen
Bethel Lodge No. 134, Ladonia, Fannin county --------W.P. Sanders
Pierce Lodge No. 144, Calvert, Robertson county --------James Murtland
Planters Lodge No. 147, Plantersville, Grimes county --------T.H. Brown, W.T.
Nobles
Eclectic Lodge No. 153, Savoy, Fannin county --------S.H. Burckhart
East Trinity Lodge 157, Rockwall, Rockwall county --------N.L. Daisey
Wm. M. Taylor Lodge No. 158, Garden Valley, Smith county --------Willis Jones
Lancaster Lodge No. 160, Lancaster, Dallas county --------Jason Case
Athens Lodge No. 165, Athens, Henderson county --------John C. Goodgame
Alamita Lodge No. 200, Helena, Karnes county --------John Rosser
Denton Lodge 201, Lewisville, Denton county --------T.J. Lott
Pine Lodge No. 203, Edom, Van Zandt county --------O.B. Belcher
Gainesville Lodge No. 210, Gainesville, Cooke county --------J.R. Hobbs, ___
Queen, John Howeth
Farmersville Lodge No. 214, Farmersville, Collin county --------Joe Stanford
Stanfield Lodge No. 217, Denton, Denton county --------G.A. Grissom
Millville Lodge No. 219, Millville, Rusk county --------A. Gibson, J.F. Robertson
Onion Creek Lodge No. 220, Lodge Room, Travis county, post office Austin
--------N. H. Watrous
Sulphur Springs Lodge No. 221, Sulphur Springs, Hopkins county --------D.W.
Manley
Butler Lodge No. 224a, Butler, Freestone county --------John T. Gill
Eutaw Lodge No. 233, Kosse, Limestone county --------C.W. Bratton, Robt.
Vincent
Torbert Lodge No. 241, Turner's Point, Kaufman county --------J.A. Inabnit
Adah Zillah Lodge No. 247, Millican, Brazos county --------Wesley Brown,
Joseph Cunningham, A. Hanneman
A. Jackson Lodge No. 249, Pine Town, Cherokee county, post office Rusk
--------S.M. Johnson
Grayson Lodge No. 265, Lost Prairie, Limestone county, post office Personville
--------C.W. Moody
Grand View Lodge No. 266, Grand View, Johnson county --------Jerry Files
Meridian Lodge No. 268, Meridian, Bosque county --------H.L. Little
Pilot Point Lodge No. 270, Pilot Point, Denton county --------J.C. Hunton, D.B.
Burks
Phoenix Lodge No. 275, Weatherford, Parker county --------L.L. Highton
Grapevine Lodge No. 288, Grapevine, Tarrant county --------John Weddle
Tyler Prairie Lodge No. 290, Pennington, Trinity county --------John H. Johnson
John Armstrong Lodge No. 291, Lodge Room on Hog Creek, Bosque county,
post office Valley Mills --------W.B. Turnipseed
Salado Lodge No. 296, Salado, Bell county --------J.E. Ferguson

Tucker Lodge No. 297, Galveston, Galveston county --------Jos. E. Peterson

Navasota Lodge No. 299, Navasota, Grimes county --------A.H. Waugh

Cedar Creek Lodge No. 300, Tryon Church, Brazos county, post office Bryan --------J.W. White, W. Hammond

Starksville Lodge No. 303, Starksville, Lamar county --------E.B. St.Clair, M. Harmon, M. Lambeth, Nat Clarke

Red Rock Lodge No. 310, Red Rock, Bastrop county --------G.W. Hendrix

Cleburne Lodge No. 315, Cleburne, Johnson county --------John B. Wright

Cedar Bayou Lodge No. 321, Cedar Bayou, Harris county --------Joseph B. Eaton

Evergreen Lodge No. 325, Oakville, Live Oak county --------H. Williams, D. Haynie

Brazoria Lodge No. 327, Brazoria, Brazoria county --------Charles Holmes

Gray Lodge No. 329, Houston, Harris county --------Jno. T. Whitfield

Carolina Lodge No. 330, Lodge Hall, Falls county, post office Landrum --------R. Morris Key

Greenville Lodge No. 335, Greenville, Hunt county --------J.J. Peters

J.H. Gurley Lodge No. 337, Waco, McLennan county --------J.F. Axling, G.A. Muller

E.M. Wilder Lodge No. 339, Power's Chapel, Falls county, post office Wilderville --------W.R. Dunlap, C.C. Cummiskey, a F.C.

Davilla Lodge No. 340, Davilla, Milam county ------H.I. Hennington, N.W. Crane

San Marcos Lodge No. 342, San Marcos, Hays county --------J.W. Stovall

Tom Anderson Lodge No. 346, Fraimville, Burleson county --------J.W. McCullough

Tulip Lodge No. 348, Tulip, Fannin county, post office Bonham --------K.P. Martin, a F.C.

Collins Lodge No. 356, Cothren's Hall, Lamar county, post office Paris --------L. Snowden

Brushy Lodge No. 367, Brushy Hall, Panola county, post office Walnut Hill --------John L. Murphey

Middleton Lodge No. 391, Christian Church, Goliad county, post office Weesatche --------J.A. Middleton

Granbury Lodge No. 392, Granbury, Hood county --------J.V. Ross

Elk Horn Lodge No. 402, Stiles School House, Red Riiver county, post office Annona --------M.D. Kennedy

Smyrna Lodge No. 407, Stephensville, Fannin county, post office Dodd City --------A.J. McGee

Oak Grove Lodge No. 408, The Grove, Coryell county --------J.A. Touchstone

Bolivar Lodge No. 418, Bolivar, Denton county --------G.A. Grissom

Rising Star Lodge No. 429, Centerpoint, Kerr county --------Geo. W. Woolls

Hiram Lodge No. 433, Collinsville, Grayson county --------W.A. Stringer

Burlington Lodge No. 440, Burlington, Montague county, post office Spanish Fort --------A.J. Morris

Golindo Lodge No. 451, Golindo, Falls county --------L.E. Hand

RETURNS OF LODGES
MASONIC YEAR A.D. 1877, A.L. 5877
DEATHS

Holland Lodge No. 1, Masonic Temple, Harris county, post office Houston --------E. H. Blake, S.L. Hohenthal, [Sol. L.] Gustav Loeffier, M.B. Abercombie, E.A., W.G. Bell, T.W. McCoombs, E.A.

Red Land Lodge No. 3, San Augustine, San Augustine county --------Thomas P. Payne, I.J. [I.I.] Roberts

St. Johns Lodge No. 5, Columbia, Brazoria county --------N.H. Johns, S.W. Perkins, W.E. Crews

Harmony Lodge No. 6, Galveston, Galveston county --------Wm. Hardy Eddins, John Jackson, Selim Rinker, Isaac Smith Warren, Thomas R. Allen, F.C.; Jacob Block, F.C.

Milam Lodge No. 11, Independence, Washington county --------Reddin Vickers

Austin Lodge No. 12, Austin, Travis county --------Otto Sandahl, W.T. Horne, Joseph Smith, W.B. Price

Constantine Lodge No. 13, Bonham, Fannin county --------M.F. Garrard [Girrard], J. Rogers [J. Rodgers], R.B. Thomas, N.A. Darnall

Trinity Lodge No. 14, Livingston, Polk county --------C.S. Douglass, W.F. Gee, W.H. Shotwell, J.D. Brown, an E.A.

Friendship Lodge No. 16, Clarksville, Red River county --------R.J. Lee, Rubin Gaines

Orphans' Friend Lodge No. 17, Anderson, Grimes county --------Edward Hobbs

Washington Lodge No. 18, Washington, Washington county --------John G. Allen

Forrest Lodge No. 19, Huntsville, Walker county --------H.M. Watkins, Elbert Clower, James A. Cabiness, Thomas R. Lindsey, B. Courtade

Graham Lodge No. 20, Brenham, Washington county --------Casper Witteborg, J.M. Whatley

Lathrop Lodge No. 21, Crockett, Houston county --------James R. Bracken, J.R. Simpson

Marshall Lodge No. 22, Marshall, Harrison county --------David McPhail, [Daniel McPhail] John Munden, [John Murden] R.C. Turner

Clinton Lodge No. 23, Henderson, Rusk county --------J.P. Grigsby, Thomas W. Slaughter

Montgomery Lodge No. 25, Montgomery, Montgomery county --------W.A. Threadgill

Paris Lodge No. 27, Paris, Lamar county --------T.J. Wood, A.E. Simmons, an E.A.

De Witt Clinton Lodge No. 29, Jasper, Jasper county --------Fabian Adams

Gonzales Lodge No. 30, Gonzales, Gonzales county --------D.B. Dillard, James C. Dilworth

Palestine Lodge No. 31, Palestine, Anderson county --------A.G. Campbell, B.F. Parker

LaFayette Lodge No. 34, LaGrange, Fayette county --------Charles Hill, G.T. Haynie, E.A.

Mount Moriah Lodge 37, Cold Springs, San Jacinto county --------Joseph T. Liles [Jos. T. Likes], Robert B. McMurry, Henry Johnson

Leona Union Lodge No. 39, Leona, Leon county --------Wm. B. Middleton

Alamo Lodge No. 44, San Antonio, Bexar county --------A. Kamp

Euclid Lodge No. 45, Rusk, Cherokee county --------W.S. Parks, G.W. Copeland, J.R. Newton

Liberty Lodge No. 48, Liberty, Liberty county --------B.T. Waring, James Rodgers

Tannehill Lodge No. 52, Dallas, Dallas county --------J.R. Conklin, Frederick Moss [Frederick Mass], W.H. Scales, Laz. Weil [Lay Weil]

St. Johns Lodge No. 53, Tyler, Smith county --------W.J. Smith

Grand Bluff Lodge No. 54, Grand Bluff, Panola county --------Edward Lewis

Larissa Lodge No. 57, Larissa, Cherokee county --------John Dewberry

Mt. Enterprise Lodge No. 60, Mt. Enterprise, Rusk county --------Daniel W. Ross

Rocky Mount Lodge No. 63, Overton, Rusk county --------J.M. Wolley [J.M. Walley]

Hubert Lodge No. 67, Chappell Hill, Washington county --------H.G. Rice, A.M.M. Upshaw [A.M.M. Upshur]

Caledonia Lodge No. 68, Columbus, Colorado county --------Asa Townsend

Temple Lodge No. 70, Mount Pleasant, Titus county, post office Titus --------N.C. Paulk, J.D. Dillard

Morton Lodge No. 72, Richmond, Fort Bend county --------S. Gilbert [G. Gilbert]

Springfield Lodge No. 74, Mexia, Limestone county --------Isaac Hendricks

Cameron Lodge No. 76, Yorktown, De Witt county --------J.H. Sikes

Concord Lodge No. 77, Concord, Harrison county, post office Jonesville --------R.D. Peobles [R.D. Peebles]

Murchison Lodge No. 80, Hallettsville, Lavaca county --------A.M. Tandy

Rio Grande Lodge No. 81, Brownsville, Cameron county --------J.M. Bailey, Richard Laycock, [Richard Saycock] Solomon Schwartz

Terrell Lodge No. 83, Alto, Cherokee county --------Daniel Henderson, J.P. Fisher

Tusculum Lodge No. 86, Pine Tree Church, Gregg county, post office Longview --------J.H. Rodgers, an E.A.

New Salem Lodge No. 87, New Salem, Rusk county --------J.F. Wiggins

Andrew Jackson Lodge No. 88, Linden, Cass county --------A.J. Henry, J.W. Griffin

San Gabriel Lodge No. 89, Georgetown, Williamson county --------W.H. Henderson, C.C. Wynne, Daniel Price

Tarrant Lodge No. 91, Lone Star Hall, Hopkins county, post office Birthright --------Wm. Moore

Waco Lodge No. 92, Waco, McLennan county --------O.J. Downs, [P.J. Downs] W.D. Eastland

Augusta Lodge No. 93, Augusta, Houston county --------J.L. Sheridan, F.D. Bodenhamer
Sharon Lodge No. 95, Pine Hill, Rusk county --------J.W. Harris, J.F. Buckner, W.M. Womack, an F.C.
Canton Lodge No. 98, Canton, Smith county, post office Troup --------Thomas W. Bell, W.W. Cooper
Danville Lodge No. 101, Kilgore, Gregg county --------S.S. Barnes, James Berry
Unity Lodge No. 102, Moscow, Polk county --------J.P. Hughs
Kickapoo Lodge No. 105, Kickapoo, Anderson county --------John Miller
Bloomfield Lodge No. 112, Kaufman, Kaufman county --------E.C. Tinnin [E.C. Tennan]
Prairie Lea Lodge No. 114, Prairie Lea, Caldwell county --------Samuel Johnson
Travis Lodge No. 117, Sherman, Grayson county --------J.S. Shackelford
Flora Lodge No. 119, Quitman, Wood county --------S.M. Flournoy [S.M. Floynoy], S.L. Houston
Mt. Hope Lodge No. 121, Mt. Hope, Tyler county, post office Chester --------Thomas J. Stewart
Texana Lodge No. 123, Texana, Jackson county --------T.B. Wilborne, J.T. Schwing, an E.A.
Madison Lodge No. 126, Orange, Orange county --------John V. Woods [John W. Woods]
Brazos Union Lodge No. 129, Bryan, Brazos county --------S.M. Hunter
Retreat Lodge No. 133, Courtney, Grimes county --------Thomas Walker
Bethel Lodge No. 134, Ladonia, Fannin county --------H.E. Stevens
Mount Horeb Lodge No. 137, Gabriel Mills, Williamson county, post office Mahomet, Burnet county --------J.W. Warden
Lexington Lodge No. 138, Lexington, Lee county --------Robert Sykes, W.C. Guthrie
Pierce Lodge No. 144, Calvert, Robertson county --------W.J. Gammill, H.S. Maddox, M.X. Brennan, an E.A.
Winnsborough Lodge No. 146, Winnsboro, Wood county --------H.T. Long
Planters Lodge No. 147, Plantersville, Grimes county --------G.W. Head
Fort Worth Lodge No. 148, Fort Worth, Tarrant county --------Constant Dodson, M.D. McCall
Marlin Lodge No. 152, Marlin, Falls county --------David Barclay
Eclectic Lodge No. 153, Savoy, Fannin county --------L.C. Whedbee, H. Bacon
Spring Hill Lodge No. 155, Spring Hill, Navarro county --------R.C. Key, [B.C. Key] S.S. Wilson, F.M. Onstott [F.M. Oustott]
Wm. M. Taylor Lodge No. 158, Garden Valley, Smith county --------A.J. Scrivner, Sloan McCurly, [McCurly Sloan] an F.C.
McClellan Lodge No. 159, Union Hill, Washington county, post office Burton --------T.R. Nunn
Lancaster Lodge No. 160, Lancaster, Dallas county --------J.W. Hill

Honey Grove Lodge No. 164, Honey Grove, Fannin county --------James Stephens, C.C. Moss

Athens Lodge No. 165, Athens, Henderson county --------James Averitt, J.M. Hatton, H.L. Gilmore, A.J. Larne [A.J. Lorne], an E.A.

Belton Lodge No. 166, Belton, Bell county --------J.M. Moore, R.P. Winnard, J.M. Pope.

San Anders Lodge No. 170, Cameron, Milam county --------Cornelius Homan, Jerre Nabors

Corsicana Lodge No. 174, Corsicana, Navarro county --------J. Cunningham

Hopkins Lodge No. 180, Black Jack Grove, Hopkins county --------W.E. Hazlewood

Post Oak Island Lodge No. 181, Post Oak Island, Williamson county, post office Elgin, Bastrop county --------J.J. Kidd [I.I. Kidd]

Hopkinsville Lodge No. 183, Hopkinsville, Gonzales county, post office Waelder --------J.J.W. Tomlinson, E.S. Allsup

Corpus Christi Lodge No. 189, Corpus Christi, Nueces county --------N.O. Vineyard, George E. Conklin, Geo. H. Lege, Thos. J. Noakes, a F.C.

Lyons Lodge No. 195, Schulenburg, Fayette county --------J.F. Barnette

Gatesville Lodge No. 197, Gatesville, Coryelle county --------R.P. Knowls, [Knowles] J.B. Dillard

Tyre Lodge No. 198, Tennessee Colony, Anderson county --------John Jackson, G.W. Stafford

Alamita Lodge No. 200, Helena, Karnes county --------T.J. Barfield

Pine Lodge No. 203, Edom, Van Zandt county --------Jonathan Ellison, W.J. Channel, J.M. Pate

Frank Sexton Lodge No. 206, Pittsburg, Camp county --------M.F. Cheney, [Cherry] Ebb Botton, [Bolton] M.L. Carswell [M.L. Caswell]

Mantua Lodge No. 209, Mantua, Collin county, post office Van Alstyne --------J.W. Morton, John Wilburn, E.A's

Gainesville Lodge No. 210, Gainesville, Cooke county --------D.L. Hayse, [Hayes] A. Brunson

Science Hill Lodge No. 211, Science Hill, Henderson county, post office Athens --------T.H. Litchfield

Blanco Lodge No. 216, Blanco, Blanco county, post office Blanco City --------Julius W. Herrman, Dudley W. McNatt

Dresden Lodge No. 218, Dresden, Navarro county --------Wm. E. Harper, A.J. Holder

Millville Lodge No. 219, Millville, Rusk county --------J.O. Eddington [J.B. Eddington]

Bellville Lodge No. 223, Bellville, Austin county --------A.E. Kopisch [Kopish]

Miller Lodge No. 224, White Rock, Hunt county --------P.W. Titus, John Stubb

Butler Lodge No. 224a, Butler, Freestone county --------G.W. Yarbro

San Saba Lodge No. 225, San Saba, San Saba county --------J.N. Estep

Brahan Lodge No. 226, La Vernia, Wilson county --------E.J. Peacock

Round Rock Lodge No. 227, Round Rock, Williamson county --------Rev. H.H. Crutcher
Newport Lodge No. 228, Newport, Walker county, post office Riverside --------John Williams, Thomas French
Sampson Lodge No. 231, Lynchburg, Harris county --------John B. Sydnor, James Langley
Lampasas Lodge No. 232, Lampasas, Lampasas county --------L.D. Nichols, W.W. Smith, H.B. Anderson
Eutaw Lodge No. 233, Kosse, Limestone county --------Griffen Bruner
Plano Lodge No. 235, Plano, Collin county --------Felix W. Furgerson
Torbert Lodge No. 241, Turner's Point, Kaufman county --------B.M. Paschall, James McCoulskey
Llano Lodge No. 242, Llano, Llano county --------E.E. Walsh
Gamble Lodge No. 244, Bastrop, Bastrop county --------L. Scarborough
Sulphur Bluff Lodge No. 246, Sulphur Bluff, Hopkins county --------R.O. Finley [R.A. Finley]
Black Point Lodge No. 250, St. Mary's, Refugio county --------John G. Maton
Hondo Lodge No. 252, Hondo Valley, Medina county, post office New Fountain --------S. Cunningham, an F.C.
J.A. Lawrence Lodge 257, Antioch Church, Smith county, post office Tyler --------W.L. Yates, J.S. Coker
Oakland Lodge No. 258, Oakland, Colorado county --------J.B. Cox, Joseph Aldridge
Whitesboro' Lodge No. 263, Whitesboro', Grayson county --------Nat Richerson, William Crenshaw, Hugh Arbuckle, J.F. Norton
Grayson Lodge No. 265, Lost Prairie, Limestone county, post office Personville --------M.V. Herring [M.V. Harrington]
Pleasant Hill Lodge No. 269, Simpsonville, Upshur county --------Benjamin Davis
Pilot Point Lodge No. 270, Pilot Point, Denton county --------Wm. B. Adams
Phoenix Lodge No. 275, Weatherford, Parker county --------Wesley Willett
Harmony Hill Lodge No. 289, Harmony Hill, Rusk county --------B. Willhelm, J.A. Coats, an E.A.
Tyler Prairie Lodge No. 290, Pennington, Trinity county --------I.H. Pennington [J.H. Pennington]
John Armstrong Lodge No. 291, Lodge Room on Hog Creek, Bosque county, post office Valley Mills --------Robert Martin
Mars Hill Lodge No. 293, Emory, Rains county --------J.E. Ray, D.R. Chamber, an F.C.
Tucker Lodge No. 297, Galveston, Galveston county --------J.W. Lang
Moulton Lodge No. 298, Moulton, Lavaca county --------Josiah Power
Navasota Lodge No. 299, Navasota, Grimes county --------W.B. Swann, G.W. Graves
Osage Lodge No. 301, Osage, Colorado county, post office Weimar --------H.S. Coble, Calvin York, [York Calvin] Thomas Slack, Sr.

81

Shiloh Lodge No. 307, Shiloh, Hunt county, post office Lone Oak --------T.C. Davis, [T.O. Davis] D. Rowley, [D. Rawley] W.S. Hart

Bryant Station Lodge No. 311, Bryant Station, Milam county, post office Ad Hall--------Thomas Hardin, an E.A.

William Foster No. 312, Fosterville, Anderson county --------James Williams

Alvarado Lodge No. 314, Alvarado, Johnson county --------William Ramsey, G.A. Bills, Joel Higgins

Cleburne Lodge No. 315, Cleburne, Johnson county --------W.S. Bledsoe

Cedar Bayou No. 321, Cedar Bayou, Harris county --------W.H. Turner

Prairieville Lodge No. 322, Prairieville, Kaufman county --------J.H. Trent, S.A. Reed, B. Reasonover, A.C. Foster, S.C. Barfield, John Long

Bandera Lodge No. 324, Bandera, Bandera county --------J.M. Phillips, S.H. Jones

Perryville Lodge No. 328, Elgin, Bastrop county --------W.B. Standifer

Gray Lodge No. 329, Houston, Harris county --------L.B. Benefield, P. Wallace

Carolina Lodge No. 330, Lodge Hall, Falls county, post office Landrum --------Robt. R. Ollinger [Olinger]

Mansfield Lodge No. 331, Mansfield, Tarrant county --------W. Hancock, Thomas O. Moody, Lewis Pyles, John Coulson

Norton Moses Lodge 336, Bagdad, Williamson county --------S.S. Evans, an E.A.

J.H. Gurley Lodge No. 337, Waco, McLennan county --------J.N. Waitt, N.H. Couger [Conger]

E.M. Wilder Lodge No. 339, Power's Chapel, Falls county, post office Wilderville --------E.M. Wilder [E.M. Welder], W.F. Marshall, S.J. Pruit

Davilla Lodge No. 340, Davilla, Milam county --------J.W. Bryant

San Marcos Lodge No. 342, San Marcos, Hays county --------Edward Burleson

Bowling Lodge No. 343, Marquez, Leon county --------W.L. Chamberlain, G.A. Winn

Fish Creek Lodge No. 344, Marysville, Cooke county --------J.L. Arrendell [Aurundall]

Jim Truit Lodge No. 345, Willow Grove, Shelby county --------S.T. Butler

Tom Anderson Lodge No. 346, Fraimville, Burleson county, post office Gause --------A.R. McGehee

White Rock Lodge No. 347, Masonic Hall, McLennan county, post office Waco -------- Monroe Moore

Bremond Lodge No. 350, Bremond, Robertson county --------T.O. Sampson

Pottersville Lodge No. 351, Pottersville, Limestone county, post office Groesbeck --------H.C. Jackson

Etam Lodge No. 353, Hempstead, Waller county --------R.M. Bozman [Bozeman]

Groesbeck Lodge No. 354, Groesbeck, Limestone county --------M.O. Hubbard

Patrick Lodge No. 359, Owensville, Robertson county, post office Englewood --------J.W. Maris [J.W. Morris]

Clifton Lodge No. 360, Clifton, Bosque county --------G. W. Helm

David Elliott Lodge No. 364, Elliott's Mills, Morris county, post office Clay Hill --------Clem C. Dickson

Sand Spring Lodge No. 365, Sand Spring, Wood county, post office Hawkins --------Oswill Hitt, E. West

Brushy Lodge No. 367, Brushy Hall, Panola county, post office Walnut Hill --------Edward R. Myrick

Ovilla Lodge No. 370, Ovilla, Ellis county --------J.Y. Witherspoon

Fannin Lodge No. 374, Ransom Butler's , Fannin county, post office Orangeville --------J.J. Patton [J.J. Patten]

Station Creek Lodge No. 376, Lodge Room, Coryell county, post office Coke, McLennan county --------Harvey Howard

Northern Star Lodge No. 377, Garrett's Chapel, Lamar county, post office Paris --------R. Thompson

Pleasant Hill Lodge No. 380, Field's Store, Waller county --------George W. Lawrence

Dodge Lodge No. 384, Dodge, Waller county --------Thomas E. Wooten, S.W. Watts

Granbury Lodge No. 392, Granbury, Hood county --------R.A. McKennon [R.A. McKinnan]

Paluxy Lodge No. 393, Lodge-room, Hood county, post office Paluxy --------J.A. Brooks

Frio Lodge No. 399, Frio City, Frio county, post office Frio Town --------A. Allen

Providence Lodge No. 400, Lodge Room, Anderson county, post office Alder Branch --------J.W. Lively

Lone Star Lodge No. 403, Denison, Grayson county --------F.R. Brown

Longview Lodge No. 404, Longview, Gregg county --------J.S. Brice

Artesia Lodge No. 406, Terrell, Kaufman county --------F.A. Dulaney, J.R. Bridges, C.S. Edwards [C.L. Edwards]

Dallas Lodge No. 412, Dallas, Dallas county --------R.C. Patton [R.O. Patten]

Montague Lodge No. 415, Montague, Montague county --------J.E. Berry [James Berry]

South Noland Lodge No. 416, Pleasant Hill, Bell county, post office Belton --------William Berry

Weimar Lodge No. 423, Weimar, Colorado county --------C.M. Brashear

Rising Star Lodge No. 429, Centerpoint, Kerr county --------J.D. Brown

Lee Lodge No. 435, Rhea's Mills, Collin county --------David Doyle

Johnson Station Lodge No. 438, Johnson Station, Tarrant county --------M.T. Coleman

Commerce Lodge No. 439, Commerce, Hunt county, post office Ashland --------D. Henslee, G.W. Keith

Duck Creek Lodge No. 441, Duck Creek, Dallas county , post office Dallas --------Peter Handley

New York Lodge No. 446, New York, Henderson county, post office New York --------James Forester [Forrester]

R.E. Lee Lodge No. 449, Oceola, Hill county, post office Covington --------James Gathings

Hemphill Lodge No. 452, Murfreesborough, Brazos county, post office Macy --------J.T. Quick

Grand Prairie Lodge No. 455, Lodge Room, Tarrant county, post office Birdville --------James Arwine [Arwure]

Palmer Lodge No. 459, Palmer, Ellis county --------F.H. Ledington

Harwood Lodge No. 468, Harwood, Gonzales county --------I.M. Shelton, [J.M. Shelton] W.G. Carpenter

Grapeland Lodge No. 473, Grapeland, Houston county --------John A. Williams

Appear in the Lodge of Sorrow 1877, but not in the Lodge Returns: S.S. Barnett, T.C. Barfield, Z.B. Bennefield, Z. Constade, Dan Dickson, Allen C. Dickson, R.N. Ely, R.P. Garnnard, J.W. Long, H.H. McGeehe, W.C. Hunter, J.O. Hughs, W.T. Hoover, J.T. Henry, J.W. Hathaway, Samuel Henderson, W.E. Hooper, F.M. Jones, M.D. Kummel, H.L. Little, J.M. Monroe, John G. Martin, J.D. McLeod, S.J. Priest, Jesse Raburn, Nat. Richardson, N.O. Yonger, B. Williams, J.C. Dickie, W.G. Caperton, J.H. West

RETURNS OF LODGES
FOR THE MASONIC YEAR
A.D. 1878, A.L. 5878
DEATHS

Holland Lodge No. 1, Held at the Masonic Temple, Harris county, post office City of Houston --------Felix Wolf, H.G. Pannell, B. Tuffly, John Kiddie, Henry Weiner, E.A.

Red Land Lodge No. 3, San Augustine, San Augustine county --------A.J. Price [A.G. Price]

St John's Lodge No. 5, Columbia, Brazoria county --------W.N. Payne, B. Swink

Harmony Lodge No. 6, Galveston, Galveston county --------Louis Gross, Ralph Levy, Henry Schaffter

Austin Lodge No. 12, Austin, Travis county --------A.B. Neumann, T.J. Markley

Constantine Lodge No. 13, Bonham, Fannin county --------John Stephenson

Friendship Lodge No. 16, Clarksville, Red River county --------D.N. Barry

Forrest Lodge No. 19, Huntsville, Walker county --------C.C. Grisham

Graham Lodge No. 20, Brenham, Washington county --------John B. Wilkin

Lathrop Lodge No. 21, Crockett, Houston county --------D.F. Campbell, [D.E. Campbell] E.E. Hail, [E.E. Hall] J.H. Saxon, J.A. Williams

Marshall Lodge No. 22, Marshall, Harrison county --------Thos. J. Kennedy, B. Smalley

Clinton Lodge No. 23, Henderson, Rusk county --------C.A. Smith, Jiles S. Boggess, Jr., Taylor Melton

Montgomery Lodge No. 25, Montgomery, Montgomery county --------J.H. Gant

Paris Lodge No. 27, Paris, Lamar county --------G.W. Wright

De Witt Clinton Lodge No. 29, Jasper, Jasper county --------Edwin Wood, a F.C.

Gonzales Lodge No. 30, Gonzales, Gonzales county --------Amasa Turner

Palestine Lodge No. 31, Palestine, Anderson county --------D.A. Calhoun

LaFayette Lodge No. 34, LaGrange, Fayette county --------John Lincecum

Mount Moriah Lodge No. 37, Cold Springs, San Jacinto county --------E. Baker

Leona Union Lodge No. 39, Leona, Leon county --------E.J. Oden

Alamo Lodge No. 44, San Antonio, Bexar county --------L.S. Owings, an E.A.

Euclid Lodge No. 45, Rusk, Cherokee county --------Robert F. Mitchell, Ira Sturdivant [Sturdevent]

St. Johns Lodge No. 51, McKinney, Collin county --------Peter R. Wallis

Tannehill Lodge 52, Dallas, Dallas county --------Joseph Bovay, [Joseph Bovey] W.L. Dunn, an E.A.; B. Lang, a F.C.; J.C. McConnell

Warren Lodge No. 56, Caldwell, Burleson county --------Wm. Wilkenson, John Johns, Stephen T. Green, John W. Carroll

Larissa Lodge No. 57, Larissa, Cherokee county --------W.B. Campbell, H. Hendon

Mt. Enterprise Lodge No. 60, Mt. Enterprise, Rusk county --------Samuel M. Boles

Rocky Mount Lodge No. 63, Overton, Rusk county --------A.M. Denton

Joppa Lodge No. 65, Elysian Fields, Harrison county --------J.W. Gibson, H.B. Mathews

Chireno Lodge No. 66, Chireno, Nacogdoches county --------Wm. B. Stivers

Hubert Lodge No. 67, Chappell Hill, Washington county --------W.T. Stone, an E.A.; J.P. Billingslea, [S.P. Billingslea] J.W. Chandler

Caledonia Lodge No. 68, Columbus, Colorado county --------Alexander Dunlavy, S.G. Marsey, [S.G. Massey] Josiah Shaw, an E.A.

Boston Lodge No. 69, Boston, Bowie county, post office New Boston --------W.E. Norris, J.C. McCopping

Temple Lodge No. 70, Mount Pleasant, Titus county --------M.L. Shuler

Springfield Lodge No. 74, Mexia, Limestone county --------Reuben Long, Hinton C. Smith

Concord Lodge No. 77, Concord, Harrison county, post office Jonesville --------E.B. Taylor

Murchison Lodge No. 80, Hallettsville, Lavaca county --------H. Holtzelaw [H. Holtzelow]

Indianola Lodge No. 84, Indianola, Calhoun county --------Jessie Blue

Pine Bluff Lodge No. 85, Rock Springs, Freestone county, post office Fairfield --------J.M. Webb

New Salem Lodge No. 87, New Salem, Rusk county --------H.S. Wiggins, [Wiggin] John Harmon

Waxahachie Lodge No. 90, Waxahachie, Ellis county --------N. Oldham, J.F. Reagor [J.T. Reagon]

Tarrant Lodge No. 91, Held at Lone Star Hall, Hopkins county, post office Birthright --------G.F. Smith

Waco Lodge No. 92, Waco, McLennan county --------Micajah Johnson

Colorado Lodge No. 96, Webberville, Travis county --------W. Wood, an E.A.

Fairfield Lodge No. 103, Fairfield, Freestone county --------E. Wallace

San Jacinto Lodge 106, Willis, Montgomery county --------G.W. Johnson, J.B. Redding

Jacksonville Lodge No. 108, Jacksonville, Cherokee county --------J.S. Shoemaker, an E.A.

Guadalupe Lodge No. 109, Seguin, Guadalupe county --------A.B. Moore, T.B. Hood, A.J.L. Sowell, E.T. Rhodes

Bloomfield Lodge No. 112, Kaufman, Kaufman county --------M.W. Sevier, C.C. Nash

Prairie Lea Lodge No. 114, Prairie Lea, Caldwell county --------Luke Allen, John C. Graham

Flora Lodge No. 119, Quitman, Wood county --------W.F. Wellons, Robert Gillom

Mt. Hope Lodge No. 121, Mt. Hope, Tyler county, post office Chester --------J.M. Halmark, [P.M. Hallmark] H.A. Willson, Martin Pascal [Pascal Martin], an E.A

Brazos Union Lodge No. 129, Bryan, Brazos county --------Wm. Davis, Jr., L. Wood, Z.M. Williams

Belmont Lodge No. 131, Belmont, Gonzales county --------A.B. Moore

Retreat Lodge No. 133, Courtney, Grimes county --------G. Stresan

Bethel Lodge No. 134, Ladonia, Fannin county --------Perry Taylor, B.B. Westbrook

Camden Lodge No. 135, Peatown, Gregg county, post office Monroe, Rusk county --------J.T. Holoway, G.T. Prothro, E.A.'s

Newton Lodge No. 136, Burkeville, Newton county --------R.P. Hext [R.P. Hert]

Mount Horeb Lodge No. 137, Gabriel Mills, Williamson county, post office Mahomet, Burnet county --------R.W. McLain, an E.A.; Jas. Ratliff, an E.A., W.C. Riggs, a F.C.

Lexington Lodge No. 138, Lexington, Lee county --------J.D. Middleton

Keechi Lodge No. 140, Centreville, Leon county --------Edward Keeton, G.M. Nash

Castillian Lodge No. 141, Canton, Van Zandt county --------W.B. Moore

Bethesda Lodge No. 142, Gilmer, Upshur county --------Pleasant Boyd, [Boyd Pleasant] J.W. Studevant

Planters Lodge No. 147, Plantersville, Grimes county --------James B. Cato

Fort Worth Lodge No. 148, Fort Worth, Tarrant county --------J.S. Hirshfield, G.F. Parman

Sam Sanford Lodge No. 149, Center, Shelby county --------George V. Lowe

Marlin Lodge No. 152, Marlin, Falls county --------H. Morris, L.A. Bledsoe

Cotton Gin Lodge No. 154, Cotton Gin, Freestone county --------W.H. Smith

Spring Hill Lodge No. 155, Spring Hill, Navarro county --------S.L. Cook

East Trinity Lodge No. 157, Rockwall, Rockwall county --------J.W. Crawley, an E.A.

Wm. M. Taylor Lodge No. 158, Garden Valley, Smith county --------K.P. Thweatt

McClellan Lodge No. 159, Union Hill, Washington county, post office Burton --------L.H. McNelly

Lancaster Lodge No. 160, Lancaster, Dallas county --------E. Elgin, George Vise

Honey Grove Lodge No. 164, Honey Grove, Fannin county --------J.A. Patrick

Athens Lodge No. 165, Athens, Henderson county --------Tandy Howeth, J.E. Thompson

Kentucky Lodge No. 167, Kentucky Town, Grayson county --------M.A. Burton

James F. Taylor Lodge No. 169, Hallville, Harrison county --------J.E. Whitehorn

San Anders Lodge No. 170, Cameron, Milam county --------N.A. Robinson

Mound Prairie Lodge No. 173, Mound Prairie, Anderson county, post office Nechesville --------J.R. Cherry

Corsicana Lodge No. 174, Corsicana, Navarro county --------Isaac Suttle, T.J. Haynes, W.H. Malone, R.A. Watkins, James Harris

St. Paul's Lodge No. 177, Port Sullivan, Milam county --------T.I. Gilbert, Z.D. Cottrell

E.J. Glover Lodge No. 178, Friendship, Marion county, post office Jefferson --------A.K. Allen

Posk Oak Lodge No. 181, Smith Springs, Lee county, post office Elgin, Bastrop county --------W. Fisher, T.J. Hughs, [T.J. Hughes] J.W. Meeks, E.A.'s

Hopkinsville Lodge No. 183, Waelder, Gonzales county --------R.D. Mullen, W.A. Terrell, D.M. Johnson

Hickory Grove Lodge No. 184, Etna, Smith county --------F.M. Williams, N. Alexander, an E.A.

White Oak Lodge No. 185, Pine Forest, Hopkins county, postofice White Oak --------J.R. Moore

Corpus Christi Lodge No. 189, Corpus Christi, Nueces county --------Wm. Gamble, M.L. Levy, an E.A.; W.L. Rogers, [W.L. Rodgers] Robt. Spence, an E.A.

Havanah Lodge No. 191, Douglassville, Cass county --------Abe Heath, J.A. Robinson

Cusseta Lodge No. 192, Cusseta, Cass county --------J.H. McCoy

Lyons Lodge No. 195, Schulenburg, Fayette county --------Alexander Byars, Henry G. Metzger

Gatesville Lodge No. 197, Gatesville, Coryell county --------J.R. Ashby

Denton Lodge No. 201, Lewisville, Denton county --------Josiah Wilkins

James A. Baker Lodge No. 202, Held at Ebenezer Church, Walker county, post office Huntsville --------W.P. Lightsey, [M.P. Lightsey] G.H. Mercer

Mount Calm Lodge No. 204, Mount Calm, Limestone county --------W.S. Oats

Gainesville Lodge No. 210, Gainesville, Cooke county --------J.M. Peery

Blanco Lodge No. 216, Blanco, Blanco county --------S.W. Hyman

Stanfield Lodge No. 217, Denton, Denton county --------Thomas Egan, James L. Stroud [Jno. L. Stroud]

Onion Creek Lodge No. 220, Held at the Lodge Room, Travis county, post office Austin --------L.J. Birdwell, J.W. Laird

Sulphur Springs Lodge No. 221, Sulphur Springs, Hopkins county --------W.W. Lanier

Bellville Lodge No. 223, Bellville, Austin county --------C.H. Faucett

Butler Lodge No. 224a, Butler, Freestone county --------N.W. Keeling

San Saba Lodge No. 225, San Saba, San Saba county --------M.H. Wadsworth

Newport Lodge No. 228, Newport, Walker county, post office Riverside --------W.M. Skein

Eutaw Lodge No. 233, Kosse, Limestone county --------W.P. Pope, T.M. Stephenson

Relief Lodge No. 236, Wadeville, Navarro county --------J.N. Smith

San Felipe Lodge No. 239, San Felipe, Austin county --------D.L. Stokes

Fayetteville Lodge No. 240, Fayetteville, Fayette county --------Jacob F. Dirr, [Jacob F. Dier] Adolph Kauffman

Gamble Lodge No. 244, Bastrop, Bastrop county --------George D. Ruport

Black Point Lodge No. 250, St. Mary's, Refugio county --------Charles Russell, an E.A.
Medina Lodge No. 252, Castroville, Medina county --------G.W. Giza, [G.W. Geza] Samuel Parsons
Homer Lodge No. 254, Homer, Angelina county --------C.H. Ballard
Oakland Lodge No. 258, Oakland, Colorado county --------T.J. Henderson
Milford Lodge No. 262, Milford, Ellis county --------D.W. Cooke [D.W. Cook]
Whitesboro' Lodge No. 263, Whitesboro', Grayson county --------Wm. H. Low, G.B. Hackleman, [H.B. Hackleman] T.J. Rogers [T.J. Rodgers]
Grand View Lodge No. 266, Grand View, Johnson county --------W.S. Quinn, [H.S. Quinn] A.W. Hightower
Stephenville Lodge No. 267, Stephenville, Erath county --------John E. Burroughs
Pilot Point Lodge No. 270, Pilot Point, Denton county --------L.K. Masters [L.T. Masters]
Dixie Lodge No. 272, Troupe Station, Smith county, post office Troupe --------J.F. Kaiser
Brownwood Lodge No. 279, Brownwood, Brown county --------O.H. Kendrick
J.D. Giddings Lodge No. 280, Giddings, Lee county --------S.H. McClellan
Grapevine Lodge No. 288, Grapevine, Tarrant county --------E.M. Jenkins
Tyler Prairie Lodge No. 290, Pennington, Trinity county --------D.W. Steele, J.M. Wilborn
John Armstrong Lodge No. 291, Rock Church, Bosque county, post office Valley Mills --------S.M. Adams, J.T. Vaughan
Tucker Lodge No. 297, Galveston, Galveston county --------Ralph Levy, F.A. Anderson
Moulton Lodge No. 298, Moulton, Lavaca county --------Thomas Walker
Cedar Creek Lodge No. 300, Tryon, Brazos county --------C.D. Owens, an E.A.
Osage Lodge No. 301, Osage, Colorado county, post office Weimar --------F.M. Burford
G.W. Foster Lodge No. 306, Nelsonville, Austin county --------Wm. Z. Dixon, W.T. Miller, an E.A.
Hull's Store Lodge No. 309, Held at Wood's Post office, Panola county, post office Wood's --------R.B. Armstrong
Wm. Foster Lodge No. 312, Fosterville, Anderson county --------M.G. Elkins [M.G. Elkin]
Zion Lodge No. 313, Stonewall Jackson Institute, Grimes county, post office Iola --------B.E. Seals
Cleburne Lodge No. 315, Cleburne, Johnson county --------W.B. Featherston, G.W. Lewis, [G.W. Louis] James H. Killough
Shuler Lodge No. 317, Monthalia, Gonzales county, post office Gonzales --------Joab Shuler
Fort Richardson Lodge No. 320, Jackboro, Jack county --------John C. Bartel, D.W. Patton
Cedar Bayou Lodge No. 321, Cedar Bayou, Harris county --------J.S. Harrell

Prairieville Lodge No. 322, Prairieville, Kaufman county --------J.J. Reasenover, [Reasenoer] an E.A.

Rockport Lodge No. 323, Rockport, Aransas county --------T.M. Dennis

Brazoria Lodge No. 327, Brazoria, Brazoria county --------Frank Willis

Perryville Lodge No. 328, Elgin, Bastrop county --------A. Clopton, Robert Wilson

Gray Lodge No. 329, Houston, Harris county --------John B. Coates

Carolina Lodge No. 330, Held at Lodge Hall, Falls county, post office Landrum --------John C. Bull, Jr.

Greenville Lodge No. 335, Greenville, Hunt county --------J.L. Hayter, [J.L. Hatter] N. McDougald

J.H. Gurley Lodge No. 337, Waco, McLennan county --------George E. Burney

E.M. Wilder Lodge No. 339, Power's Chapel, Falls county, post office Wildersville --------A.J. Phillips

Davilla Lodge No. 340, Davilla, Milam county --------H.W. Guynes

Tom Anderson Lodge No. 346, Fraimville, Burleson county, post office Gause --------J.T. Newman

Tulip Lodge No. 348, Tulip, Fannin county --------Robert Darnall

Bremond Lodge No. 350, Bremond, Robertson county --------Jacob Burnett, [Jacob Bennett] W.G. Coons

Etam Lodge No. 353, Hempstead, Waller county --------H.B. Waller [H.W. Waller]

Groesbeck Lodge No. 354, Groesbeck, Limestone county --------J.C. Welch, Wm. J. Alexander

Clifton Lodge No. 360, Clifton, Bosque county --------Wm. Moss [William Mass]

Golden Rule Lodge No. 361, Hearne, Robertson county --------W.W. McCollum, an E.A.

Oenaville Lodge No. 363, Oenaville, Bell county --------J.C. Veazey

Sand Spring Lodge No. 365, Sand Spring, Wood county, post office Hawkins --------J.J. Camby, E.M. Sego, W.B. Tompson [Thompson]

Salem Lodge No. 368, Lodge Hall, Lee county, post office Ledbetter --------D.B. Cowan

Ovilla Lodge No. 370 Ovilla, Ellis county --------M.L. McElroy

Eureka Lodge No. 371, Held at Veal's Station, Parker county --------John P. Hill

Dexter Lodge No. 372, Dexter, Cook county --------J.M. English

Fannin Lodge No. 374, Ransom Butler's, Fannin county, post office Orangeville --------A.W. Stapp

Northern Star Lodge No. 377, Held at Garrett's Chapel, Lamar county, post office Garrett's Bluff --------S.C. Farris, an E.A.

Morales Lodge No. 378, Morales, Jackson county --------Henry Pruss

Halesboro Lodge No. 381, Halesboro, Red River county --------J.H. Bloodworth, Joel Terrell

Reily Springs Lodge No. 382, Reily Springs, Hopkins county --------Wm. Gray

Cooper Lodge No. 383, Cooper, Delta county --------E.H. Threlkill

Snow River Lodge No. 385, Town Bluff, Tyler county --------J.S. Ratcliff [James Ratliff]

Bald Prairie Lodge No. 387, Bald Prairie, Robertson. county --------L.P. Cooke, [L.P. Cook] L.M. Hicks, an E.A.

LaFayette Lodge No. 388, LaFayette, Upshur county --------T.J. Black

Beckville Lodge No. 389, Beckville, Panola county --------J.T. Wall

Frio Lodge No. 399, Frio City, Frio county --------M.W. Watkins, J.J. Elam

Elk Horn Lodge No. 402, Stiles' Schoolhouse, Red River county, post office Clarksville --------M.G. Pipkins

Lone Star Lodge No. 403, Denison, Grayson county --------A. Matzdorf [A. Matzorf]

Longview Lodge No. 404, Longview, Gregg county --------J.H. Phelps [J.H. Philips]

Artesia Lodge No. 406, Terrell, Kaufman county --------Ed. Hudson, G.W. Ridgen

Oak Grove Lodge No. 408, The Grove, Coryell county --------M. Cross

Trespalacios Lodge No. 411, Trespalacios Hall, Matagorda county, post office Deming's Bridge --------Norman Savage

Dallas Lodge No. 412, Dallas, Dallas county --------G.L. Parsons, Mathew Bone

Blazing Star Lodge No. 413, Lodge Room Burnet county, post office Shovel Mount --------A.M. Pharis

Rock House Lodge No. 417, Rock House, Hamilton county --------Charles D. Burton

Wills Point Lodge No. 422, Willis Point, Van Zandt county --------Robert Doyal, [Robert Doyel] James M. Wagg

Weimar Lodge No. 423, Weimar, Colorado county --------H.W. Hollensworth [H.W. Hollingsworth]

Rising Star Lodge No. 429, Centerpoint, Kerr county --------Joseph M. Denton

Acacia Lodge No. 434, Union Church, Gonzales county, post office Cuero, De Witt county --------Patrick Cannon

Johnson Station Lodge No. 438 Johnson Station, Tarrant county --------Wm. L. Burney [William M. Burney]

Los Moras Lodge No. 444, Brackett, Kinney county, post office Bracketville --------James B. Ballantyne

Decatur Lodge No. 447, Decatur, Wise county --------S.J. Gibbs [S.I. Gibbs]

R.E. Lee Lodge No. 449, Oceola, Hill county, post office Covington --------John Hammonds, a F.C.

Palmer Lodge No. 459, Palmer, Ellis county --------John Hardy

Red Oak Lodge No. 461, Lodge Room, Ellis county, post office Red Oak --------G.C. Parks [Park]

Sherman Lodge No. 464, Sherman, Grayson county --------H.T. Galt

Hope Lodge No. 471, Rio Grande City, Starr county --------Henry S. Pearce

Aurora Lodge No. 479 Aurora, Wise county --------C.W. Smith

Hope Lodge No. 481, Comanche, Comanche county --------George L. Todd, J.F. Little

St. Joe Lodge No. 483, St. Joe, Montague county --------C.W. Wyatt
Douglass Lodge U.D., Douglas, Nacogdoches county --------J.W. Baxter
Young County Lodge No. 485, Graham, Young county --------Arthur J. Ernest

Appear in Lodge of Sorrow 1878, but not in the Lodge returns: Wharton Bates, John F. Berry, Jacob Bennett, M.A. Burton, David Denny, Geo. W. Fitzhugh, A.F. Hunt, H.M. Levy, Ben Long, L.M. Logan, W.C. Moore, M. Marcus, Sam Mather, J.P. Martin, O.L. Poole, --F. Prothra, D.M. Perry, E.N. Phillips, John H. Shaw, R. Sowers, T.R. Walker, J.F. Whetchom, R.B. Welch

RETURNS OF LODGES
FOR THE MASONIC YEAR
A.D. 1879, A.L. 5879
DEATHS

Holland Lodge No. 1, Masonic Temple, Houston, Harris county --------Thomas W. Marshall, James B. Likens, H.C. Parker, W.C.O. Driscoll, R.M. Dechene, E.H. Cushing, J.D. Johnson, F.C.

Red Land Lodge No. 3, San Augustine, San Augustine county --------Joseph T. Childers, Inloe Matthews, C.B. Powell

St. Johns Lodge No. 5, Columbia, Brazoria county --------H.P. Dance, C.J. Foster, E.H. Cushing

Harmony Lodge No. 6, Galveston, Galveston county --------John Dean, Abraham Levy, J.B. Sable, S.C. Wilson

Austin Lodge No. 12, Austin, Travis county --------J.T. Alexander

Constantine Lodge No. 13, Bonham, Fannin county --------Z.B. Sims, C.J. Fuller

Trinity Lodge No. 14, Livington, Polk county --------Kirk Augustin

Friendship Lodge No. 16, Clarksville, Red River county --------I.D. Lawson

Orphans' Friend Lodge No. 17, Anderson, Grimes county --------L.Y. Maddox

Forrest Lodge No. 19, Huntsville, Walker county --------J. Polk Moore

Graham Lodge No. 20, Brenham, Washington county --------J.D. Giddings, P.G.M.; Kinney Krug, Simeon Harrison, Theodore Giesecke

Lathrop Lodge No. 21, Crockett, Houston county --------Neil McLean, Wm. Johnson

Marshall Lodge No. 22, Marshall, Harrison county --------John F. Williams, John J, Graham, G. Wall, E.A.

Montgomery Lodge No. 25, Montgomery, Montgomery county --------J.E. White, Johnson Abbott

Paris Lodge No. 27, Paris, Lamar county --------J.E. Henley, C.H. Massey, N.K. Record, W.A. Dickson, C.L. Wilhite, J.H. Hall, an E.A.; W.J. Sneed, an E.A.; John St.Clair, an E.A.

De Witt Clinton Lodge No. 29, Jasper, Jasper county --------G.W. Causey [S.W. Causey]

Gonzales Lodge No. 30, Gonzales, Gonzales county --------W.D.S. Cook, Green Hastings, F.L. Laird

Palestine Lodge No. 31, Palestine, Anderson county --------A.G. Cantley, I.M. Hughes, R.H. Lacey

LaFayette Lodge No. 34, LaGrange, Fayette county --------Theo. Schmidt, W.B. Turnage

Lavaca Lodge No. 36, Port Lavaca, Calhoun county --------Joe Rosetto, James Gardner

Mount Moriah Lodge No. 37, Cold Springs, San Jacinto county --------J.C. Hall, A.F. Sprott

Leona Union Lodge No. 39, Leona, Leon county --------J.G. Gilmore

Alamo Lodge No. 44, San Antonio, Bexar county --------William Vance, Jacob Linn
Euclid Lodge No. 45, Rusk, Cherokee county --------J.M. Tullis
Liberty Lodge No. 48, Liberty, Liberty county --------Joseph Richardson, T.S. Boone, an E.A.
Tannehill Lodge No. 52, Dallas, Dallas county --------G.W. Penn, S.A. Gallagher
Grand Bluff Lodge No. 54, Grand Bluff, Panola county --------W.C. Bowen
Warren Lodge No. 56, Caldwell, Burleson county --------George Rowland
Rocky Mount Lodge No. 63, Overton, Rusk county --------R.J. McDavid, Wm. L. Bealle
Joppa Lodge No. 65, Elysian Fields, Harrison county --------W.B. Cooke, J.L. Shepherd, B. Birmingham, an E.A.
Hubert Lodge No. 67, Chappell Hill, Washington county --------C. Henland
Caledonia Lodge No. 68, Columbus, Colorado county --------George B. Halyard; J.R. Brooks, an E.A.
Boston Lodge No. 69, Boston, Bowie county --------W.D. Swain, M.G. Braswell
Morton Lodge No. 72, Richmond, Ft. Bend county --------Achile Ferris, S.D. Everett, Wm. H. Voss
Springfield Lodge No. 74, Mexia, Limestone county --------B.Y. Hayter, an E.A.
Oasis Lodge No. 79, Daingerfield, Morris county --------Jasper Goolsby
Murchison Lodge No. 80, Hallettsville, Lavaca county --------E. Sumerlin, A.B. Kilpatrick
Rio Grande Lodge No. 81, Brownsville, Cameron county --------Edward Downey, Jose Ravesse
Terrell Lodge No. 83, Alto, Cherokee county --------A.A. Brown, Shelby Cook
Andrew Jackson Lodge No. 88, Linden, Cass county --------W.S. Eddins, an E.A.
Waxahachie Lodge No. 90, Waxahachie, Ellis county --------George L. Williams
Waco Lodge No. 92, Waco, McLennan county --------J.W. Cannon, J. Long, F. Jones, H.J. Lyon
Augusta Lodge No. 93, Augusta, Houston county --------K.D. Bradshaw
Goliad Lodge No. 94, Goliad, Goliad county --------R. Miller, T.J. Henderson
Sharon Lodge No. 95, Pine Hill, Rusk county --------J.A. Jones
Colorado Lodge No. 96, Webberville, Travis county --------R.S. Riggle
Canton Lodge No. 98, Canton, Smith county --------N.A. Pace
Unity Lodge No. 102, Moscow, Polk county --------H. McCormick
Fairfield Lodge No. 103, Fairfield, Freestone county --------Jesse B. Evans
San Jacinto Lodge No. 106, Willis, Montgomery county --------W.S. Rodgers
Jacksonville Lodge No. 108, Jacksonville, Cherokee county --------W.J. McGowan
Bloomfield Lodge No. 112, Kaufman, Kaufman county --------H.B. Boykin
Red River Lodge No. 116, Pine Creek Church, Red River county, post office Tomaha --------J.J. Shrigley, H. Ford, B.H. Gear
Starr Lodge No. 118, Starrville, Smith county --------Henry Smith

Flora Lodge No. 119, Quitman, Wood county --------S.A. Bottoms, N.T. Dickenson [A.T. Dickenson], C.B. Willingham
Mt. Hope Lodge No. 121, Mt. Hope, Tyler county, post office Chester --------S.H. Barnes
Baylor Lodge No. 125, Gay Hill, Washington county, post office Brenham --------Y.S. Veazy
Brazos Union Lodge No. 129, Bryan, Brazos county --------J.P. Mitchell, Sr.
Bethel Lodge No. 134, Ladonia, Fannin county --------Arch Dillingham
Camden Lodge No. 135, Peatown, Gregg county, post office Iron Bridge --------J.P. Gladney
Lexington Lodge No. 138, Lexington, Lee county --------D.H. Browder
Keechi Lodge No. 140, Centreville, Leon county --------Henry Weir, T.A. Womack
Castillian Lodge No. 141, Canton, Van Zandt county --------M.M. Stover
Planters Lodge No. 147, Plantersville, Grimes county --------W.E. Moseley, A.B. Easley
Fort Worth Lodge No. 148, Fort Worth, Tarrant county --------C.J. Neal
Cibolo Lodge No. 151, Selma, Bexar county --------Wm. Sabine
Eclectic Lodge No. 153, Savoy, Fannin county --------L. Cleaveland
Cotton Gin Lodge No. 154, Cotton Gin, Freestone county --------J.F. Rutherford
Spring Hill Lodge No. 155, Spring Hill, Navarro county --------R.H. Hight
Hickory Hill Lodge No. 156, Avinger, Cass county --------G.W. Booker
East Trinity Lodge No. 157, Rockwall, Rockwall county --------J.R. Bryant
Athens Lodge No. 165, Athens, Henderson county --------B.G. Pate
Kentucky Lodge No. 167, Kentucky Town, Grayson county --------J.C. Marshal, T.J. Francis; P. Crouch, an E.A.
James F. Taylor Lodge No. 169, Hallville, Harrison county --------A.P. Davis; R.H. Leary, an F.C.
San Anders Lodge No. 170, Cameron, Milam county --------J.A. Ward
Bosque Lodge No. 171, Bosqueville, McLennan county --------W.F. Compton
Mound Prairie Lodge No. 173, Mound Prairie, Anderson county, post office Nechesville --------W.B. Thomas
Valley Lodge No. 175, Burnet, Burnet county --------D.C. Cowan [David C. Cowen], Wm. H. Magill, Sr., E. Sampson
St. Paul's Lodge No. 177, Port Sullivan, Milam county --------J.M. Payne
E.J. Glover Lodge No. 178, Friendship Church, Marion county, post office Jefferson --------W.T. Baker, [W.L. Baker] John Ferrel
Post Oak Island Lodge No. 181, Sam Smith Springs, Lee county, post office McDade --------J.H. Lawrence, M. Gardner
Hickory Grove Lodge No. 184, Etna, Smith county --------J.L. Dabbs [J.L. Dabbe], B.W. Thompson, Sr.
White Oak Lodge No. 185, Pine Forest, Hopkins county, post office Carroll Prairie --------W.W. Gay
Tyrian Lodge No. 187, Sabine Pass, Jefferson county --------S.L. Mackan

Corpus Christi Lodge No. 189, Corpus Christi, Nueces county --------Chris. H. Ley

Leon Lodge No. 193, Lodge Room, Bell county, post office Moffat --------Wm. Robinson, L.F. Bryan

Lyons Lodge No. 195, Schulenburg, Fayette county --------James C. Porter

Aquilla Lodge No. 196, Hillsboro, Hill county --------J.F. Tander, S.S. Cannon, an E.A.

Tyre Lodge No. 198, Tennessee Colony, Anderson county --------R.A. Tamplin

Denton Lodge No. 201, Lewisville, Denton county --------J.W. Burge, W.H. Gatewood

James A. Baker Lodge No. 202, Ebenezer Baptist Church, Walker county, post office Huntsville --------K. Cooper, V.H. Pace

Pine Lodge No. 203, Edom, Van Zandt county --------J.P. Youngblood

Mount Calm No. 204, Mount Calm, Limestone county --------W.B. Thompson, A. DeBorde [Abel DeBoard]

Frank Sexton Lodge No. 206, Pittsburg, Camp county --------Wm. Dickson

Mantua Lodge No. 209, Mantua, Collin county, post office Van Alstyne --------J.C. Cooper

Gainesville Lodge No. 210, Gainesville, Cooke county --------Phineas Cox, J.E. McCraw, J.W. Wilkerson, F.M. Townsen

Farmersville Lodge No. 214, Farmersville, Collin county --------M.H. Turner, H.C. Harless, E.B. Wingo

Dresden Lodge No. 218, Dresden, Navarro county--------W.A. Haden, J.R. Weaver, J.C. Lemmons, Rev. W.J. Grant, L.P. Campbell, an E.A.

Millville Lodge No. 219, Millville, Rusk county --------W.A.J. Robertson

Sulphur Springs Lodge 221, Sulphur Springs, Hopkins county --------Z.G. Matthews

Parsons Lodge No. 222, Manor, Travis county --------A.B. Townsend

Miller Lodge No. 224, At or near White Rock, Hunt county --------G.C. Perrin, an E.A.; John Hazel, an E.A.

Brahan Lodge No. 226, Lavernia, Wilson county --------F.M. Fennell

Round Rock Lodge No. 227, Round Rock, Williamson county --------W.M. Melburn, Nelson Merrill

Newport Lodge No. 228, Newport, Walker county, post office Riverside --------Jas. M. Evans

Eutaw Lodge No. 233, Kosse, Limestone county --------J.L. Conoly, B.F. Burns [B.E. Burns] J.H. Price, W.F. Williams, W.L. Brown, S.R. Lampkin, H. Arnett

White Rock Lodge No. 234, Frankfort, Collin county, post office Richardson --------Wm. McCollough, N.B. Pearce, Samuel Scott

Plano Lodge No. 235, Plano, Collin county --------Henry Dye, Benjamin F. Mathews, W.W. Wade, John M. Salmons, A.S. Chandler, D.C. Forman

San Felipe Lodge No. 239, San Felipe, Austin county --------Lewis Cooper, Enos Cooper, L. Duncan, A. McKinney, T. Whitworth

Gamble Lodge No. 244, Bastrop, Bastrop county --------Alford Moore

A. Jackson Lodge No. 249, Pine Town, Cherokee county, post office Jacksonville --------W.H. Bane, David Rainey

Homer Lodge No. 254, Homer, Angelina county --------John Granberry, Jas. Thomson

Beeville Lodge No. 261, Beeville, Bee county --------G.A. Craven

Whitesboro' Lodge No. 263, Whitesboro', Grayson county --------J.R. Brown, A.S. Hightower, N.J. McElroy

Grayson Lodge No. 265, Lost Prairie, Limestone county, post office Personville --------J. W. Neely, T.J. Pierce, G.W. Baldwin

Grand View Lodge No. 266, Grand View, Johnson county --------Wm. McFarland

Stephensville Lodge No. 267, Stephensville, Erath county --------Wm. Gordon

Meridian Lodge No. 268, Meridian, Bosque county --------A.C. Pearce, D.A. Gardner

Pilot Point Lodge No. 270, Pilot Point, Denton county --------S.P. Brown

Phoenix Lodge No. 275, Weatherford, Parker county --------John H. Ross, B.M. Martin, O.L. Harden, B.G. Lanhams

Mountain Lodge No. 277, Hopewell, Williamson county, post office Hopewell, Burnet county --------J.B. Arnett

Brownwood Lodge No. 279, Brownwood, Brown county --------J.R. Brown, Geo. Hogue

J.D. Giddings Lodge No. 280, Giddings, Lee county --------J. Moore, Wm. Wolf, J.F. Harmon

Winchester Lodge No. 282, Winchester, Fayette county --------W.J. Allsop

Pleasanton Lodge No. 283, Pleasanton, Atascosa county --------Robert E. Neill, Daniel McKinzie

Eastern Star Lodge No. 284, Centralia, Trinity county --------W.R. Gaston

Beaumont Lodge No. 286, Beaumont, Jefferson county --------R.H. Leonard

John Armstrong Lodge No. 291, Lodge Room, on Hog Creek, Bosque county, post office Vaughan --------F.M. Snider

Kimball Lodge No. 292, Kimball, Bosque county --------T.J. Robinson, J.W. Holland

Mars Hill Lodge No. 293, Emory, Rains county --------J.A. Smith, P.T. Taylor, Henry Turney, S.B. Dyer

Scyene Lodge No. 295, Scyene, Dallas county, post office Mesquite --------Thomas D. Coats, James A. Coats

Salado Lodge No. 296, Salado, Bell county --------W.R. Kemp, J.P. Barr

Tucker Lodge No. 297, Galveston, Galveston county --------T.W. Slade, M.H. Swartz, J. Vineyard, R.M. Tevis, W. Rutherford

Cedar Creek Lodge No. 300, Tryon, Brazos county, post office, Bryan --------W.F. Mintz

Starksville Lodge No. 303, Blossom Prairie, Lamar county --------W.B. Harrison, W.A. Childers

Littleton Fowler Lodge No. 305, Hemphill, Sabine county --------S.N. Beckcorn, S.E. Goodman, a F.C.

G.W. Foster Lodge No. 306, Nelsonville, Austin county --------E. Wangemann
Shiloh Lodge No. 307, Shiloh Hall, Hunt county, post office Lone Oak --------J.D. Donnell, W.M. Moxley, W.S. Norris
Cedar Grove Lodge No. 308, Cedar Grove, Kaufman county, post office Wills' Point --------A. Caro
Wm. Foster Lodge No. 312, Fosterville, Anderson county --------G.F. Richards
Alvarado Lodge No. 314, Alvarado, Johnson county --------W.R. Bounds, Sr. [W.R. Bonds], Moses Graham
Cleburne Lodge No. 315, Cleburne, Johnson county --------M. Dixon [Mike Dixon], J.A. Young, Levi Stewart
Shuler Lodge No. 317, Monthalia, Gonzales county --------J.W. Lemmond
Cedar Bayou Lodge No. 321, Cedar Bayou, Harris county --------E. Arvidson [Emil Arvidson], J.C. Kelly
Prairieville Lodge No. 322, Prairieville, Kaufman county, post office Kemp --------I. Spikes, John Johnson
Victoria Lodge No. 326, Victoria, Victoria county --------W.J. Whitehead, Wm. Jahn
Perryville Lodge No. 328, Elgin, Bastrop county --------J.P. Reynolds, J.E. Standifer
Gray Lodge No. 329, Houston, Harris county --------Frank Superville
Mansfield Lodge No. 331, Mansfield, Tarrant county --------R.F. Blackwell, J.D. Spencer, J.B. Cope, C.P. Yarborough
Birdston Lodge No. 333, Birdston, Navarro county --------J.M. Harris, R.G. Manning
Leesburg Lodge No. 334, Leesville, Gonzales county --------G.B. Poland
E.M. Wilder Lodge No. 339, Power's Chapel, Falls county, post office Wilderville --------Hugh Judkins, J.T. McDonald
Davilla Lodge No. 340, Davilla, Milam county --------W.F. Bunting
San Marcos Lodge No. 342, San Marcos, Hays county --------L.H. Armstrong [S.H. Armstrong]
Bowling Lodge No. 343, Marquez, Leon county --------E.A. Powell
Fish Creek Lodge No. 344, Marysville, Cooke county --------R.A. Brooks [B.A. Brooks]
Tulip Lodge No. 348, Tulip, Fannin county --------S.G. Jennings
Wm. C. Young Lodge No. 349, Elizabeth, Denton county --------T.J. Bates, Wm. A. Vickers, Iraneous Neace
Pottersville Lodge No. 351, Pottersville, Limestone county, post office Groesbeck --------Ed. Roberts, W.M. McGill
Caddo Grove Lodge No. 352, Caddo Grove, Johnson county --------Bolivar Cook
Prairie Valley Lodge No. 355, Prairie Valley, Hill county --------W.A. Turner, J.H. Goodman, Phillip Smith, an E.A.
Collins Lodge No. 356, Cothran's Hall, Lamar county, post office Paris --------M.A. White, H.B. Hadden
Colita Lodge No. 357, Colita, Polk county --------W.P. Rogers

Tehuacana Lodge No. 358, Tehuacana, Limestone county --------T.M. Purtell
Patrick Lodge No. 359, Englewood, Robertson county --------E. Baker
Oenaville Lodge No. 363, Oenaville, Bell county --------J.A. Black
Sand Spring Lodge No. 365, Sand Spring, Wood county, post office Hawkins --------J.C. Turlington
Brushy Lodge No. 367, Masonic Hall, Panola county, post office Walnut Hill --------W.W. Miller, James M. Smith, D.M. Sullivan
Ennis Lodge No. 369, Ennis, Ellis county --------N. Paterson
Eureka Lodge No. 371, Veal's Station, Parker county --------J.L. Shown, J. Hill, M.L. Scott
Rainey's Creek Lodge No. 375, Coryell, Coryell county --------J.M. Beene
Morales Lodge No. 378, Morales, Jackson county --------J.J. Bell
Halesboro Lodge No. 381, Halesboro, Red River county --------J.A. Humpreys, Squire Allen
Reily Springs Lodge No. 382, Reily springs, Hopkins county --------J.C. Blankenship
Cooper Lodge No. 383, Cooper, Delta county --------F.G. Ewing
Dodge Lodge No. 384, Dodge, Walker county --------J.B. Hemphill
Brooklyn Lodge No. 386, Forney, Kaufman county --------J.C. Garrison
Bald Prairie Lodge No. 387, Bald Prairie, Robertson county --------J.F. Hardy, M.W. McDaniel, an E.A.
Beckville Lodge No. 389, Beckville, Panola county --------G.W. Lentz
Millerton Lodge No. 390, Millerton, Milam county, post office Rockdale --------T.B. Guthrie
Middleton Lodge No. 391, Christina Church, Goliad county, post office Weesatche --------J.P. Harryman, J.J. Ratliff
Granbury Lodge No. 392, Granbury, Hood county --------W.B. Rayburn
Paluxy Lodge No. 393, Lodge Room, Hood county, post office Paluxy --------B.M. Cowan
Providence Lodge No. 400, Providence Church, Anderson county, post office Alder Branch --------W.R. Anglin
Little River Lodge No. 401, Pleasant Valley, Bell county, post office Birdsdale --------W.M. Wood
Lone Star Lodge No. 403, Denison, Grayson county --------A.J. Poff, D.W. Kirk, J.J. Brenner, J.J. Newdorfer
Longview Lodge No. 404, Longview, Gregg county --------W.H. Cunyus [W.H. Cunyes], W.D. Simmons
Artesia Lodge No. 406, Terrell, Kaufman county --------J.L. Franklin
Lindale Lodge No. 410, Lindale, Smith county --------T.J. Barron [T.J. Barrow]
Trespalacios Lodge No. 411, Trespalacios Hall, Matagorda county, post office Deming's Bridge --------B.K. Moore
Blazing Star Lodge No. 413, Shovel Mount, Burnet county --------W.N. Hays
Rockdale Lodge No. 414, Rockdale, Milam county --------W.C. Waldrop
South Noland Lodge No. 416, Pleasant Hill, Bell county, post office Noland Valley --------A.J. Fleming

Colthorp Lodge No. 419, Colthorp, Houston county --------Thos. Payne, Jas. M. Hager

J. Nixon Lodge No. 421, Post Oak Grove, Bastrop county, post office Smithville --------John P. Jones

Wills Point Lodge No. 422, Wills Point, Van Zandt county --------T.F. Scott

Anchor Lodge No. 424, San Antonio, Bexar county --------W.A. T. R. Spaulding

Jewett Lodge No. 427, Jewett, Leon county --------__ Compton, M.M. Hagard

Rising Star Lodge No. 429, Centerpoint, Kerr county --------A. Surber

Flatonia Lodge No. 436, Flatonia, Fayette county --------Geo. G. Fees

Golden Drain Lodge No. 437, Caledonia, Rusk county --------J.L. Long

Johnson Station Lodge No. 438, Johnson Station, Tarrant county --------S.A. Daniels

Burlington Lodge No. 440, Burlington, Montague county, post office Spanish Fort --------John Weems, E.O. Driskill

Coryell Lodge No. 442, Jonesboro, Coryell county --------Chas. Parsons

Los Moras Lodge No. 444, Brackett, Kinney county --------S.C. Crowell]L.C. Crowell], Chas. M.C. Rivers, R.E. Robinson, an E.A.

New York Lodge No. 446, New York, Henderson county --------C. Browning

Decatur Lodge No. 447, Decatur, Wise county --------J.J. Criner

Johnsonville Lodge No. 448, Johnsonville, Somervell county, post office George's Creek --------D. Womack

R.E. Lee Lodge No. 449, Oceola, Hill county --------B.P. Wooldridge

Grand Prairie Lodge No. 455, Smithfield, Tarrant county --------J.W. Washborn, Eli Smith

Hill City Lodge No. 456, Austin, Travis county --------T.D. Manning

John Sims Lodge No. 458, New Waverly, Walker county --------G.A. Vick, an E.A.

Sherman Lodge No. 464, Sherman, Grayson county --------T.J. Heady

Eastland Lodge No. 467, Eastland, Eastland county --------N.K. Tracy, Jesse A. Smith

Hope Lodge No. 471, Rio Grande City, Starr county --------E.T. Peck, J.O. Thompson

Uvalde Lodge No. 472, Uvalde, Uvalde county --------R.T. Creigler [B.T. Creigler]

Hico Lodge No. 477, Hico, Hamilton county --------B.F. Chenault, S.S. Rigsby, Isaac Malone

Mammoth Springs Lodge No. 478, Center Point, Ellis county, post office Mountain Peak --------H.A. Riddle

Aurora Lodge No. 479, Aurora, Wise county --------F.M. Kenneday

Jim's Bayou Lodge No. 491, Kildare, Cass county --------C.E. Moore

Dublin Lodge No. 504, Dublin, Erath county --------M.D. Robertson

RETURNS OF LODGES
FOR THE MASONIC YEAR A.D. 1880
DEATHS

Holland Lodge No. 1, Masonic Temple, Houston, Harris county --------Mortimer J. Massie, J.W. Allen

Milam Lodge No. 2, Nacogdoches, Nacogdoches county --------Isaac Meeks, Isaac Meeke] John Forbes

St. Johns Lodge No. 5, Columbia, Brazoria county --------Andrew J. Burke, Jr.

Harmony Lodge No. 6, Galveston, Galveston county --------Geo. H. Delesdernier, Robt. J. Hughes, Weston R. Howard, C.C. Lund, Henry Lowell, J.J. McBride, A.C. McKeen, [A.C. McKean] F.G. Moelling, J.F. Magale, David Wakelee

Austin Lodge No. 12, Austin, Travis county --------W.H. Sharp

Constantine Lodge No. 13, Bonham, Fannin county --------W.R. Stewart [W.A. Stewart]

Friendship Lodge No. 16, Clarksville, Red River county --------J.L. Carroll

Orphan's Friend Lodge No. 17, Anderson, Grimes county --------David C. Dickson

Washington Lodge No. 18, Washington, Washington county --------A.J. Hall, [A.T. Hall] B.F. Rucker

Forrest Lodge No. 19, Huntsville, Walker county --------J.J. Elkins

Graham Lodge No. 20, Brenham, Washington county --------H. Mouldenhauer

Lathrop Lodge No. 21, Crockett, Houston county --------Kenneth Murchison, John Spence, A.M. Hallmark

Marshall Lodge No. 22, Marshall, Harrison county --------Thomas S. Langley

Clinton Lodge No. 23, Henderson, Rusk county --------J.L. Wester

Paris Lodge No. 27, Paris, Lamar county --------Samuel Long

Palestine Lodge No. 31, Palestine, Anderson county --------M.L. Majors, T.S. Parker, Henry Nathan, [H. Nathens] Thomas M. Hogue

Jefferson Lodge No. 38, Jefferson, Marion county --------N.P. Modrall [L.P. Modrall]

Leona Union Lodge No. 39, Leona, Leon county --------R.M. Ewing

Alamo Lodge No. 44, San Antonio, Bexar county --------J.C. Burnett, Wm. Stone, A. Stowe

Euclid Lodge No. 45, Rusk, Cherokee county --------T.L. Philleo

St. Johns Lodge No. 51, McKinney, Collin county --------R.M. Rudolph

Tannehill Lodge No. 52, Dallas, Dallas county --------J.M. Brown, I.N. Simmons

St. Johns Lodge No. 53, Tyler, Smith county --------P.W. Warriner [F.W. Warrener], J.C. Hill [Jas. C. Hill], W.S. Walker

Grand Bluff Lodge No. 54, Grand Bluff, Panola county --------James A. Alexander

Larissa Lodge No. 57, Larissa, Cherokee county --------T. Ford, J.D. Long

Mt. Enterprise Lodge No. 60, Mt. Enterprise, Rusk county --------Thomas M. Attaway, J.M. Welch

Caledonia Lodge No. 68, Columbus, Colorado county --------E.L. Beeman, E.A.
Boston Lodge No. 69, Boston, Bowie county --------Jerry Washington
Springfield Lodge No. 74, Mexia, Limestone county --------Harrison Moody, B.R. Tyrus, R.G. Miller, H.H. Young, S.W. Holman
Murchison Lodge No. 80, Hallettsville, Lavaca county --------J.W. Whitfield
Rio Grande Lodge No. 81, Brownsville, Cameron county --------A.R. Nesmith, Zenon Garcia, E.A.'s
Terrell Lodge No. 83, Alto, Cherokee county --------C. Bell
Indianola Lodge No. 84, Indianola, Calhoun county --------H. Sheppard
New Salem Lodge No. 87, New Salem, Rusk county --------Alexander Gray
San Gabriel Lodge No. 89, Georgetown, Williamson county --------W. Adams [Walter Adams], E. Cole, D.S. Cook, R. Sansom
Waxahachie Lodge No. 90, Waxahachie, Ellis county --------R.S. Bynum, Benj. Pendleton
Waco Lodge No. 92, Waco, McLennan county --------B.T. Duval, S.B. Trice, J.J. French, L.N. Cassady, W.A. Boren, B.P. Loftin, [B.T. Loftin] J.E. Harrison
Canton Lodge No. 98, Canton, Smith county, post office Omen --------J.C. Moore
Unity Lodge No. 102, Moscow, Polk county --------A.J. Willcox
Fairfield Lodge No. 103, Fairfield, Freestone county --------Frank G. Gullette [F.C. Gullette]
San Jacinto Lodge No. 106, Willis, Montgomery county --------T.W. Hoy, J.J. Casey
Prairie Lea Lodge No. 114, Prairie Lea, Caldwell county --------L. Washburn, J.J. Trammell [J.J. Trommell]
Red River Lodge No. 116, Pine Creek, Red River county, post office Tomaha --------J.H.B. Dinwidie [J.H.R. Dinwidie]
Flora Lodge No. 119, Quitman, Wood county --------J.H. Saxon, W.L. Willingham
Madison Lodge No. 126, Orange, Orange county --------Jas. Woods, F.A. Davis
Brazos Lodge No. 129, Bryan, Brazos county --------J.A. Patterson, J.R. Evans, Thos. S. Gathright
Retreat Lodge No. 133, Courtney, Grimes county, post office White Hall --------W.K. McAlpin, M.S. Jeffers
Bethel Lodge No. 134, Ladonia, Fannin county --------R.B. Kennedy, J.M. Clinton
Newton Lodge No. 136, Burkeville, Newton county --------H. Hunter
Mount Horeb Lodge No. 137, Gabriel Mills, Williamson county, post office Mahomet, Burnet county --------B.M. Smart
Lexington Lodge No. 138, Lexington, Lee county --------D.A. Castleberry [D.W. Castleberry]
Keechi Lodge No. 140, Centreville, Leon county --------Aaron Barnes
Castillian Lodge No. 141, Canton, Van Zandt county --------David Chappell
Bethesda Lodge No. 142, Gilmer, Upshur county --------J.M. Gilbert, N.M. Harrison

Pierce Lodge No. 144, Calvert, Robertson county --------P.H. Talbot [B.H. Talbot], Frank Sims

Winnsborough Lodge No. 146, Winnsboro, Wood county --------W.W. Lommuck [W.N. Lemmuck] J.J. Kennedy

Planters Lodge No. 147, Plantersville, Grimes county --------H.J. Phalen [H.J. Phaton]

Fort Worth Lodge No. 148, Fort Worth, Tarrant county --------J.N.B. Williams

Eclectic Lodge No. 153, Savoy, Fannin county --------R.S. Ford, R.W. Galahar, J.E. Kearns [J.E. Karnes]

Cotton Gin Lodge No. 154, Cotton Gin, Freestone county --------C.W. Colgin

Wm. M. Taylor Lodge No. 158, Garden Valley, Smith county --------A.C. Allen

McClellan Lodge No. 159, Union Hill, Washington county, post office Burton --------J.E. Murray [J.F. Murray]

Lancaster Lodge No. 160, Lancaster, Dallas county --------James M. Sawyers

Athens Lodge No. 165, Athens, Henderson county --------R.H. Day

Belton Lodge No. 166, Belton, Bell county --------E.J. Sluder, W.P. Haymond, A.A. Haggard

J.F. Taylor Lodge No. 169, Hallville, Harrison county --------A.C. Williams, Sr.

San Anders Lodge No. 170, Cameron, Milam county --------J.W. Hood

Bosque Lodge No. 171, Bosqueville, McLennan county --------I.R. Woodard

Corsicana Lodge No. 174, Corsicana, Navarro county --------O.J. Meador, E.H. Forman

Valley Lodge No. 175, Burnet, Burnet county --------James M. McDonald, S.W. Snodgrass

St. Paul's Lodge No. 177, Port Sullivan, Milam county --------John E. Tyson

E.J. Glover Lodge No. 178, Marion, Marion county, post office Lodwick --------H. Whitehead

Hardeman Lodge No. 179, Luling, Caldwell county --------R.A. Gray

Post Oak Island Lodge No. 181, Sam Smith Spring, Lee county, post office McDade, Bastrop county --------R.C. Smith

Concrete Lodge No. 182, Concrete, De Witt county --------P. Watson

Hopkinsville Lodge No. 183, Waelder, Gonzales county --------E.P. Kindred

Hickory Grove Lodge No. 184, Etna, Smith county --------R.R. Roddy, W.L. Campbell

White Oak Lodge No. 185, Pine Forest, Hopkins county, post office Carroll's Prairie --------A.J. Lowe

Tyrian Lodge No. 187, Sabine Pass, Jefferson county --------T.B. Whiting

Refugio Lodge No. 190, Refugio, Refugio county --------Wm. E. McCampbell

Aquilla Lodge No. 196, Hillsboro, Hill county --------George Cope [Geo. Cape]

Gatesville Lodge No. 197, Gatesville, Coryell county --------S.B. Raby, H.P. Bone, [H.R. Bone] Jackson Smith

Tyre Lodge No. 198, Tennessee Colony, Anderson county --------J.M. Brown

Alamita Lodge No. 200, Helena, Karnes county --------J.A. Edmiston, an E.A.

Denton Lodge No. 201, Lewisville, Denton county --------J.G. Scarbrough [J.G. Scarborough]

103

Mount Calm Lodge No. 204, Mount Calm, Limestone county --------N.S. Middleton

Frank Sexton Lodge No. 206, Pittsburg, Camp county --------W.T. Baily, a F.C.; Rufus Sikes, an E.A.

Gainesville Lodge No. 210, Gainesville, Cooke county --------E. Couch, N. Gilbert, J.C. Gibson

Farmersville Lodge No. 214, Farmersville, Collin county --------E. King

Blanco Lodge No. 216, Blanco, Blanco county --------Andrew J. Cockrum

Stanfield Lodge No. 217, Denton, Denton county --------J.M. McNeal, F.B. French, W.R. Baker

Dresden Lodge No. 218, Dresden, Navarro county --------Squire Smith, Jas. M. Wood

Onion Creek Lodge No. 220, Lodge Room, Travis county, post office Bluff Springs --------James P. McKinney

Sulphur Springs Lodge No. 221, Sulphur Springs, Hopkins county --------Reuben Withers, [Reuben Wethers] F.A. Cochran

Bellville Lodge No. 223, Bellville, Austin county --------M.H. Chatham, James E. Morris

Miller Lodge No. 224, At or near White Rock, Hunt county --------J.C. Kiser, J.L. Kennedy

Butler Lodge No. 224a, Butler, Freestone county --------John Tippen

San Saba Lodge No. 225, San Saba, San Saba county --------G.B. Cook

Round Rock Lodge No. 227, Round Rock, Williamson county --------Jesse Womack

Eutaw Lodge No. 233, Kosse, Limestone county --------Joseph Jones

Plano Lodge No. 235, Plano, Collin county --------Sam M. Wilkins, Jas. M. Williamson

Fayetteville Lodge No. 240, Fayetteville, Fayette county --------W.R. Pollard [W.R. Poland]

Torbert Lodge No. 241, Turner's Point, Kaufman county, post office Poetry Bluff --------M.E. Allen, S.M. Davis

Sulphur Bluff Lodge No. 246, Sulphur Bluff, Hopkins county --------R.M. Maxwell, James Burkham

Adah Zillah Lodge No 247, Millican, Brazos county --------Geo. D. Haswell; Peter Bowling, W.R. Ellis, E.A.'s

A. Jackson Lodge No. 249, Pine Town, Cherokee County, post office Jacksonville --------G.W. Thomison, Johnsey Ball

Sexton Lodge No. 251, Milam, Sabine county --------Robt. K. Goodloe

Oakland Lodge No. 258, Oakland, Colorado county --------E.H. Edwards, J.H. Simpson, E.B. Fowlkes

Milford Lodge No. 262, Milford, Ellis county --------L.H. Gideon, J.C. Wilson, A. Wright

Whitesboro' Lodge No. 263, Whitesboro', Grayson county --------J.R. Diamond

Grayson Lodge No. 265, Lost Prairie, Limestone county, post office Personville --------T.W. Nealy

Grand View Lodge No. 266, Grand View, Johnson county --------D.S. Files
Stephensville Lodge No. 267, Stephensville, Erath county --------C.H. Walker
Pilot Point Lodge No. 270, Pilot Point, Denton county --------J.E. Sheegog, H. Pebley, [H. Pebly] J.G. Plemmons
Phoenix Lodge No. 275, Weatherford, Parker county --------R.A. Denham, J.E. Britton [J.E. Brittan]
Brownwood Lodge No. 279, Brownwood, Brown county --------Horace M. Fry, W.S. Nolan
Pleasanton Lodge No. 283, Pleasanton, Atascosa county --------Wright Williams
Eastern Star Lodge No. 284, Centralia, Trinity county --------J.W. Bowman
Acton Lodge No. 285, Acton, Hood county --------J.B. Little
Grapevine Lodge No. 288, Grapevine, Tarrant county --------J.M. Buckhalter
Harmony Hill Lodge No. 289, Harmony Hill, Rusk county --------J.M. Robertson
Tyler Prairie Lodge No. 290, Pennington, Trinity county --------J.H. Dill
John Armstrong Lodge No. 291, Lodge room, Hog Creek, Bosque county, post office Vaughan --------E.P. Booth
Mars Hill Lodge No. 293, Emory, Rains county --------I.B. Dement
Salado Lodge No 296, Salado, Bell county --------E.S.C. Robertson
Tucker Lodge No. 297, Galveston, Galveston county --------S.H. Kimball, F. Fabj, [Frank Fabj] B.B. Richardson, S. Carter
Navasota Lodge No. 299, Navasota, Grimes county --------D.P. Everett
Starksville Lodge No. 303, Blossom Prairie, Lamar county --------Eli Harris, T.H. St.Clair
Live Oak Lodge No. 304, Live Oak Academy, Hays county, post office Mountain City --------J.M. Breedlove [I.M. Breedlove], Thomas Gray
Littleton Fowler Lodge No. 305, Hemphill, Sabine County --------Solomon Arthur [Author]
Wm. Foster Lodge No. 312, Fosterville, Anderson county --------John Reynolds, F.C.
Zion Lodge No. 313, Stonewall Jackson Institute, Grimes county, post office Iola --------B.J. Ross
Alvarado Lodge No. 314, Alvarado, Johnson county --------C. Laramore, W.W. Bockman, S. Ramsey
Cleburne Lodge No. 315, Cleburne, Johnson county --------J.M. Legg, D.F. Hoyler [Horler]
Cedar Bayou Lodge No. 321, Cedar Bayou, Harris county --------Barney Weiser
Victoria Lodge No. 326, Victoria, Victoria county --------G.F. Rogers
Brazoria Lodge No. 327, Brazoria, Brazoria county --------John M. Prewitt
Leesburg Lodge No. 334, Leesville, Gonzales county --------James P. Collins [Jas. R. Collins]
Florence Lodge No. 338, Florence, Williamson county --------J. Rodgers
Davilla Lodge No. 340, Davilla, Milam county --------H.G. Shrock
San Marcos Lodge No. 342, San Marcos, Hays county --------Richard L. Breeding

Bowling Lodge No. 343, Marquez, Leon county --------C.H. Chamberlain, C.G. Walker

Fish Creek Lodge No. 344, Marysville, Cook county --------Wm. N. Savage

Jim Truit Lodge No. 345, Willow Grove, Shelby county, post office Tomday --------J.M. Robertson

Tom Anderson Lodge No. 346, Fraimville, Burleson county, post office Gause --------G.C. Lovelace

Tulip Lodge No. 348, Tulip, Fannin county --------S.F. Darnell, [S.F. Darnall] J.W. Sherrard

Bremond Lodge No. 350, Bremond, Robertson county --------S. Durham

Golden Rule Lodge No. 361, Hearne, Robertson county --------Dr. J.M. Morrison

David Elliott Lodge No. 364, Elliott's Mills, Morris county, post office Clay Hill --------J.W. Coffey

Salem Lodge No. 368, Lodge Room, Lee county, post office Ledbetter --------W.B. Hildebrand

Ennis Lodge No. 369, Ennis, Ellis county --------B.L. Ham, S.R. Stephenson

Ovilla Lodge No. 370, Ovilla, Ellis county --------V.G. Rust

Dexter Lodge No. 372, Dexter, Cooke county --------S. Albright

Fannin Lodge No. 374, Ransom Buttler's, Fannin county, post office Pilot Grove --------P.A. Hunt

Rainey's Creek Lodge No. 375, Coryell, Coryell county --------I.W. Miller

Northern Star Lodge No. 377, Garrett's Chapel, Lamar county, post office Garrett's Bluff --------Jasper Reid [Reid Jasper]

Pleasant Hill Lodge No. 380, Field's store, Waller county --------T.B. Holder [Holden]

Reiley Springs Lodge No. 382, Reiley Springs, Hopkins county --------W.S. McMichael

Dodge Lodge No. 384, Dodge, Walker county --------W.K. Spaulding, F.C.

Brooklyn Lodge No. 386, Forney, Kaufman county --------J.H. Sorey [I.H. Sorey]

Granbury Lodge No. 392, Granbury, Hood county --------Abel Nutt

Reevesville Lodge No. 396, Reevesville, Grayson county, post office Pottsboro --------B.F. Smith

Lamar Lodge No. 398, Friendship Church, Lamar county, post office Paris --------R.P. Ratliff

Knobb Creek Lodge No. 401, Pleasant Valley, Bell county, postoffce Birdsdale --------F. Fleming

Longview Lodge No. 404, Longview, Gregg county --------T.M. Coleman

Artesia Lodge No. 406, Terrell, Kaufman county --------T.B. Finley [F.B. Finley]

Oak Grove Lodge No. 408, The Grove, Coryell county --------G.W. Touchstone, B.D. Galispie

Dallas Lodge No. 412, Dallas, Dallas county --------P. Hamilton

South Noland Lodge No. 416, Pleasant Hill, Bell county, post office Noland Valley --------J.J. Meek, Wm. Wright

106

Rock House Lodge No. 417, Hamilton, Hamilton county --------W.T. Claunch
J. Nixon Lodge No. 421, Post Oak Grove, Bastrop county, post office Smithville --------J.C. Watts
Wills Point Lodge No. 422, Wills Point, Van Zandt county --------J.M. Starnes
Weimar Lodge No. 423, Weimar, Colorado county --------S.M. Gladney [J.M. Gladney]
Anchor Lodge No. 424, San Antonio, Bexar county --------George Chamberlain, P. Wolfinger, [Phil. Wolfinger] M.R. Clark [W.R. Clark]
Farmington Lodge No. 430, Farmington, Grayson county --------B.F. White, George Hardin
Hiram Lodge No. 433, Collinsville, Grayson county --------H. Wells [H. Willis]
Flatonia Lodge No. 436, Flatonia, Fayette county --------W.R. Ragsdale, P.M.
Johnson Station Lodge No. 438, Johnson Station, Tarrant county --------J.S. Strayhan [J.S. Strahan]
Commerce Lodge No. 439, Commerce, Hunt county, post office --------G. Jackson
Burlington Lodge No. 440, Burlington, Montague county, post office Spanish Fort, Texas --------M.S. McNatt
Los Moras Lodge No. 444, Brackett, Kinney county --------Wm. McCabe
New York Lodge No. 446, New York, Henderson county --------C.L. McGill, E.A. Decatur Lodge No. 447, Decatur, Wise county --------John Holden
Johnsonville Lodge No. 448, Johnsonville, Somerville county, post office George's Creek --------H.C. Stevens
R.E. Lee Lodge No. 449, Osceola, Hill county --------D. Matthews
Lone Star Lodge No. 450, Bundick School House, Gonzales county, post office Zedler's Mills --------Wm. Bundick
Noland's River Lodge No. 453, Noland's River, Johnson county --------H.B. Gatewood
Henrietta Lodge No. 454, Henrietta, Clay county --------C.A. James
Grand Prairie Lodge No. 455, Smithfield, Tarrant county --------J.G. Walker [J.C. Walker]
Hill City Lodge No. 456, Austin, Travis county --------W.G. Thomas
Ferris Lodge No. 460, Ferris, Ellis county --------J.M. Andrews
Atlanta Lodge No. 463, Atlanta, Cass county --------E.A. Mason
Sherman Lodge No. 464, Sherman, Grayson county --------Jas. A. Long, V.R. Evans, W.A. Pullen [W.H. Pullen]
Harwood Lodge No. 468, Harwood, Gonzales county --------John F. Williams, J.C. Brenton [J.G. Brenton]
Grapeland Lodge No. 473, Grapeland, Houston county --------T.J. Keen
Liberty Grove Lodge No. 475, Liberty Grove, Hill county --------Stephen Jackson
Mullins Creek Lodge No. 476, William's Ranch, Brown county --------O.B. Huckelby
Hico Lodge No. 477, Hico, Hamilton county --------J.Q. Anderson

TEXAS MASONIC DEATHS WITH SELECTED BIOGRAPHICAL SKETCHES

Aurora Lodge No. 479, Aurora, Wise county --------J.M. McCright [J.M. McGright]
Thornton Lodge No. 486, Thornton, Limestone county --------W.G. Hudson, W.C. Jones
Cryer Creek Lodge No. 497, Cryer Creek, Navarro county --------Geo. Levens, Wm. Stokes
Mineola Lodge No. 502, Mineola, Wood county --------C.A. Estes, A.J. Turman
Desdemonia Lodge No. 506, Eastland county --------W.N. Noel, A.L. Ross
Valley View Lodge No. 507, Valley View, Cook county --------Dan McGee
Mountain Creek Lodge No. 511, Grand Prairie, Dallas county --------David Jordan, [David Jordon] H.W. Caho
Audubon Lodge No. 512, Audubon, Wise county --------W.E. Akin
Belle Plain Lodge No. 522, Belle Plain, Callahan county --------C.L. Terry

Appear in Lodge of Sorrow, but not in the Lodge returns for 1880: L.W. Coon, E.M. Delk, W.R. Campbell, G.D. Howard, G.G. Kennedy, G.C. Love, C. Lawrence, B. Murchison, R.C. Montgomery, John McKenna, J.A. Odell, J.S. Nolen, T.B. Payne, J. Rogers, J.W. Robertson, S.H. Sluder, Eugene Smith, W.W. Stone, J.F. Walker

RETURNS OF LODGES
FOR THE MASONIC YEAR
A.D. 1881, A.L. 5881
DEATHS

Holland Lodge No. 1, Houston, Harris county --------Jas. W. Henderson, J.C.C. Winch, Chas. Granger Collins, C.S. Longcope, E.A.

Milam Lodge No. 2, Nacogdoches, Nacogdoches county --------Frederick Voight, John A. Shanks, E.A.

Harmony Lodge No. 6, Galveston, Galveston county --------Thos. M. Jack, S.C. Woodrow, F.W. Clayton, E.L. Collins

Austin Lodge No. 12, Austin, Travis county --------O. Fisher, J.M. Tibaut

Trinity Lodge No. 14, Livingston, Polk county --------J.O. Stevens, C.J. Fields, J.B. Agnew, F.J. Williams, E.A.

Friendship Lodge No. 16, Clarksville, Red River county --------C. H. Fassett, J.W.P. McKinzie

Washington Lodge No. 18, Washington, Washington county --------L.W. Spann, E.A.

Forrest Lodge No. 19, Huntsville, Walker county --------Jas. L. Reid, P. Singleton

Graham Lodge No. 20, Brenham, Washington county --------A.G. Beaumont, A.H. Rippetoe

Lathrop Lodge No. 21, Crockett, Houston county --------Wm. Morrow

Marshall Lodge No. 22, Marshall, Harrison county --------G.B. Lipscomb, A. Bernstein, Sam. F. Sexton, C.H. Pepper, E.A.

Clinton Lodge No. 23, Henderson, Rusk county --------J.S. Boggess, Sr. D.W. Rogers

Montgomery Lodge No. 25, Montgomery, Montgomery county --------H.R. Bell

Palestine Lodge No. 31, Palestine, Anderson county --------J.H. McKnight, T.D. Shehan, W.H. Bowen, Ed. Davis

LaFayette Lodge No. 34, LaGrange, Fayette county --------J.R. Fenner, T.J. Martin, T.J. Walker

Jefferson Lodge No. 38, Jefferon, Marion county --------Thos. Browrigg, John M. Fay, J.C. Gray, all E.A.'s

Leona Union Lodge No. 39, Leona, Leon county --------John T. Adkisson, W.H. Waltman

Alamo Lodge No. 44, San Antonio, Bexar county --------J.H. Lyons, James Vance

Euclid Lodge No. 45, Rusk, Cherokee county --------James C. Francis, J.B. Smith

Liberty Lodge No. 48, Liberty, Liberty county --------W.D. Williams, H.C. Moss, A.N.B. Tompkins

St. Johns Lodge No. 51, McKinney, Collin county --------John Wagner, J.M. Benge

Tannehill Lodge No. 52, Dallas, Dallas county --------L.P. Garrison. Wesley Overend

St. Johns Lodge No. 53, Tyler, Smith county --------G.W. McDougal, O. Smith E.A.'s; M.M. Coulter, J.T. Griffin, F.C.'s

Grand Bluff Lodge No. 54, Grand Bluff, Panola county --------J.R. Smith, F.C.

Warren Lodge No. 56, Caldwell, Burleson county --------L.W. Wilkinson, H.C.A. King

Mt. Enterprise Lodge No. 60, Mt. Enterprise, Rusk county --------Dan. Bartlett

Rocky Mount Lodge No. 63, Overton, Rusk county --------T.F. Herring

Hubert Lodge No. 67, Chappell Hill, Washington county --------B.R. Thomas, D.E. Silas, Gid. Keesee

Caledonia Lodge No. 68, Columbus, Colorado county --------W.J. Darden, M.T. Gentry

Morton Lodge No. 72, Richmond, Fort Bend county --------Harman Boness, R.A. Weston

Cameron Lodge No. 76, York Town, De Witt county --------W.R. Wallace, David Murray, Sr.

Oasis Lodge No. 79, Daingerfield, Morris county --------George W. Beasley, D.J. Porter

Rio Grande Lodge No. 81, Brownsville, Cameron county --------Henry L. Howlett

Indianola Lodge No. 84, Indianola, Calhoun county --------Martin Reynolds, I.T.W. Mitchell

New Salem Lodge No. 87, New Salem, Rusk county --------W.C. Caison

Andrew Jackson Lodge No. 88, Linden, Cass county --------J.L. Jeter

San Gabriel Lodge No. 89, Georgetown, Williamson county --------George A. Scott, J.J. Stubblefield, Sam. Mankins

Waxahachie Lodge No. 90, Waxahachie, Ellis county --------C.D. Pickett

Tarrant Lodge No. 91, Lone Star Hall, Hopkins county, post office Birthright --------Jesse Beason

Waco Lodge 92, Waco, McLennan county --------J.J. Riddle

Augusta Lodge No. 93, Augusta, Houston county --------A.M.B. Glover, J.J. Allen

Goliad Lodge No. 94, Goliad, Goliad county --------J.A. Dill

Sharon Lodge No. 95, Pine Hill, Rusk county --------L.M. Rausseau

Canton Lodge No. 98, Canton, Smith county, post office, Omen --------J. J. Flinn, R.R. Collier, M.V. Arnold, F.C.

Danville Lodge No. 101, Kilgore, Gregg county --------W.H. Leach

Unity Lodge No. 102, Moscow, Polk county --------John E. Parrish

San Jacinto Lodge No. 106, Willis, Montgomery county --------J.V. Reese

Guadalupe Lodge No. 109, Seguin, Guadalupe county --------Jacob Kubler

Red River Lodge No. 116, Pine Creek Church, Red River county, post office Tomaha --------Isham East

Travis Lodge No. 117, Sherman, Grayson county --------N.C. Cunningham, John A. Fitch, John E. Perry

Starr Lodge No. 118, Starrville, Smith county --------J.R. Noler, E.A.
Mount Hope Lodge No. 121, Mount Hope, Tyler county, post office Chester --------James C. Riley
Texana Lodge No. 123, Texana, Jackson county --------J.T. White
Madison Lodge No. 126, Orange, Orange county --------S.M. Milburn, Robert Whiting, Robert B. Russell
Brazos Union Lodge No. 129, Bryan, Brazos county --------N.B. Davis, George C. Gentry, L.D. Stockton, H. Todd
Belmont Lodge No. 131, Belmont, Gonzales county --------P. Dilworth, J.A. Mayfield, W.A. Caragin, visiting brother
Bethel Lodge No. 134, Ladonia, Fannin county --------S.M. Dillingham
Castillian Lodge No. 141, Canton, Van Zandt county --------J.L. Turner, A.M. Reece
Bethesda Lodge No. 142, Gilmer, Upshur county --------V.H. Vivion
Winnsborough Lodge No. 146, Winnsboro, Wood county --------Jesse Odom, Benj. Williams
Fort Worth Lodge No. 148, Fort Worth, Tarrant county --------Geo. Birdwell, C.L. Pigman, Henderson Thornton
Spring Hill Lodge No. 155, Spring Hill, Navarro --------J.A. Stansell, L.W. Spence
Lancaster Lodge No. 160, Lancaster, Dallas county --------M.P. Everts
Honey Grove Lodge No. 164, Honey Grove, Fannin county --------J.J. Faulk, J.W. Piner
Kentucky Lodge No. 167, Kentucky Town, Grayson county --------Jesse A. Brown, Henry P. Fitch
J.F. Taylor Lodge No. 169, Hallville, Harrison county --------J.W. Whipple, J.R. Renfro
San Anders Lodge No. 170, Cameron, Milam county --------W.M. James
Bosque Lodge No. 171, Bosqueville, McLennan county --------Robt. A. Ford
Valley Lodge No. 175, Burnet, Burnet county --------W.L. Chesser
St. Paul's Lodge No. 177, Port Sullivan, Milam county --------J.C. Coward
Hardeman Lodge No. 179, Luling, Caldwell county --------J.H. Mitchell, A. Henning
Post Oak Island Lodge 181, Sam Smith Springs, Lee county, post office McDade, Bastrop county --------S.M. Rawls, Winslow Turner
Hopkinsville Lodge No. 183, Waelder, Gonzales county --------T.J. Tomlinson, Frank W. Smith
White Oak Lodge No. 185, Pine Forest, Hopkins county, post office Carroll's Prairie --------J.A. Post
Havana Lodge No. 191, Douglassville, Cass county --------John T. Draper
Gatesville Lodge No. 197, Gatesville, Coryell county --------W.W. Jones
Tyre Lodge No. 198, Tennesse Colony, Anderson county --------A.B. Fitzgerald
James A. Baker Lodge No. 202, Ebenezer Baptist Church, Walker county, post office, Huntsville --------O.G. Ross, J.M. Wynne
Pine Lodge No. 203, Edom, Van Zandt county --------C.C. Sims

Frank Sexton Lodge No. 206, Pittsburg, Camp county --------A. Carpenter, F.C.
Mantua Lodge No. 209, Mantua, Collin county, post office Van Alstyne --------W.M. Derrick
Gainesville Lodge No. 210, Gainesville, Cooke county --------John Chadwell, J.W. Truelove
Stanfield Lodge No. 217, Denton, Denton county --------Thomas E. Hogg
Sulphur Springs Lodge No. 221, Sulphur Springs, Hopkins county --------W.S. Petty, E.T. Goodson, H.H. Hargrave
Parsons Lodge No. 222, Manor, Travis county --------James Manor
Bellville Lodge No. 223, Bellville, Austin county --------Julius Schonert, J.H. Catlin, Sr.
Miller Lodge No. 224, White Rock, Hunt county --------G.W. Tatom, Harvey Young
Butler Lodge No. 224a, Butler, Freestone county --------Joe Ivy
Round Rock Lodge No. 227, Round Rock, Williamson county --------T.V. Strode
Sampson Lodge No. 231, Lynchburg, Harris county --------C.P. Karcher, David Duncan
Eutaw Lodge No. 233, Kosse, Limestone county --------T.J. Davis, G.B. Duncan
Plano Lodge No. 235, Plano, Collin county --------E.D. Hogge
Torbert Lodge No. 241, Turner's Point, Kaufman county, post office Poetry --------A.C. Luis
Llano Lodge No. 242, Llano, Llano county --------J.J. Bogarth, M.A. Harvey
Gamble Lodge No. 244, Bastrop, Bastrop county --------R.E. Hill
Adah Zillah Lodge No. 247, Millican, Brazos county --------J.W. Harington, J.H. Millican, E.A.
A. Jackson Lodge No. 249, Pinetown, Cherokee county, post office Jacksonville --------H. McKnight
Homer Lodge No. 254, Homer, Angelina county --------Sam Rich, J.F. Richardson
Beeville Lodge No. 261, Beeville, Bee county --------O.P. Crosby
Grayson Lodge No. 265, Lost Prairie, Limestone county, post office Personville --------J.C. Morton, J.H. Reeves
Stephenville Lodge No. 267, Stephenville, Erath county --------J.R. Pickard, S.T. Evans
Dixie Lodge No. 272, Troupe, Smith county --------A.F. Dorsett
Phoenix Lodge No. 275, Weatherford, Parker county --------J.L. Oldham
Brownwood Lodge No. 279, Brownwood, Brown county --------Isaac Mullins
J.D. Giddings Lodge No. 280, Giddings, Lee county --------W.L. Bracken
Winchester Lodge No. 282, Winchester, Fayette county --------B.C. Stroud
Eastern Star Lodge No. 284, Centralia, Trinity county --------J.W. Hamilton
Action Lodge No. 285, Action, Hood county --------Jo. Robinson
Mars Lodge No. 293, Emory, Rains county --------R.W. Spradling
Salado Lodge No. 296, Salado, Bell county --------E.N. Good
Tucker Lodge No. 297, Galveston, Galveston county --------W. Sandall, I. Fedder, R. Tommins, A. Bradford, H.C. Freeland, F.W. Clayton, G. Dowell

Moulton Lodge No. 298, Moulton, Lavaca county --------John Walker, M.J. Duff, John McKinney

Navasota Lodge No. 299, Navasota, Grimes county --------Ignatz Kohn

Cedar Creek Lodge No. 300, Tryon Church, Brazos county, post office Bryan --------J.T. Bowman, Joseph Terry, J.S. Marlow, E.A.

Osage Lodge No. 301, Osage, Colorado county, post office Weimar --------W.W. Walker

Starksville Lodge No. 303, Masonic Hall, Lamar county, post office Blossom Prairie --------J.W. Harmon, H.H. Rheudacil, B.P. Lambert, E.A.

G.W. Foster Lodge No. 306, Nelsonville, Austin county --------J.H. Catlin, J. Henry Shelburne

Shiloh Lodge No. 307, Shiloh Hall, Hunt county, post office Lone Oak --------G.W. Adair

Hull's Store Lodge No. 309, Woods Post office, Panola county --------J.C. Moore, Van Swearingen, E.A.

Wm. Foster Lodge No. 312, Fosterville, Anderson county --------John W. Cantrell

Alvarado Lodge No. 314, Alvarado, Johnson county --------W.H. Harris, Nathaniel Davis, S.J. Brown

Cleburne Lodge No. 315, Cleburne, Johnson county --------J.T. Orear, A. Vancleave

Palo Pinto Lodge No. 319, Palo Pinto, Palo Pinto county --------Mat Veale

Fort Richardson Lodge No. 320, Jacksboro, Jack county --------G.W. Wingate

Rockport Lodge No. 323, Rockport, Aransas county --------W.C. Casterline

Bandera Lodge No. 324, Bandera, Bandera county --------J.H. White

Brazoria Lodge No. 327, Brazoria, Brazoria county --------Henry Luedecker

Gray Lodge No. 329, Houston, Harris county --------R. Greene

Leesburg Lodge No. 334, Leesville, Gonzales county --------A.R. Morris

Greenville Lodge No. 335, Greenville, Hunt county --------J.C. Gill

Florence Lodge No. 338, Florence, Williamson county --------J.M. Moore

E.M. Wilder Lodge No. 339, Power's Chapel, Falls county, post office Wilderville --------Miles Gregory

San Marcos Lodge No. 342, San Marcos, Hays county --------G.W. Crank, Wm. Barbee

Bowling Lodge No. 343, Marquez, Leon county --------John S. Garrett

White Rock Lodge No. 347, White Rock, McLennan county, post office Bold Springs --------E.R. Williams

Bremond Lodge No. 350, Bremond, Robertson county --------T.S. Kirven, S.T. Price, S.H.D. Warren, J.S. Snellings

Caddo Grove Lodge No. 352, Caddo Grove, Johnson county --------C.W. Clark

Groesbeck Lodge No. 354, Groesbeck, Limestone county --------Richard Andrews, A. Levingston

Prairie Valley Lodge No. 355, Prairie Valley, Hill county, post office Whitney --------A.F. Walling

Golden Rule Lodge No. 361, Hearne, Robertson county --------W.J. Hale, Chas. Lewis, Larkin Echols

Sand Springs Lodge No. 365, Sand Springs, Wood county, post office Hawkins --------G.W. Francis

Brushy Lodge No. 367, Brushy, Panola county, post office Clayton --------Andrew T. Davis, Sr.

Ennis Lodge No. 369, Ennis, Ellis county --------Q.N. Hall, A.R. Strother, E.A.

Dexter Lodge No. 372, Dexter City, Cooke county --------J.W. Donalson

Atascosa Lodge No. 379, Benton, Atascosa county, post office Somersett --------Aaron Kambie, George W. Williams, E.A.

Halesboro Lodge No. 381, Halesboro, Red River county --------Wm. Humphreys

Snow River Lodge No. 385, Town Bluff, Tyler county --------C. Davis

Brooklyn Lodge No. 386, Forney, Kaufman county --------D.H. Peed

Bald Prairie Lodge No. 387, Bald Prairie, Robertson county --------J.D. McCutcheon

Granbury Lodge No. 392, Granbury, Hood county --------Wm. R. Brown

Poluxey Lodge No. 393, Lodge Room, Hood county, post office Poluxey --------D. Shipman

Little River Lodge No. 397, Little River Church House, Milam county, post office Jones' Prairie --------J.M. Cargill, M. Hildreth

Longview Lodge No. 404, Longview, Gregg county --------W.N. Jones, M.S. Durham

Artesia Lodge No. 406, Terrell, Kaufman county --------John G. Moore, S.E. Wilson, R.A. Terrell

Oak Grove Lodge No. 408, The Grove, Coryell county --------W.C. Ridling, T.J. Tremier

Tres Palacios Lodge No. 411, Tres Palacios Hall, Matagorda county, post office Deming's Bridge --------J.J. Loudermilk

Montague Lodge No. 415, Montague, Montague county --------D.L. Poiner

Rock House Lodge No. 417, Hamilton, Hamilton county --------Isaac H. Steen

Wills Point Lodge No. 422, Wills Point, Van Zandt county --------G.L. Ellis

Weimar Lodge No. 423, Weimar, Colorado county --------T.J. Grace, A.L. Pettus, L.W. Ulrich

Elmo Lodge No. 425, Elmo, Kaufman county --------J.J. Jordan, D.H. Mallory, E.A.

Longbottom Lodge No. 428, Worthham, Freestone county --------J.P. Pugh

Liberty Hill Lodge No. 432, Liberty Hill, Williamson county --------W. Hampton Poole

Hiram Lodge No. 433, Collinsville, Grayson county --------B.S. Mitchell

Flatonia Lodge No. 436, Flatonia, Fayette county --------J.M. Davis, W.P. Ivy

Johnson Station Lodge No. 438, Johnson Station, Tarrant county --------Sam D. Kelley

Commerce Lodge No. 439, Commerce, Hunt county --------Wm. Jernigan, D.E. Byrd

Duck Creek Lodge No. 441, Duck Creek, Dallas county --------W.F. McCullough
Coryell Lodge No. 442, Jonesboro, Coryell county --------John Beckett
Las Moras Lodge No. 444, Brackett, Kinney county --------Joshua Cox, James Murphy
New York Lodge No. 446, New York, Henderson county --------A.T. Johnson, Wm. Burns
Johnsonville Lodge No. 448, Johnsonville, Somervell county, post office George's Creek --------L. Lafon
Lone Star Lodge No. 450, Bundick's School House, Gonzales county, post office Zedler's Mill --------D. Ramsay
Palmer Lodge No. 459, Palmer, Ellis county --------Robert Curry
Atlanta Lodge No. 463, Atlanta, Cass county --------A.J. Newton
Harwood Lodge No. 468, Harwood, Gonzales county --------J.C. Barkly
Hope Lodge No. 471, Rio Grande City, Starr county --------Joseph M. Hart
Rosston Lodge No. 474, Rosston, Cooke county --------George W. Medley
Reagan Lodge No. 480, Reagan, Falls county --------G.T. Robinson
Albany Lodge No. 482, Albany, Shackelford county --------J.N. Masterton
Solomon Lodge No. 484, Taylor, Williamson county --------D.F. Ramsaur
Thornton Lodge No. 486, Thornton, Limestone county --------J.S. Ellis
Litton Springs Lodge No. 487, Litton Springs, Caldwell county, post office Ophelia --------W.L. Cartar, Z.R. Jourdan
Fort Griffin Lodge No. 489, Fort Griffin, Shackelford county --------E. Woosley, J.F. Bozeman
Blue Ridge Lodge No. 490, Blue Ridge, Collin county --------R.O.N. Osburn, Lot Bruton
Magnolia Lodge No. 495, Woodville, Tyler county --------J.S. Riley
Coleman Lodge No. 496, Coleman, Coleman county --------M.A. Henry
Dublin Lodge No. 504, Dublin, Erath county --------A.J. Morrison
Valley View Lodge No. 507, Valley View, Cooke county --------D.T. Shirley
Deer Creek Lodge No. 510, Oak Grove, Tarrant county --------B.F. Birdwell
Mountain Creek Lodge No. 511, Grand Prairie, Dallas county --------J.R. Lassater
Carlton Lodge No. 519, Carlton, Hamilton county --------W.W. Weeks, S.F. Tibout
Carthage Lodge No. 521, Carthage, Panola county --------Drew Simmons
Glen Rose Lodge No. 525, Glen Rose, Somervell county --------A.C. West
Junction City Lodge No. 548, Junction City, Kimble county --------J.C. Wagner

115

PROCEEDING GRAND LODGE OF TEXAS 1882
RETURNS OF LODGES
FOR THE MASONIC YEAR 1882
DEATHS

Milam Lodge No. 2, Nacogdoches, Nacogdoches county --------Benj. Rusk

Red Land Lodge No. 3, San Augustine, San Augustine county --------Geo. F. Border

St. Johns Lodge No. 5, Columbia, Brazoria county --------Chas. S. Bennett

Harmony Lodge No. 6, Galveston, Galveston county --------I.C. Owings, S.S. Whittemore, E.S. Wood, M. Strickland, B.R. Davis

Milam Lodge No. 11, Independence, Washington county --------J.A. McCrocklin, J.M. Williams, John Crowley

Austin Lodge No. 12, Austin, Travis county --------Ed. Finnin, E. Raven, F.M. Fincher, W.J. Russell, H. Persinger

Constantine Lodge No. 13, Bonham, Fannin county --------J.R. Russell

Trinity Lodge No. 14, Livington, Polk county --------William C. Meece

Friendship Lodge No. 16, Clarksville, Red River county --------John A. Bagby, Chas. Duffie

Washington Lodge No. 18, Washington, Washington county --------J.J. Wyatt, J.C. Evans

Graham Lodge No. 20, Brenham, Washington county --------B.D. Dashield, S.S. Hosea, W.W. Hackworth, J.J. Wilburn, N. Kavenaugh

Lathrop Lodge No. 21, Crockett, Houston county --------W.A. Watson

Marshall Lodge No. 22, Marshall, Harrison county --------A. Kahn, R.S. James

Clinton Lodge No. 23, Henderson, Rusk county --------J.N. Still, Levi Compton

Montgomery Lodge No. 25, Montgomery, Montgomery county --------J.F. Luckey, A.J. Matthews

Paris Lodge No. 27, Paris, Lamar county --------J.N. Adams, A.S. Johnson, L.H. Williams, J.S. Ormby

De Witt Clinton Lodge No. 29, Jasper, Jasper county --------R.C. Doom

Gonzales Lodge No. 30, Gonzales, Gonzales county --------Arthur Chance

Palestine Lodge No. 31, Palestine, Anderson county --------J.W. Bray, S.P. Doss, E.D. Thompson

Mount Moriah Lodge No. 37, Cold Springs, San Jacinto county --------Daniel Byrd

Jefferson Lodge No. 38, Jefferson, Marion county --------P.M. Graham

Leona Union Lodge No. 39, Leona, Leon county --------E.F. Heard, Thomas B. Gates, L. Keeling

Alamo Lodge No. 44, San Antonio, Bexar county --------M.G. Cotton, D.C. Knox

Euclid Lodge No. 45, Rusk, Cherokee county --------George Davidson

Liberty Lodge No. 48, Libery, Liberty county --------E.B. Pickett

Tannehill Lodge No. 52, Dallas, Dallas county --------N.B. McKinnon, M.M. Pharis, J.H. Stephens, J.F. Rowe

St. Johns Lodge No. 53, Tyler, Smith county --------S.H. Boren, Wm. Hill

116

Warren Lodge No. 56, Caldwell, Burleson county --------T.H. Chestnut, Joseph Jackson

Mt. Enterprise Lodge No. 60, Mt. Enterprise, Rusk county --------J.F.M. Hall

Rocky Mount Lodge No. 63, Overton, Rusk county --------Nat Geurin

Caledonia Lodge No. 68, Columbus, Colorado county --------George Obrecht, N.C. Spencer, A.L. Townsend

Boston Lodge No. 69, Boston, Bowie county --------H.L. Bryant, T.C. Busick

Cameron Lodge No. 76, Yorktown, De Witt county --------L.B. Wright

Rio Grande Lodge No. 81, Brownsville, Cameron county --------F.J. Parker, Wm. E. Whitehead

Terrell Lodge No. 83, Alto, Cherokee county --------A.V. Singletarry, W.J. Windham

Indianola Lodge No. 84, Indianola, Calhoun county --------S.D. Clark, Wm. P. Milby

Andrew Jackson Lodge No. 88, Linden, Cass county --------J.F. Tune

Waxahachie Lodge No. 90, Waxahachie, Ellis county --------J.B. Allen, A.J. Rosson

Augusta Lodge No. 93, Augusta, Houston county --------Samuel Robinson

Colorado Lodge No. 96, Webberville, Travis county --------W.S. Fowler

Danville Lodge No. 101, Kilgore, Gregg county --------Reuben Goforth, A.B. Hudson, J.C. Wilson

Fairfield Lodge No. 103, Fairfield, Freestone county --------James R. Seeley

Kickapoo Lodge No. 105, Kickapoo, Anderson county --------George Hollingsworth, A.B. Oldham, O.O. Lee

San Jacinto Lodge No. 106, Willis, Montgomery county --------J.M. Sandel, Thos. Tomlison

Guadalupe Lodge No. 109, Seguin, Guadalupe county --------D.R. Freeman

Prairie Lea Lodge No. 114, Prairie Lea, Caldwell county --------J.A. Glenn

Red River Lodge No. 116, Held at Pine Creek Church, Red River county, post office Tomaha --------M.J. Mullins

Flora Lodge No. 119, Quitman, Wood county --------J.T. Adiar

Baylor Lodge No. 125, Gay Hill, Washington county --------J.T. McLeod

Brazos Union Lodge No. 129, Bryan, Brazos county --------Albert Paris, L. Spring, Wm. Davis, Sr.

Retreat Lodge No. 133, Courtney, Grimes county --------W.S. Kennon

Bethel Lodge No. 134, Ladonia, Fannin county --------Wm. Cozby, S.F. Montgomery

Newton Lodge No. 136, Burkeville, Newton county --------Ira Stephenson

Castillian Lodge No. 141, Canton, Van Zandt county --------J.H. Evans

Pierce Lodge No. 144, Calvert, Robertson county --------F.J. Sink

Winnsborough Lodge No. 146, Winnsboro, Wood county --------J.P. Anderson, R.C. Huie

Fort Worth Lodge No. 148, Fort Worth, Tarrant county --------W.E. Orgain, M.S. Matheney, Thos. B. Haygood

Marlin Lodge No. 152, Marlin, Falls county --------J.B. Billingsley

Eclectic Lodge No. 153, Savoy, Fannin county --------E.S. Aston
Hickory Hill Lodge No. 156, Held in Lodge Room, Cass county, post office Avinger --------H.J. Avinger, David Keasler, John Wilson, J.W. Orr
East Trinity Lodge No. 157, Rockwall, Rockwall county --------John Butler
Wm. M. Taylor Lodge No. 158, Garden Valley, Smith county --------T.B. McAdams, G.W. Childers
Athens Lodge No. 165, Athens, Henderson county --------Eph. Burton, D.M. Mabray, C.W. Ingram, W.P. Evans
Belton Lodge No. 166, Belton, Bell county --------John Owens, Wm. Elliott
San Anders Lodge No. 170, Cameron, Milam county --------Jordan Hill
Bosque Lodge No. 171, Bosqueville, McLennan county --------Geo. R. Steel
Corsicana Lodge No. 174, Corsicana, Navarro county --------J.B. Jones, S.C. Liscomb, G.W. Tankersly, C.M. Winkler
Valley Lodge No. 175, Burnet, Burnet county --------L.J. Conner
St. Paul's Lodge No. 177, Port Sullivan, Milam county --------I.P. Sneed
Hardeman Lodge No. 179, Luling, Caldwell county --------E.S. Binns
Hopkins Lodge No. 180, Black Jack Grove, Hopkins county --------W.Y. Box
Post Oak Lodge No. 181, held at Smith Springs, Lee county, post office Beaukiss, Williamson county --------N.B. Scott
Hopkinsville Lodge No. 183, Waelder, Gonzales county --------G.W. Bartlett
White Oak Lodge No. 185, Pine Forest, Hopkins county, post office Carroll's Prairie --------W.H.C. Johnson, J.T. Hancock, G.W. White
Corpus Christi Lodge No. 189, Corpus Christi, Nueces county --------E.D. Sidbury, D.M. Hastings, W.C. Dickey, J.S. Millstead
Refugio Lodge No. 190, Refugio, Refugio county --------J.R. Harrison
Havana Lodge No. 191, Douglassville, Cass county --------Rev. W.L. Heath
Leon Lodge No. 193, Held at Lodge Room, Bell county, post office Moffatt --------J.R. Augustus, J.W. Abbott, Miles Ashburn, M.A.O. Moore
Jack Titus Lodge No. 194, Held at Coleman's Springs, Red River county, post office Walker Station --------John Coleman
Tyre Lodge No. 198, Tennessee Colony, Anderson county --------G.P. Wallace
Pine Lodge No. 203, Edom, Van Zandt county --------J.W. Webb
Farmersville Lodge No. 214, Farmersville, Collin county --------L.D. Smith
Dresden Lodge No. 218, Dresden, Navarro county --------A.M. Maddox
Onion Creek Lodge No. 220, Held at Lodge Room, Travis county, post office Bluff Springs --------Enoch Martin
Sulphur Springs Lodge No. 221, Sulphur Springs, Hopkins county --------J.P. Connally, C.P. Connally
Bellville Lodge No. 223, Bellville, Austin county --------F.C. Hober
San Saba Lodge No. 225, San Saba, San Saba county --------M.C. Williamson
Round Rock Lodge No. 227, Round Rock, Williamson county --------G. McClure
Sampson Lodge No. 231, Lynchburg, Harris county --------A.K. Jemison
Eutaw Lodge No. 233, Kosse, Limestone county --------J.H. Harbison
White Rock Lodge No. 234, Frankford, Collin county --------E.P. McKamy

San Felipe Lodge No. 239, San Felipe, Austin county --------G.D. Parker, T.S. Reneau
Medina Lodge No. 252, Castroville, Medina county --------Jos. Ney
Beeville Lodge No. 261, Beeville, Bee county --------Roswell Gillett
Milford Lodge No. 262, Milford, Ellis county --------James Gilbreath
Whitesboro' Lodge No. 263, Whitesboro', Grayson county --------E.J. Cravin
Grand View Lodge No. 266, Grand View, Johnson county --------J.M. Gunn
Meridian Lodge No. 268, Meridian, Bosque county --------C. Pederson
Pleasant Hill Lodge No. 269, Simpsonville, Upshur county --------D.E. Calvert
Pilot Point Lodge No. 270, Pilot Point, Denton county --------N.M. Dollins, Levi Webster
Dixie Lodge No. 272, Troupe, Smith county --------Wm. Norris
McCulloch Lodge No. 273, Mason, Mason county --------David Brown
Brownwood Lodge No. 279, Brownwood, Brown county --------James H. Gideon, J.P. Allison, A. Anderson, Wm. Connell
Acton Lodge No. 285, Acton, Hood county --------R.A. Duncan, W.T. Lusk
Grapevine Lodge No. 288, Grapevine, Tarrant county --------G.M. Morison, D.W. Bulock
Tyler Prairie Lodge No. 290, Pennington, Trinity county --------N. Dial
Mars Hill Lodge No. 293, Emory, Rains county --------J.W. Montgomery
Nathan Corley Lodge No. 294, Magnolia Springs, Jasper county --------G.B. Gandy, Wm. Jones
Scyene Lodge No. 295, Scyene, Dallas county --------W.L. Knox
Tucker Lodge No. 297, Galveston, Galveston county --------J.P. Evans, T.C. Shearer, M. Strickland
Moulton Lodge No. 298, Moulton, Lavaca county --------John McKinney
Navasota Lodge No. 299, Navasota, Grimes county --------M. Callanan, A. Kuhnerdt
Cedar Creek Lodge No. 300, Held at Tryon Church, Brazos county, post office Bryan --------J.W. Sparks
Osage Lodge No. 301, Osage, Colorado county, post office Weimar --------Jeff Shiver
Shiloh Lodge No. 307, Held at Hefner Chappel, Hunt county, post office Lone Oak --------T.P. Bright, J.W. Cryer
Cedar Grove Lodge No. 308, Cedar Grove, Kaufman county, post office Wills Point --------Wm. Bennison, W.M. Osburn
Red Rock Lodge No. 310, Red Rock, Bastrop county --------T.L. Clifton
Zion Lodge No. 313, Iola, Grimes county --------Henry Neeley
Alvarado Lodge No. 314, Alvarado, Johnson county --------J.F. Golding, E.L. Smith, W.C. Mahanay, Wallace Bills, B.B. House, Samuel Ramsey
Cleburne Lodge No. 315, Cleburne, Johnson county --------N.H. Cook, A.J. Brown, W.J. Hayes
Palo Pinto Lodge No. 319, Palo Pinto, Palo Pinto county --------J.M. Harris
Prairieville Lodge No. 322, Prairieville, Kaufman county --------H.M. Barfield
Bandera Lodge No. 324, Bandera, Bandera county --------Louis Hillman

Evergreen Lodge No. 325, Oakville, Live Oak county --------S.S. Mapes
Victoria Lodge No. 326, Victoria, Victoria county --------M.F. Holton
Gray Lodge No. 329, Houston, Harris county --------C.B. Kettringham
Mansfield Lodge No. 331, Mansfield, Tarrant county --------Edward T. Teague
Birdston Lodge No. 333, Birdston, Navarro county --------David Burleson
Greenville Lodge No. 335, Greenville, Hunt county --------H.B. Simonds
E.M. Wilder Lodge No. 339, Held at Power's Chapel, Falls county, post office Wilderville --------A.G. Tarver
San Marcos Lodge No. 342, San Marcos, Hays county --------H.B. Coffield
Tulip Lodge No. 348, Tulip, Fannin county --------Sam'l Pratt
Wm. C. Young Lodge No. 349, Held at Elizabeth, Denton county, post office Roanoke --------John Robins
Bremond Lodge No. 350, Bremond, Robertson county --------J.O. Chamberlin
Caddo Grove Lodge No. 352, Caddo Grove, Johnson county --------Benj. Bransom, E. Cook
Prairie Valley Lodge No. 355, Prairie Valley, Hill county, post office Whitney --------J.M. Grisham, H.C. Couch
Patrick Lodge No. 359, Franklin, Robertson county --------A.J. Guinn
Clifton Lodge No. 360, Clifton, Bosque county --------R.J. Singleton
Golden Rule Lodge No. 361, Hearne, Robertson county --------H.P. Hale
Eagle Lake Lodge No. 366, Eagle Lake, Colorado county --------R.W.B. Frazar, H.B. Stockings, an E.A., T.C. Tartt
Salem Lodge No. 368, Held at their Hall in Lee county, post office Ledbetter --------W.H. Foster
Ovilla Lodge No. 370, Ovilla, Ellis county --------E.D. Sullivan
Eureka Lodge No. 371, Springtown, Parker county --------Jos. S. Amos, Ezra Clark
Reily Springs Lodge No. 382, Reily Springs, Hopkins county --------J.C. Coker, Nat. Clifton
Dodge Lodge No. 384, Dodge, Walker county --------Milton Estill, R.P. Jennings
Snow River Lodge No. 385, Town Bluff, Tyler county --------E.B. Rudd, J.J. Swearingen
Brooklyn Lodge No. 386, Forney, Kaufman county --------J.H. McIntyre
Bald Prairie Lodge No. 387, Bald Prairie, Robertson county --------J.E. Thompson, J.D. Franks
Lamar Lodge No. 398, Held at Friendship Church, Lamar county, post office Biard's --------N.S. Liddell
Providence Lodge No. 400, Held at Providence Church, Anderson county, post office Alder Branch --------Samuel Robertson
Elk Horn Lodge No. 402, Held at Stiles' School House, Red River county, post office Clarksville --------C.B. Bush
Lone Star Lodge No. 403, Denison, Grayson county --------Julius Jasper, Jas. Beer, N.R. Barnes, H. Kinnel
Longview Lodge No. 404, Longview, Gregg county --------A. Cohn, J.M. Whitehead, Nick Hoyler

Iredell Lodge No. 405, Iredell, Bosque county --------A.M. Trimble
Artesia Lodge No. 406, Terrell, Kaufman county --------G.W. Carter
Rock House Lodge No. 417, Hamilton, Hamilton county --------E. Manning
Bolivar Lodge No. 418, Bolivar, Denton county --------R.B. Markham, Isaac Griffith
Weimar Lodge No. 423, Weimar, Colorado county --------H.C. Thomas
Anchor Lodge No. 424, San Antonio, Bexar county --------Erastus Reed, I.A. Steagall
Longbottom Lodge No. 428, Wortham, Freestone county --------Mathew Gleghorn
Farmington Lodge No. 430, Farmington, Grayson county --------W.C. Davis
Hiram Lodge No. 433, Collinsville, Grayson county --------W.P. Stone, G.T. Shivel
New York Lodge No. 446, New York, Henderson county --------Jas. Edins
R.E. Lee Lodge No. 449, Osceola, Hill county --------R.S. Johnson
Lone Star Lodge No. 450, Held at Bundick School House, Gonzales county, post office Zedler's Mill --------John A. King
Ferris Lodge No. 460, Ferris, Ellis county --------J.T. Hussey
Sonora Lodge No. 462, Near Martindale, Caldwell county --------J.A. Killian
Sherman Lodge No. 464, Sherman, Grayson county --------Chas B. Keep, an E.A.
Hope Lodge No. 471, Rio Grande City, Starr county --------John Decker, Noah Cox, L.H. Box
Grapeland Lodge No. 473, Grapeland, Houston county --------Zack Horn
Mullins Creek Lodge No. 476, William's Ranch, Brown county --------D.J.M. Danniel
Saint Joe Lodge No. 483, Saint Joe, Montague county --------J.J. Wilson
Young County Lodge No. 485, Graham, Young county --------Robt. Dickens
Litton Springs Lodge No. 487, Litton springs, Caldwell county, post office Ophelia --------A.W. Wright, L.C. Sims
Fort Griffin Lodge No. 489, Fort Griffin, Shackelford county --------S.J. Ward
Magnolia Lodge No. 495, Woodville, Tyler county --------Jesse Stewart
Chambers' Creek Lodge No. 499, Rankin Chapel, Ellis county, post office Astonia --------John Jackson
Centennial Lodge No. 500, Cannon, Grayson county --------R.D. Turner
Mineola Lodge No. 502, Mineola, Wood county --------J.P. Williams, C.R. Donnelly
Excelsior Lodge No. 505, Wolf's Mill, Hunt county, post office Hickory Creek --------Wm. Cozby
Desdemonia Lodge No. 506, Desdemonia, Eastland county --------J.R. Shuler
Chico Lodge No. 508, Chico, Wise county --------E.B. Youngblood
Audubon Lodge No. 512, Audubon, Wise county --------T.J. McNeely
Tivoli Lodge No. 513, Forrest's Store, Ellis county --------G.H. Fort
East Point Lodge No. 516, East Point, Wood county, post office Winnsboro --------G.L. Turner, J.M. Cain

Irene Lodge No. 517, Irene, Hill county --------L.O. Jones

Carthage Lodge No. 521, Carthage, Panola county --------J.M. Lawrence

Belle Plain Lodge No. 522, Belle Plain, Callahan county --------O.M.L. Parker

Glen Rose Lodge No. 525, Glen Rose, Somervell county --------J.H. Montgomery

Rosalie Lodge No. 527, Rosalie, Red River county --------V.J. Carter, B.F. Dinwiddie

Tressle Board Lodge No. 534, Cannon's School House, Hunt county, post office Payne's Store --------John Humpreys

Cottondale Lodge No. 538, Cottondale, Wise county --------W.P. Edwards

Lovelady Lodge No. 539, Lovelady, Houston county --------A.R. Chilcoat

Wayland Lodge No. 542, Wayland, Stephens county --------D. Brazos Smith

Laredo Lodge No. 547, Laredo, Webb county --------A.A. Johnston

Cross Timber Lodge No. 557, Tom Campbell's, Hunt county, post office Campbell --------John A. Ramsey

Center City Lodge No. 558, Center City, Hamilton county --------D.J. McDaniel

Abilene Lodge No. 559, Abilene, Taylor county --------E.H. Hillton

Paige Lodge No. 562, Paige, Bastrop county --------R.J. McKinney, W.G. Bauchman, S.B. Chirchill

~~~~~~

PART 2

BIOGRAPHICAL SKETCHES

SELECTED
OBITUARIES AND BIOGRAPHICAL SKETCHES OF
TEXAS MASONS

John E. Cravens----J.E. Cravens was Past Master of Palestine Lodge No. 31; at Labor in 1855, Junior Grand Warden; in 1856, Senior Grand Warden; in 1857, Deputy Grand Master; at refreshment 13 May 1860. A Faithful Workman Gone To Sleep.

Charles G. Keenan----C.G. Keenan of Huntsville came to Texas during the Republic and was in the Legislature 1846-1850. He was the Treasurer of the Grand Lodge of Texas for ten years as well as Past Grand Junior Warden. C.G. Keenan died in 1870.

Archibald St.Clair Ruthven----A.S. Ruthven, Past Grand Master, was born in Edinburgh, Scotland, in 1813, and died in Glasgow, Scotland, in 1865. His wife was named Annie Jane Coates. Ruthven came to Texas in 1839. He was initiated in Holland Lodge No. 1 on 12 September 1841; elected Senior Warden in 1843; W.M. in 1844/45/46/47; Grand Master in 1845; Grand Secretary 1846 to 1860 -- fifteen consecutive years. He was a member of Temple Lodge No. 4.

Thomas J.H. Anderson---- T.J.H. Anderson of Port Sullivan was born in Pike county, Alabama, 26 November 1828, and died in Houston, Harris county, Texas, 29 August 1871. In 1854, he was raised a Master Mason, and in 1858 he was elected W.M. of St. Paul's Lodge No. 177, in which capacity he served twelve consecutive years. He was Grand Senior Warden in 1869, Deputy Grand Master in 1870. He was elected Grand Master in 1871, but lived only a few weeks after his induction.----"Tell my brethren," he said in his last moments, "tell my brethren that I die at my post." Anderson was buried at Port Sullivan.

J.A. Greer and Joseph C. Harrison----J.A. Greer, P.G.M., and J.C. Harrison, P.D.G.M., were given a Tribute of Respect in 1856: "Whereas, it has pleased an all-wise Creator to remove from their worldly labors our much loved and worthy Brethren, P.G.M. J.A. Greer and P.D.G.M. Joseph C. Harrison, with whom we were wont to meet in time gone by, and labor together in our works of love and charity. We tender our heartfelt sympathies to the bereaved family of our deceased Brother J.C. Harrison, in their deep affliction, and to the friends of our departed Brother J.A. Greer, and trust that in their sorrow they may find consolation in the thought that our mutual loss is their eternal gain."

William M. Taylor----W.M. Taylor of Crockett, Houston county, was born 17 April 1817, and died 23 September 1871. He was Past Grand Master, initiated, passed and raised, 1845; Deputy Grand Master, 1850; Grand Master, 1854; High Priest of Trinity Chapter No. 4, 1850; Grand High Priest, 1853; M.E. Grand High Priest of the Order of High Priesthood for many years to the time of his death. He was created a Knight Templar in 1849; first Commander of Palestine Commandery No. 3, remaining so several years; Eminent Grand Commander in 1856. "It can always be truly said of our departed brother, that his life was one of active labor, no less than of honor. In every station he was a diligent workman, filling his post with credit to himself and benefit to his fellows and mankind."

William B. Ochiltree----W.B. Ochiltree, Past Grand Master, was born in Cumberland county, North Carolina, 18 October 1811. He died 25/27 December 1868 at his residence in Jefferson, Texas, aged fifty-six years. He had for some time been in feeble health, but his death was unexpected. Ochiltree was Secretary to Treasurer of the Republic in 1845 and was for twenty-five years a prominent man in Texas.

Henry Cartmell----Henry Cartmell was born in the town of Winchester, Virginia, on 22 September 1800. At an early day he emigrated to the state of Tennessee and made the city of Nashville his home. He continued a true and faithful member of Cumberland Lodge until 19 March 1836, when he moved to the State of Texas. He was Past Grand Junior Warden. He was a honest man and a zealous Mason whose simplicity of manners won all hearts. He was one of the oldest members of the Masonic Fraternity in the state. Cartmell died at his residence in Washington on 3 March 1868.

John R. Reid----Rev. J.R. Reid died in December 1841 or February 1842 in Houston. His funeral sermon was preached by the Rev. Mr. Sommers at 11 o'clock at the Presbyterian Church in Houston. The Masonic and Odd Fellows were requested to attend.

Alvan Reed/Reid----Judge Alvan Reed died 27 August 1867 in Galveston. He was among those who had fallen victim to this fatal epidemic (yellow fever) after having lived through similar visitations in former years. Judge Reed was formerly Sheriff of this county, but more recently one of our magistrates. He was a citizen of a great many years and was well known in the community. He was born in New York and was forty-four years old at his death. He was a member of Harmony Lodge No. 6.

Richard Bache----Hon. Richard Bache was born in Pennsylvania in 1784, the grandson of Benjamin Franklin. He came to Texas in 1836. He died in Austin on 17 March 1848 at 4 o'clock p.m. He was Senator from the Galveston district. Bache was buried with Masonic Honors.

Edward Hopkins Cushing---- E.H. Cushing died of pneumonia in Houston on 15 January 1879. He was born at Royalton, Vermont, 1 June 1829; graduated Dartmouth College, New Hampshire, in 1850; and came to Texas the same year. He taught school. He engaged in publishing the *Columbia Democrat* at Columbia, Brazoria county. In 1856, he went to Houston and assumed control of the *Houston Telegraph*, which he continued to edit with marked ability and success until the close of the Civil War. After that, he engaged in commercial pursuits. In every relation of life, Bro. Cushing was eminently a useful man. In his death those with whom he was associated in everyday life realized the loss of a citizen whose place could not be easily supplied; a friend who had a kind word for all, whose ready purse was open to the needy; a Christian gentleman, and an honorable business man.

Mrs. E.H. Cushing, wife of the editor of the *Houston Telegraph,* died in late September or early October 1857.

Bro. Cushing was made a Mason in St. Johns Lodge No. 5 at Columbia in 1851, and served as W.M. of that Lodge in 1854; took the Chapter Degrees in Columbia Chapter in 1856; received the Orders of Knighthood in Ruthven Commandery No. 2 in 1857; served as Eminent Commander in 1859. He filled the several stations in the Grand Commandery and was R.E. Grand Commander in 1862. The services of this lamented Brother in this Grand Body are too well known and appreciated by the members of the Grand Lodge to require any extended notice. He was emphatically a working member. Zealous and devoted in his attachment to the Order, and the noble principles inculcated by its teaching, he never flagged in the discharge of his duties as a Mason. He never was a candidate for any position, but worked faithfully and effectively in whatever place he was assigned. He served several times as Chairman of the Committee on Foreign Correspondence, and was distinguished as one of our soundest and ablest writers. We feel well assured that he received his reward as a Mason and a Christian.

Kenneth L. Anderson----K.L. Anderson, last Vice President of the Republic, was born 1 September 1805 in Hillsboro, North Carolina. In 1829, he moved to Tennessee, and in 1837 he came to San Augustine, where he was appointed customs collector. He was a member of the House, and was Speaker 1841-1842. Col. Anderson was uniformly distinguished as a warm advocate of the popular measure of annexation. He departed this life on the evening of the 3 July 1845 at one quarter before 3:00 p.m. at Fanthorp's in the county of Montgomery, and was there buried with Masonic Honors. The cause of death was fever. The cemetery where he was buried is across the road from Fanthorp Inn, Anderson, Grimes county. He left a widow and children.

George W. Harrison----G.W. Harrison was born in Virginia, where he resided until about the year 1845, when he emigrated to Washington county, Arkansas. In 1846, he removed to Texas. He died in October 1850, after a protracted illness, aged about fifty years, leaving a large family. He was a member of Victoria Lodge No. 40, and he was buried with Masonic Honors.

J.J. McBride----J.J. McBride, Past Deputy Grand Master, Past Grand Lecturer, and member of the Committee on Work, departed this life at Oak Woods, in Leon county, of congestive chills on 14 July 1879. He was a native of Virginia, but had been a resident of Texas for more than thirty years. He was engaged in planting until the beginning of the war between the states, when he entered the Army and commanded a company in Hood's Brigade for three years. By his courage and coolness he distinguished himself on all the principal battlefields of Virginia in defense of the cause which he had earnestly and honestly espoused. In camp among his comrades, he was noted for his quiet, modest demeanor, as in battle for his gallantry and daring, and during the whole war he maintained the character of the moral and Christian gentleman. He was wounded in the second Battle of Manassas, and again in the memorable Battle of the Wilderness, from the effects of which he never recovered. There was probably not a day from 6 May 1864 to the time of his death that he did not suffer excruciating pain; yet not a murmur was ever known to escape him.

Bro. McBride was initiated, passed and raised in Palestine Lodge No. 31 in 1850; was made Royal Arch Mason at that place the next year; afterwards served as High Priest of the Chapter. The Orders of Knighthood were conferred upon him in Palestine Commandery in 1853, and he afterwards served as Eminent Commander. He was an active working member of all the Masonic Grand Bodies for several years. He was Grand Commander of the Grand Commandery of the State in 1859; served through the several stations of the Grand Lodge; was Deputy Grand master in 1858, when his innate modesty would not allow him to accept the higher station, and he declined further promotion. He served as Grand Lecturer two years before the war, and has since been a member of the Committee on Work.

It has well been said of him that he was "a man distinguished among brave men for courage; among patient men for fortitude; among true men for fidelity; among honest men for singleness of purpose, and simplicity of character; and among patriots for a love of country so beautiful, steadfast and sincere that it seemed to grow brighter and purer in the face of disaster, suffering and death."

E.T. Bonney----Dr. E.T. Bonney died on the night of 6 August 1869 at Bellville. He was a good physician and exemplary Mason. A Tribute of Respect was given by Bellville Lodge No. 223, held at the Lodge Room in Bellville, on 21 August 1869. Bonney left a little orphan son, mother, sister, and brother.

D.A. Perry----Dr. D.A. Perry lived near Washington, and in July 1845 he rode from his residence to his plantation, a distance of half a mile. Several hours after his departure his horse returned. His family instituted a search and his body was found, his head horribly mutilated. A negro, formerly the property of Dr. Perry, was believed to have perpetrated the murder. He confessed and was hung. Dr. Perry left a widow and a large family. Dr. Perry was buried with Masonic Honors.

Isaac VanZandt---- Isaac VanZandt was born in Franklin county, Tennessee, 10 July 1813, the son of Jacob and Mary VanZandt. His mother's father was Samuel Isaacs. He came to Panola county in 1838, and in 1839 he moved to Marshall, where he began the practice of law. VanZandt was appointed Charge d' Affaires in 1842 by Sam Houston, and was a member of the convention of 1845 that completed the work of annexation and framed the first constitution on the "Lone Star" State. He was a Christian and a member of the Baptist Church. At the age of twenty he married Miss Fannie Lipscomb. Hon. Isaac VanZandt died of yellow fever in Houston, 2 October 1847, and was buried 11 October. His funeral was at the Baptist Church. He was buried with Masonic Honors. He left a wife and children. He was a member of Holland Lodge No. 1.

H.B. Kelsey----Dr. H.B. Kelsey of Marshall was an editor, minister, and Mason. He died in October or November 1848 at the age of fifty. He was editor of the *Marshall Patriot* and *State Star Patriot*. Kelsey, a native of New York, came to Texas in 1839.

John W. Hall----Capt. J.W. Hall was a native of South Carolina, whence he removed to Louisiana with his father, and came to Texas in 1812. Hall was in the Battle of Salado and in the Battle of New Orleans. He settled with his family in 1822 on the spot where he died and where he encamped in 1812. He founded the town of Washington. He died at his residence on 1 January 1845 and was interred with Masonic Honors. Both houses of Congress adjourned as a mark of respect.

T. B. Ives----Col. T.B. Ives, formerly of Yallabusha county, Mississippi, was a member of the Masonic Fraternity and the Methodist Church. At one time, he was lapped in the luxury of a wealth which was dissipated in a lavish and prodigal charity as much as by unfortunate speculation. At another time, we see him the leader of his political party in Mississippi. Ives died at Corpus Christi, 27 October 1852, in the fifty-second year of his age.

Henry L. Kinney----H.L. Kinney was the founder of Corpus Christi. He was killed by Mexicans at Matamoros in July 1861.

George Wages----George Wages died, at the home of Mrs. Northway, after a painful illness, suffered from a severe pain in his toe, which was superinduced by trimming a corn. He died on 17 October 1876, leaving a wife and children.

Levi W. Young ----L.W. Young, a citizen of Bastrop county, was waylaid and shot on 14 September 1853, about five miles from home as he was going from his residence to the town of Bastrop. He left a wife and five children. The Masonic Fraternity offered a reward.

William E. Finch----W.E. Finch's funeral took place at the residence of Mrs. Stephen Locke, Washington, on 7 December 1855. He was buried with Masonic Honors.

Henry V. Robertson----H.V. Robertson was a member of Milam Lodge No. 11 in the town of Independence, and at a meeting in the Lodge on 20 May 1856 Brothers H. Clark, G.J. Duncan and J.B. Robertson were appointed a committee to draft resolutions expressing the sense of the Lodge on the loss it had sustained in the death of Henry V. Robertson. Robertson died at his residence at a quarter past 2 o'clock p.m. on 19 June 1856.

Wilson M. Low----W.M. Low was born 9 March 1836 and died on 8 August 1874. He was a Master Mason and a member of Sunshine Lodge No. 341, Bell county. He was buried in the Post Oak cemetery, near Holland, Bell county.

J.N. Williams----Dr. J.N. Williams died in Bastrop, at his residence, on 14 November 1868. He was a member of the Masonic and Odd Fellows Fraternity.

Martin Ruter----Rev. Martin Ruter was buried by the Masons on 29 March 1853.

John Allcorn---John Allcorn was born in Franklin county, Georgia, 20 May 1799, and emigrated with his parents, Elijah and Nancy Allcorn, in 1822, when Texas was under Mexico. His parents were one of Austin's Old Three Hundred. He died of typhoid fever on 7 June 1853, after an illness of twenty-two days, and after nearly thirty years of dangers and hardships of the frontier, leaving a wife and child. He was a devoted Baptist and Mason. His funeral sermon was preached by Rev. Rufus C. Burleson, at his residence, after which his corpse was carried to the family burying ground, near Jefferson Allcorn's, and buried with Masonic Honors.

Horace B. Hurlburt----H.B. Hurlburt died on Monday, 26 June 1854, of pulmonary consumption at the age of thirty-six years. Hurlburt was buried by the Masons.

John H. Dunham----J.H. Dunham was born in Tennessee on 19 September 1828, and emigrated to Texas at an early age with the family of Dunhams. He died at his residence, in Grimes county, on Monday, 14 November 1853, of yellow fever, in the twenty-sixth year of his age. Dunham left a wife and two little children.

J.C. Habermehl ----J.C. Habermehl/Hobermehl died at his residence in San Jacinto, 14 April 1865 of dropsy at the age of fifty-four years. He was buried with Masonic Honors.

William C. Gould----Capt. W.C. Gould died Wednesday morning, 18/19 July 1854, in the vicinity of Washington, of dropsy and disease of the throat, in the forty-first year of his age. He was a native of Baltimore and for thirteen years had been a resident of Texas, the latter part of which he was engaged in the mercantile business. He was a member of the Washington Lodge No. 18 and was conveyed to the tomb by the Masons in Galveston.

W.O. Wilson----W.O. Wilson was buried with Masonic Honors on the third Sunday in April 1855 eight miles east of Caldwell.

Mr. Weinert----Mr. Weinert was one of the persons drowned in the Colorado river Sunday, 1 February 1863, in attempting to cross in a skiff. His body was found below LaGrange on Friday and his remains were interred in the cemetery by the Masons the next Saturday.

Samuel D. Mills ---S.D. Mills, a respected citizen of Galveston, was killed in March 1866 at his home fifteen miles from Houston by a German named Snyder, sometimes called Grodecker. He was shot twice in the breast. Samuel Mills' funeral took place at the residence of his uncle, Robert Mills, in Galveston, under the direction of the Masonic Fraternity.

Paul Helterich----Paul Helterich was a native of Hesse Cassel. For many years he was a highly respected resident of Galveston, where he was a surveyor of the county and a civil engineer. He died at 11 a.m., 20 July 1866, after a brief illness, said to be bilious fever. Helterich was buried with Masonic Honors.

J.B. Patrick ----J.B. Patrick, who was a native of Missouri, came to Texas with De Witt's colony in the fall of 1828, and he lived almost the whole time in Gonzales. Patrick died in July 1866.

J.H. Darnell---J.H. Darnell was an old and respected merchant of Clarksville. He died in late April or early May 1867, in the fifty-third year of his age. Darnell was a member of the Masonic and Odd Fellows Societies.

W.D. Mitchell----Judge W.D. Mitchell died at Tuxpan, Mexico, on 22 April 1867, and was buried with Masonic Honors on 13 May 1867 in Richmond, Texas.

George W. Glasscock---- Hon. G.W. Glasscock died at Webberville, Travis county, on 28 February 1868, in consequence of injuries received by being thrown from a mule. Glasscock was buried at Austin on 1 March 1868 with Masonic Honors.

W.S. Stephens----On Sunday morning between eight and nine o'clock, a barkeeper by the name of C.I. Tripp entered the store of W.S. Stephens, and after a few words were passed between the parties, Tripp discharged two barrels of a six-shooter, the contents taking effect in either side of Mr. Stephens' breast. After committing the deed, Mr. Tripp made his escape. Mr. Stephens' remains were followed to the grave on Monday morning by his relatives, the Masons and a large number of sympathizing friends. Mt. Pleasant, July 1867.

William Voight---- William Voight, a useful citizen and Mason, was the brother of the editor of the *Chronicle*. Voight died 28 July 1867.

Oliver Loring----Oliver Loring, Dean of Cattle Drives, left Parker county the summer of 1867 for New Mexico with a drove of beeves. After proceeding about six hundred miles he was attacked by Indians near the Pecos river on 6 August and mortally wounded. He was not found until the 12th and then was taken to Ft. Sumner, where he died on 25 September. His remains were brought back and reinterred at Weatherford on 8 March 1868 by the Masonic Fraternity. His funeral was the largest procession ever witnessed at that place. He was an old and much esteemed citizen. Loring's last request was "Take me back to Texas. Don't leave me on foreign soil."

William N. Sparks----W.N. Sparks, who had been confined to his bed with rheumatism for nearly fourteen years, died at his residence in Galveston on 23 June 1868. His funeral took place the next morning at 9 o'clock from his late residence and was conducted by the Masonic Fraternity.

Robert Barr----Robert Barr, born 1802 in Ohio, was Post Master General during the Republic of Texas, having been appointed by Sam Houston. Barr came to Texas before 1833, and was a hero of San Jacinto. He died at his residence in Houston on Friday, 11 October 1839, at half past nine a.m. Barr was a member of Holland Lodge No. 1.

Edward Burleson----Edward Burleson, born 26 November 1826, died at the home of his sister, in Austin, 12 May 1877. He was buried near Kyle. Burleson was in the Mexican War and the Civil War.

131

William T. Hunt----W.T. Hunt was a member of the Baylor Lodge No. 125, Gay Hill, and the Lodge paid a Tribute of Respect to him on 9 November 1856.

Thomas W. Blakey----Tribute of Respect on the death of Thomas W. Blakey was given by Milam Lodge No. 11 in May 1854.

Asa Hoxey----Dr. Asa Hoxey, who was born 22 February 1800, died 20 May 1863 at Independence. He was a member of Consultation of 1835. His home, built in 1833, has a historical marker.

James Morrow----James Morrow died at his residence in Fayette county on 25 June 1866 after an illness of two years. Tribute of Respect was given by Lyons Lodge No. 195, Fayette county.

Blackstone B. Sullivan----B.B. Sullivan died in Caldwell county on 26 April 1852. A Tribute of Respect was given by Lockhart Lodge No. 59.

Martin Forehand---- Martin Forehand died 29 December 1853 and a Tribute of Respect was given by Colorado Lodge No. 96.

Henry Dunlavy----Henry Dunlavy was born in New York on 23 April 1811, and died 5 May 1873. His wife's name was Elizabeth Shaver.

George D. Flood----G.D. Flood was Charge d' Affairs United States to Texas. He built the Tremont Hotel in Galveston. He died in Galveston on 6 August 1841.

Dewitt Clinton Baker----D.C. Baker was born 23 November 1832 in Portland, Maine, and died 17 April 1881 in Austin. He was married 28 May 1861 to Mary Elizabeth Graham, at the residence of her father, Dr. Beriah Graham, who was from Logan county, Kentucky. D.C. Baker was a member of Austin Lodge No. 12. His son, William Graham Baker, a salesman for McKean, Eilers and Company in Austin, was also a member of Austin Lodge No. 12. Dewitt Clinton and Mary Elizabeth were buried at Oakwood cemetery in Austin.

Logan Vandiver----Logan Vandiver/Vanderver was born in Cass county, Kentucky, on 8 January 1815. He came to Texas at the age of eighteen, settling in Mina. In 1836, he joined the Bastrop Volunteers under the command of Capt. Jesse Billingsly, and was severely wounded at San Jacinto. He married Miss Lucinda Mayes, of Bastrop county, in 1838 and they had four daughters and one son, William Andrew. Logan and his brother, Zachary, who were in Louisiana with a herd of cattle, died in Plaquemines, Louisiana, in September 1855 of yellow fever. A Tribute of Respect was given by Valley Lodge at Hamilton on 13 November 1855.

Henry K. Holland----H.K. Holland was secretary of the Masonic Lodge at San Marcos when the Lodge paid a Tribute of Respect on 23 October 1855. He died while nobly defending his country's rights as a volunteer under command of Capt. Benton.

James M. Cook----J.M. Cook was given a Tribute of Respect by Constantine Lodge No. 13, Bonham, Fannin county, on 13 January 1869.

C.A. Nash----C.A. Nash was given a Tribute of Respect by the Masonic Hall, Columbia, 16 August 1856.

Jesse Cornelius Tannehill----J.C. Tannehill was born 30 December 1797 in Kentucky. In 1827, he came to Texas with his wife and two children, and settled near Caney in Matagorda county. He built one of the first houses in Bastrop. Tannehill, who was active in the development of Travis county and was a member of Austin Lodge No. 12, died 17 March 1863.

Darius Gregg----Darius Gregg, the son of Andrew and Martha Jane Gregg, was born 8 November 1804 in Jessamine county, Kentucky. On 6 April 1831, he was granted a one-fourth league of land near Anderson. Gregg, who participated in the Grass Fight and seize of Bexar, died 28 March 1870.

John R. Boon----Rev. J.R. Boon was born in Louisiana in 1818. At the age of nineteen, he became religious and joined the Baptist Church. He was ordained a preacher in 1848. He died at his residence, in Harrison county, in the thirty-sixth year of his age after a short but painful illness. Boon was a member of good standing, and by his request was buried with the usual Masonic ceremonies.

Henry Fanthorp----Henry Fanthorp, born in England, 20 November 1790, was the owner of Fanthorp Inn, a well known inn during the Republic, in Anderson. Fanthorp built the inn in 1834 and it became the first post office as well as the first mercantile establishment in the area. Fanthorp applied for land in the Stephen F. Austin and Samuel M. Williams Colony in 1832, when he testified that he was a widower with a son in England. He married Rachael Kennard in 1834. In 1851, he was agent for the United States mail coaches. Fanthorp died 31 October 1867 and was buried across the road from his inn, which is now a state park. He is called the Father of Masonry in Grimes county.

Norman Hurd Couger----N.H. Couger/Conger was born in Western New York on 18 August 1829, and died in Waco on 15 December 1876. He was buried at the First Street cemetery. He had lived in Illinois before coming to McLellan county in 1870. Clara Harvey was his daughter.

Michael B. Menard----Col. M.B. Menard was born in the village of La Prairie, Montreal, 5 December 1805, his parents being French. At the age of nineteen, he went to Missouri at the solicitation of his uncle, Pierre Menard. About 1833 or 1834 he came to Texas and settled at Nacogdoches. He was a signer of the Texas Declaration of Independence. His date of death was 2 September 1856. Menard was a member of the Grand Lodge, 14 November 1840, and Harmony Lodge No. 6.

William B. Anderson----W.B. Anderson died 13 May 1869 at his residence in Port Sullivan, Milam county. A Tribute of Respect from St. Paul's Lodge No. 177 was given by the Lodge.

Thomas Marshall Duke----T.M. Duke was born in Lexington, Kentucky, in 1795. Duke came to Texas in 1822 as one of Austin's Original 300. On 24 July 1824, he received a league grant on Caney creek in present Matagorda county. He was attacked on about 24 May 1867 with yellow fever and died a few days later. He was married three times and had seven children. He was a member of Matagorda Lodge No. 7.

James Washington Guinn---J.W. Guinn was born 11 June 1804 in Green county, Tennessee, the son of John Guinn and Rachael Shields. Before coming to Texas in 1858, he lived in Randolph county, Alabama. He was a lawyer and Senator for Angelina, Nacogdoches, and San Augustine counties. Guinn was married to Catherine Ann Dobson, who was the daughter of John Dobson and Nancy Parks. Catherine Ann was a doctor. She died in Homer, Angelina county, and was buried in the Homer cemetery. James W. was a member of the M.E. Church; a Douglas Democrat; opposed succession. He had five sons in the Confederate Army. One lost an arm, another was captured and imprisoned twice. James Washington Guinn died in Austin, Texas, on 17 August 1866, after an illness of a few days, and was buried in the State cemetery in Austin. Judge Guinn was a charter member of Homer Lodge No. 254, which was organized in February 1860. He was J.W. in 1862, and Treasurer in 1865 and 1866.

The younger brother of J.W. Guinn, Robert Henry Guinn, was born 19 December 1822 in Greene county, Tennessee, and was married to Sarah Hearne. The Guinns came to Texas in 1846 and lived near Rusk, where Robert Henry practiced law. He was a noted criminal lawyer. Robert Henry Guinn died of pneumonia while holding court in Homer, Texas, and was buried in Rusk.

Jobes York----Jobes York departed this life on 24 May 1874 and the resolutions commemoration of his death were published by the Masonic Fraternity of Calhoun county.

John P. Clements----J.P. Clements died 18 October 1875 at the age of thirty-two years and two months. Clements was in the Civil War. He was buried in the First Street cemetery in Waco.

Jabez B. Johnson----J.B. Johnson died 13 September 1874 at the age of forty-nine years and eleven months. He was in the Civil War. He was buried in the First Street cemetery in Waco.

Minor Bawsell----Mr. Bawsell, Assistant Postmaster of Houston, died in Houston, September 1867, of yellow fever at the age of thirty-five. His life was insured in the St. Louis Cornelius Tannehill Mutual for $2,500. His wife died ten days later of yellow fever at the age of twenty-three, leaving three orphan children.

Michael Cronican---- Michael Cronican was a native of Boston and by profession a practical printer, employed in some of the principle offices in New Orleans up to November 1835, when he embarked in the cause of Texas for independence. He joined Captain Cooke's company of the "Louisiana Greys." At the close of the Revolution, Cronican returned again to his profession at which he continued until the invasion of 1842, when once more he joined the standard of his adopted country. He participated in the Battle of Mier and was among the few who escaped. He established the *Galveston News*, *Austin Democrat*, and the *Western Texan*. He was Junior Deacon Holland Lodge No. 1 in 1840. On 27 April 1849, he died in San Antonio of cholera.

John D. Williams----J.D. Williams was given a Tribute of Respect by Gilmer Lodge No. 61 on 10 April 1856.

B.E. Jamison----B.E. Jamison, a well known citizen of Houston, was found dead in his chair in early January of 1867. His death was doubtless caused by apoplexy.

Hugh T. Scott----Capt. Hugh Scott was well known in Houston, where during and subsequent to the war he made a large number of acquaintances. He was probably a native of Tennessee, and came here during the war as an officer and was assigned to duty in Houston by Gen. Magruder. Before the war closed he was married to Miss Milby, a daughter of Wm. Milby. Scott died either 7 or 9 October 1867 in Houston and was buried there.

J.Y. Allen----J.Y. Allen was born 21 June 1819. Allen was in the Civil War. He died 21 June 1881 and was buried in the First Street cemetery in Waco.

W.D. Bedwell----W.D. Bedwell was born 11 December 1821. Bedwell was in the Civil War. He died on 18 December 1867 and was buried in the First Street cemetery in Waco.

A.P. Pruitt----A.P. Pruitt, an attache of the H.& T.C.R.R., and Edward Brown, of the firm of Harrell & Brown, two young men well known in Houston, met near the corner of Congress and Fannin streets and, it is said, after a brief altercation of words were drawn into a personal encounter which resulted in the death of the former and the dangerous wounding of the latter. The next day, young Pruitt, who was so severely wounded in his recontre with Ed. Brown, was not expected to recover as he was said to be suffering under brain fever caused by a severe contusion of the head. Mr. Pruitt died at about 11 a.m. on 10 October 1867 in Houston and was buried there.

Zeb M.P. French----Zeb French died in LaGrange of yellow fever on 6 September 1867. He was County Clerk.

Lorin Kent----Gen. Lorin Kent was born in Illinois. He was Collector of Customs, port of Galveston. Gen. Kent died of yellow fever on 28 August 1867 in Galveston. He, by his obliging disposition and gentlemanly deportment, was held in the highest estimation by all. His funeral took place at his residence on Broadway at 10 o'clock a.m. on the 29th. The office of the Internal Revenue was closed out of respect to Gen. Kent.

Rev. Thomas Wooldridge, Hon. James W. McDade, J.A. Haynie, J.R. Moore, E.W. Rodgers, W.D. Crockett, J.E. Crockett, and T.J. Jackson----Tribute of Respect from the Masonic Hall, Chappell Hill, Texas, to the memory of our deceased Brethren. 21 February 1868.

Edward S. Hine----E.S. Hine was born in 1824 in Limestone county, Alabama. He died 5/25 November 1866 after an illness of fifteen days in LaGrange, which he had recently adopted as his home. He spent his life in Alabama till a few months before his death, when he was induced to emigrate to Texas with a view of recuperating his fortunes, which the late war so sadly shattered. In 1858, he became a member of the M.E. Church. His death was calm and peaceful. He was former Junior Warden. A Tribute of Respect was given in February 1867 by the Athens, Alabama Lodge.

James Nicholson----James Nicholson died in LaGrange of yellow fever on 29 August 1867.

A.G. Perry-----Judge A.G. Perry, an old settler of Falls county, died 29 March 1874. He was a Christian and Mason.

Capt. Sylvanus Hatch----Capt. Sylvanus Hatch of Chocolette, near Indianola, was the oldest Mason in Texas in March 1874, when he was eighty-seven years old. He became a Mason in 1809 in Maine, and in 1874 had been a Mason for sixty-five years. Even though eighty-seven years old, he read newspapers and kept up with the times.

Frank J. Trusty----F.J. Trusty died 24 May 1874. He was seriously ill in February. Waco Lodge No. 92 accompanied his remains to the railroad train which was to carry them to his loved relatives in Mississippi. Mississippi Lodge No. 340.

J.H. Banton----Judge J.H. Banton was educated at Austin College, was admitted to the Supreme Court in 1857, and began his practice in Huntsville. He was not a native of Texas. He died 14 July 1874 at the age of about forty years, and his funeral was the largest Masonic procession ever seen in Waco. Dr. R.H. Bush, of Huntsville, was his brother-in-law.

V. Korn----V. Korn died in LaGrange of yellow fever on 12 September 1867. He left a helpless family.

Benjamin Shropshire----Benjamin Shropshire died at his residence in La Grange, Texas, on Sunday, 22 September, aged forty-one years. He was a native of Bourbon county, Kentucky, but a resident of Texas for sixteen years. He was left an orphan at the age of seven years, with limited means. At the age of about eighteen years, he entered Cumberland College, at Princeton, Kentucky, and by spending all of his patrimony completed his collegiate education. Shropshire prepared himself for the practice of law, and came to Texas in 1851, locating at La Grange, where he practiced his profession successfully until the unfortunate political troubles commenced in our country, when he warmly espoused the Southern cause, and served most of the four years of the war in the Southern Army. He left a wife and four children.

David H. Grove----D.H. Grove was a native of North Carolina. In 1847, he moved to Galveston, where he had mostly resided with his family. He died in Galveston on the night of 9 January 1867, in his fiftieth year.

Patrick Gorman----Patrick Gorman was given a Tribute of Respect by Baylor Lodge No. 125 in September 1854.

D.B. Carson----D.B. Carson, who died 30 June 1854, was given a Tribute of Respect by Chappell Hill Lodge.

George Rottenstein----Rev. George Rottenstein, of Houston, died in February 1868. A noble Masonic brother.

Alexander Wray Ewing----Dr. A.W. Ewing was born in Londonderry, Ireland, in 1809. Ewing came to Texas in 1830 from Erie, Pennsylvania. He fought at San Jacinto. Dr. Ewing married first to Susan Henrietta Smiley Reid and after she died in 1842 he married Elizabeth Graham. He was a member of Holland Lodge No. 1, and an original member of the Grand Lodge of Texas. He died 1 November 1853.

TEXAS MASONIC DEATHS WITH SELECTED BIOGRAPHICAL SKETCHES

W. H. Fowler----On 10 August 1867 at Jefferson, Judge Davis B. Bonfoey, Collector of U.S. Internal Rev., killed Col. W.H. Fowler, Deputy U.S. Internal Rev. Collector. Judge Bonfoey entered the office of Colonel Fowler and placed a pistol to his head and fired, killing him instantly. Col. Fowler was an Alabamian, and removed to this state last winter. He left a wife and three daughters. Rumor says that a negro woman was the only witness of the murder, and that after Fowler fell, Bonfoey placed a cocked pistol in his hand and left the room announcing that he had killed Fowler in self defense.

J.S. Gillespie----J.S. Gillespie, born in Pennsylvania, died in Galveston of an abscess in the neck. He was interred by the Masonic Fraternity in Galveston on 26 August 1867.

C.R. Marchmann----C.R. Marchmann died in LaGrange on 28 August 1867 of yellow fever.

Micajah Johnston----Micajah Johnston was an old citizen of McClellan county. He died 12 February 1878 and was interred at Robinsonville by Waco Lodge No. 92. Johnston lived four miles from Waco.

O.J. Downs----O.J. Downs, the son of Maj. W.W. Downs, died 27 August 1876 at the residence of his father on 3rd Street in Waco. He died from voluntary abstinence from strong drink.

Sam Houston----Samuel Houston was born in Rockbridge county, Virginia, on 2 March 1793. He was a signer of the Texas Declaration of Independence; Commander-in-Chief of Texas Army; in command at San Jacinto; President of the Republic of Texas; Governor of the State of Texas. He was married first to Eliza H. Allen. This marriage ended in divorce. Houston went to Arkansas and there he had an Indian wife, Tiana Rogers. His third wife was Margaret Moffette Lea, whom he married in Alabama. They had eight children. In 1854, Sam Houston was baptized by Dr. R.C. Burleson in the waters of Rocky Creek south of Independence Baptist Church. Margaret Lea Houston and her mother were buried across the street from the church. After the Civil War, Houston retired to Huntsville, where he died 26 July 1863. His last words were "Texas, Texas, Margaret." Houston was a member of Cumberland Lodge No. 8, Nashville, Tennessee, Commandery No. 1, Knights Templar, Washington, D.C., Holland Lodge No. 36, Forest Lodge No. 19, and an original member Grand Lodge of Texas.

Thomas G. Western----T.G. Western was a Major in the Army of the Republic. Western, who delivered oration over remains of the Alamo victims, died 20 December 1847. Original member of the Grand Lodge of Texas.

John S. Black----J.S. Black , who was at the storming and capture of Bexar in 1835, was a member of Holland Lodge No. 1. Original member of the Grand Lodge of Texas.

Christopher Dart----Christopher Dart was a slave trader and a soldier in the Army of 1836. Original member of the Grand Lodge of Texas.

T. J. Hardeman----Col. T.J. Hardeman died at his residence in Bastrop county on 11 January 1854 at the age of sixty. Prairie Lea Lodge No. 114 held a Tribute of Respect on 31 January 1854. Original member of the Grand Lodge of Texas.

Charles S. Taylor----C.S. Taylor was born in London, England, in 1808. He came to America in 1823, and was a signer of the Texas Declaration of Independence. Taylor participated In the Battle of Nacogdoches. He was licensed to practice law in the Republic in 1839. His wife was Anna Maria Rudoff, from Esslingen, Germany, a sister of Adolphus Sterne. Taylor was the first man "raised" in Milam Lodge No. 40. He was one of the founders of Milam Lodge No. 2 in the year 1839, acted as Junior and Senior Warden and was Worshipful Master in 1843 and 1844, and was a member of said Lodge until his death on 1 November 1865. Rest, Brother, Rest! Thy work is done. Original member of the Grand Lodge of Texas.

William Fairfax Gray----W.F. Gray was born in Fairfax county, Virginia, in 1787. He was married to Milly Richards Stone and they had twelve children. Gray moved his family to Texas in 1837 and settled in Houston. He was a lawyer and served as Clerk of the House of Representatives in 1837. Upon the creation of the Texas Supreme Court, he was named Clerk. He was District Attorney of the Republic of Texas. He died in Houston on 16 April 1841. Gray Lodge No. 329 was named for him. Gray was a member of Temple Lodge No. 4, and was an original member of the Grand Lodge of Texas.

Anson Jones----Dr. Anson Jones was born in Massachusetts on 20 January 1798 and reared in Pennsylvania. He came to the then Provence of Texas in October 1833 and settled near Brazoria, where he engaged in the profession of medicine. He fought at San Jacinto and in 1844 he was elected President of the Republic of Texas and held this office until annexation in February 1846, when he retired to Washington on the Brazos, Washington county. Jones shot himself in a room in the Capitol Hotel in Houston at 3:00 a.m. on 9 January 1858, having suffered with depression all his life. He married Mary Smith McCrory, who was first married to Hugh McCrory in Lawrence county, Arkansas, in 1819. He was the first Grand Master in 1838, and is called the Father of Texas Masonry. Original member of the Grand Lodge of Texas.

Thomas J. Rusk----T.J. Rusk fought at San Jacinto, was Secretary of War, and was a signer of the Texas Declaration of Independence. Rusk came to Texas in 1835. Mrs. Mary F. Rusk, wife of Hon. Thos. J. Rusk, died at her residence near Nacogdoches on 26 April 1856 at the age of forty-six years, eight months and twelve days, of consumption. She was born in Habersham county, Georgia, and was the daughter of Benj. Cleveland. On 29 July 1857, Thomas J. Rusk was no more. The cause of death was a gun shot (rifle) wound on the fore part of the head inflicted from a rifle gun held in his own hands and discharged by himself. Being separated from his wife was more than he could bear. Mr. and Mrs. Rusk were buried in Nacogdoches. Original member of the Grand Lodge of Texas and Milam Lodge No. 40.

Adolphus Sterne----Adolphus Sterne was born in Germany on 5 April 1801. He came to Texas in the mid 1820's. Sterne held several offices in Nacogdoches from 1831 to 1833 and was a delegate to the Convention in 1833. In the Fredonian Rebellion, Sterne's sympathies were with Ben. W. Edwards' party, which he aided with munitions secured in New Orleans and secreted in bales of dry goods and coffee barrels. When discovered by the Mexican authorities, he was charged with treason and ordered to be shot. Pending approval of the sentence by the military commandant at Saltillo, he was confined at the Old Stone Fort. Meanwhile, the Masons, for which he had joined in New Orleans, interceded in his behalf and he was released on parole. He was Post Master at Nacogdoches during the Republic. He commanded a company in the Cherokee War and fought in the Battle of Neches. Adolphus Sterne helped finance the Texas Revolution. He died in New Orleans on the night of 27 March 1852, his age was about forty-eight years. Original member of the Grand Lodge of Texas.

William G. Cooke----W.G. Cooke was born in Fredericksburg, Virginia, the son of Adam Cooke and Martha Riddle. In 1835, he came to Texas to aid in the revolution and organized the "New Orleans Grays." He took part in the storming of Bexar, the "Council House Fight," fought at San Jacinto, and in 1841 took part in the Santa Fe Expedition and as a prisoner marched to Mexico City. His wife was Angela Navarro, a niece of Juan Antonio Navarro, a signer of the Texas Declaration of Independence. Cooke died in 1847. His wife married Abram G. Martin in 1851. Cooke was a member of Holland Lodge No. 1 and Deputy Grand Master 1839-1840. Original member of the Grand Lodge of Texas.

Henry Matthews----Henry Matthews was an early minister of the pioneer days of Houston. He was a member of Holland Lodge No. 36. Original member of the Grand Lodge of Texas.

Littleton Fowler----Littleton Fowler was first Chaplain Congress Republic of Texas and First Grand Chaplain Texas Grand Lodge. Original member of the Grand Lodge of Texas.

Henry Millard----Henry Millard was born in Mississippi in 1807. He fought at San Jacinto, Lieutenant Colonel commanding regular infantry. On 24 August 1826, he married Mary Dewburleigh Borlace Warren Beaumont at Natchez. In 1835, Millard laid out a town at the site of Trevis Bluff and named it Beaumont. In 1843, Millard moved to Galveston and died there in 1844. He was a member of Harmony Lodge No. 6 and was secretary of the Grand Lodge in 1840. Original member of the Grand Lodge of Texas.

Kelsey H. Douglass----K.H. Douglass was in Army of 1836 and was in command of troops in the Cherokee War in 1839. He was a member of Milam Lodge No. 40. Original member of the Grand Lodge of Texas.

Asa Brigham----Asa Brigham was born about 1790 in Massachusetts. He arrived in Texas from Louisiana with his first wife Elizabeth S. and two sons in April 1839. He was a signer of the Texas Declaration of Independence and he was the first Treasurer of the Republic of Texas. He became an Alderman of the city of Houston in February 1839, holding the office at the same time that he was State Treasurer. He retired as State Treasurer in 1840, but at the end of 1841 was reappointed by Houston. In 1842, he was Mayor in Austin. He was a merchant in Brazoria and Junior Warden of Holland Lodge No. 36 at Brazoria in 1836. He died at his residence in Washington, Texas, after a long and painful illness on 3 July 1844 at the age of fifty-six. Original member of the Grand Lodge of Texas.

Jefferson E. Wright----J.E. Wright was a painter of portraits and miniatures who was known as the semiofficial Artist of the Republic of Texas. He painted at least two portraits of Samuel Houston. He was a Captain Volunteer Army of 1837. In Houston, February 1842, he was made Vice-President of the Friends of Temperance. He was Master of Holland Lodge No. 1 in 1837. Original member of the Grand Lodge of Texas.

Isaac Watts Burton----I.W. Burton was born in 1805 in Clark county, Georgia, and came to Texas in 1832. Burton fought at San Jacinto, and was Commander of the "Horse Marines." Burton and his wife, Mary Lacy, had two children. He practiced law in Nacogdoches and in Crockett, where he died in January 1843. Member Milam Lodge No. 40. Original member of the Grand Lodge of Texas.

Algeron S. Thurston----A.S. Thurston was born in Kentucky in 1806 and died in 1865. Affiliated with Holland Lodge No. 1, 8 November 1837, demitted 13 April 1842. Original member of the Grand Lodge of Texas.

TEXAS MASONIC DEATHS WITH SELECTED BIOGRAPHICAL SKETCHES

John Shea----John Shea, who was in the Army in 1836, died 21 June 1870. Original member of the Grand Lodge of Texas.

Thomas J. Gazley----Dr. T.J. Gazley was born 8 January 1801 in Dutchess county, New York, and came to Texas in 1829 from Louisiana. Gazley was a signer of the Texas Declaration of Independence. He was a member of Holland Lodge No. 36. Original member of the Grand Lodge of Texas.

J.C. Veazey----J.C. Veazey was born 5 October 1831. He was a member of the Oenaville Lodge, Bell county. He died 23 August 1877 and was buried in the Oenaville cemetery.

W.Y. McFarland----W.Y. McFarland was a resident of Belton, Bell county. He was a lawyer and a Mason. He died at his residence in Belton on 21 February 1872 in his sixty-fourth year.

R.S. Spencer----R.S. Spencer was born 26 December 1832. He was a member of the Oenaville Lodge, Bell county. He died 23 November 1874. His wife, Elizabeth, was born 20 December 1822 and died 17 November 1891. They were buried at the Oenaville cemetery, Bell county.

William W. Goode----W.W. Goode was born 15 November 1827. He died 14 September 1863 and was buried in Bell county.

Richard M. Johnson----R.M. Johnson was born 9 October 1819. He died 5 November 1875 and was buried in Bell county.

Williamson Daniels----Williamson Daniels was one of Captain Isaac Watts Burton's "Horse Marines." He died 30 December 1870.

Hardin Richard Runnels----H.R. Runnels was born 30 August 1820 in Mississippi. He came to Texas in about 1843 with his mother and brothers. He was elected Governor in 1857, defeating Sam Houston. Runnels died 23 May 1870.

J. Heath----J. Heath died 7 March 1862, while in defense of the liberties of his country and while charging the enemy's battery on the Battle of Elkhorn, Arkansas. He was a member of the Lancaster Lodge No. 160, Lancaster, Dallas county.

John Laprelle----John Laprelle died at the age of forty-seven on 23 December 1855. He was buried at the cemetery across from Fanthorp Inn in Anderson, Grimes county.

TEXAS MASONIC DEATHS WITH SELECTED BIOGRAPHICAL SKETCHES

James Webb----James Webb died 1 November 1856. In his death, Masonry has lost of her earliest, most useful and most zealous supporters. He was Judge of the Federal and State Courts and Grand Master.

Ezekiel Curd----Ezekiel Curd was born in 1823 in North Carolina. He came to Texas in the 1830's with his parents, Isaiah and Mary Curd. On 13 October 1857, he married Martha Jane Weeks and they were the parents of six children. He died 19 March 1875 at the age of fifty-two years and was buried at Peach Tree cemetery, Grimes county.

W.W. Evans----W.W. Evans was born in Kentucky in 1833 and died 4 May 1872. He was a cabinet maker and a member of Austin Lodge No. 12.

Col. Terry----The obsequies of Col. Terry. The remains arrived by train from Beaumont, 30 December 1861. He was a member of Holland Lodge No.1.

Henderson Yoakum----Henderson Yoakum was the first historian of Texas, won for himself a fame that will long last after his mortal remains were moldered into dust. He was a most faithful and learned Mason, and patriotic and excellent citizen. He never held any official position in the Grand Lodge, yet he attended several of its Communications. He was a distinguished member of the Bar. He died in 1856.

William McFarland----William McFarland was born in Lancaster, Pennsylvania, in 1774, and died 16 August 1840 at Belgrade on the Sabine. He was in the Battle of Nacogdoches in 1832, and represented Ayish Bayou District in the Conventions of 1832 and 1833. He was first Worshipful Master of McFarland Lodge, the third Masonic Lodge in Texas.

John B. Jones----J.B. Jones was Past Grand Master. He was every inch a Mason.

Jesse Kincheloe Davis----J.K. Davis was born in Alabama in 1802. He fought at San Jacinto. His wife watched the battle from a tree. Davis died 28 November 1869 and was buried at the Masonic cemetery in Gonzales.

Marmion Henry Bowers----M.H. Bowers was born at Moore's Hill, Dearborn county, Indiana, on 29 April 1823. He died on 4 March 1872 of consumption. He was an editor and lawyer. He was a member of Austin Lodge No. 12.

A.L. Hudiburgh----A.L. Hudiburgh lived in Angelina county. His wife was named Mary and his daughter was named Mary Catherine. Mary Catherine Hudiburgh married Jacob Heflin Polk Simon Guinn, the son of James Washington Guinn. Hudiburgh was a member of Homer Lodge No. 254.

143

Alexander J. Russell----Alexander Russell, who built and owned first store in Austin, was a writer and publisher. He was Grand Junior Warden in 1840 and a member of Austin Lodge No. 12. He died in 1842.

Stephen F. Austin----S.F. Austin, the Father of Texas, was born 3 November 1793 in Virginia. He was a member of St. Louis Lodge No. 3, St. Louis, Missouri. In 1828, he was one of the men who met at San Felipe, on the Brazos, for the first Masonic Convention ever held in Texas. He died 27 December 1836 of pneumonia, which had lingered since his Mexico City imprisonment. His remains are at the State cemetery in Austin. He was not only the "Father of Texas" but he was the truest, purest, noblest, most loyal soul that ever died for the Lone Star of Texas. The closest research has never revealed a single spot to mar the cleanliness of his white apron.

William H. Cushney----W.H. Cushney was born in 1824 and came to Texas in 1840. He was a publisher. He married Mary Ann Harrell in Austin, and was a member of Austin Lodge No. 12. He died in Independence in 1852.

Elijah Sterling C. Robertson----E.S.C. Robertson, known as the "Father of Salado", was born 23 August 1820 in Nashville, Tennessee, the son of the Empersario Sterling C. Robertson and his wife Sarah. At the age of nineteen, he became the acting Postmaster General of the Republic of Texas. In 1840, he was elected Secretary of the Senate of the Republic. He was an Entered Apprentice at age of twenty-one in Milam Lodge No. 11 at Independence. He was charter member of Olive Branch Lodge No. 26. After moving to Salado, Bell county, in 1852, he was the first Worshipful Master of Belton Lodge No. 166, in Belton. He died in Bell county on 8 October 1879.

William Robinson----William Robinson was born in Virginia about 1785 and came to Texas about 1828. Robinson was at a Battle of San Jacinto and the War of 1812. He was a charter member of Forest Lodge No. 19, where he was first Junior Warden.

James Manor----James Manor was born 17 November 1804 in North Carolina. He came to Texas in about 1833, having been chosen by Sam Houston to negotiate treaties with the Indians. In 1836, he settled land along Gilliand creek near Manor. He served in the Texas Army in 1838. His sister, Kitty G. Manor, married Thomas Benton Wheeler, who was a member of Austin Lodge No. 12. Manor was a member of Austin Lodge No. 12 in 1842. His death occurred 17 May 1881. His brother was Joseph J. Manor.

Archibald S. Lewis----A.S. Lewis was born in New York. He fought at San Jacinto. He died 3 December 1839 in Houston.

144

G.F. Dorsett----On 1 March 1881, Dixie Lodge was called to meet for the purpose of burying G.F. Dorsett, whose funeral was preached by Albert Little in the Methodist Church.

William Norris----On 20 November 1881, Dixie Lodge was called to meet for the purpose of burying William Norris, father of Mrs. Dora Shaw.

William Keigwin----William Keigwin was an early settler of Bremond. He was born 15 April 1821 and died 19 November 1872. Keigwin was buried in the Bremond cemetery, Robertson county.

George Elliott Hunter----G.E. Hunter was born in Kentucky in 1797. He came to Texas in 1837 and settled in Cincinnati. He was a charter member of Forest Lodge No. 19 and Olive Branch Lodge No. 26. He died from burns received in a steamboat explosion in 1853.

George Preston Finlay----G.P. Finlay was six feet, four inches in height and weighed 190 pounds. He stood easily in the front rank as a lawyer, legislator and statesman. His paternal grandfather and grandmother were of Scotch descent, though natives of the North of Ireland. His mother was Cada Lewis, daughter of Joel Lewis, a highly respected and venerated citizen of Brandon, Mississippi, and a sister of Everett and Hugh Lewis of Gonzales county. George P. had two brothers, Luke W. Finlay, a lawyer of Memphis, Tennessee, and Oscar E. Finlay, a lawyer of Graham, Young county. George P. was born in Augusta, Perry county, Mississippi, 16 November 1829. He came to Texas in 1853, settled at Lavaca, Calhoun county, where he engaged in the practice of his profession. He married Carrie Rea in Lavaca on 16 November 1854. She was a native of Boonville, Missouri, and was born 13 May 1836. Carrie was the daughter of Horsley Rea and Pamelia Ewing, who was the daughter of Rev. Finis Ewing, the founder of the Cumberland Presbyterian Church. Mrs. Pamelia Ewing Rea died in Austin in 1881. George P. was made a Mason in 1854 at Lavaca, and a Knight Templar in 1873 at Austin.

Edward D. Sidbury----E.D. Sidbury was born in Wilmington, North Carolina, in 1838, and was reared in that city. His father John Edward Sidbury died in 1839, leaving his widowed wife, Miranda, and two sons, John, age three, and Edward D., aged one year. In 1862, Edward entered the Confederate Army. Owing to exposure during the war, he contracted rheumatism, from which he never fully recovered. On 29 January 1875, he married Charlotte M. Cook Scott, who was first married to John W. Scott. Mr. Sidbury was a member of the Masonic Fraternity for fifteen years, and at the time of his death was a member of Corpus Christi Lodge No. 189, and held the office of Worshipful Master for four years. He was a Royal Arch Mason and filled a number of the highest offices known to that degree.

145

S.M. Hunter----S.M. and J.W. Hunter had a dry goods store in Bryan and received their goods by train.

Alexander McDonald----Alexander McDonald was born in 1820 in Canada. He came to Texas in 1837. His wife was named Margaret S. Roberts. They had three sons. He was raised a Master Mason in Harmony Lodge No. 6 in Galveston in 1841, and drafted and signed the petition for Forest Lodge No. 19 in Huntsville. Alexander McDonald died in Houston on 21 December 1850.

James E. Harrison----Gen. J.E. Harrison was born 24 April 1815, and died 23 February 1875 at the age of fifty-nine years, nine months and twenty-nine days. He served as a Brigadier General, 15 TX Inf CSA. Harrison was buried in the First Street cemetery in Waco.

Edward Thomas Branch----E.T. Branch was born 11 December 1811 in Richmond, Virginia, and died on 24 September 1861. He represented Liberty county in the First and Second Congresses. He married Annie Cleveland Wharton in Brazoria county in 1838. In addition to being a Mason, he was a Methodist, and a charter member of the Philosophical Society of Texas.

Aaron Shannon----Aaron Shannon was born in South Carolina in 1796, and moved to Alabama in 1820, settling in Tuscaloosa county. He became a slave owner and operated a large plantation on the Tombigbee River. His wife was Elizabeth Kilpatrick, a granddaughter of General Charles Brandon of Tennessee. Aaron Shannon was commissioned a Colonel in the United States Army by Andrew Jackson and was a member of the board of regents of the University of Alabama. He came to the Republic and settled in what is now Grimes county. He was a loyal Baptist and was interested in all enterprises of the Baptist denomination. He was a charter member of the board of trustees of Baylor University and remained in that position twenty years. He was always a loyal supporter of and large contributor to Baylor. He died on his plantation in Grimes county in July 1865.

Terrell J. Jackson----T.J. Jackson was born in Green county, Georgia, in 1805, but was raised chiefly in Alabama. He married Julia A. Coleman in 1832. In 1838, he made a profession of religion and united with the church at Mt. Enon in Pickens county, Alabama. In 1841, he removed with his family to Texas and settled a few miles from Chappell Hill. He was a Deacon in the Providence Baptist Church in Chappell Hill for over twenty years until his death on 21 October 1867. He was a man of broad views and a large heart - a public benefactor as well as a good citizen. His house was a home for the stranger and a resting place for his brethren. A daughter, Mary, married a Mr. Justice; another daughter was Mrs. R.J. Sledge; another daughter was Mrs. Chappell. He was buried in the Mason cemetery at Chappell Hill.

George Tyler Wood----G.T. Wood was born in Georgia and came to Texas in 1839 on the sloop *Marshall*. He was a lawyer, Congressman, Senator, and the second Governor of Texas. He died at his plantation near Point Blank in 1858. He was a member of Forest Lodge No. 19.

Patrick C. Jack----P.C. Jack, a lawyer, came to Texas in 1832. In 1840, he was appointed district attorney of the First Judicial District. He died in Houston at the hour of 6 o'clock p.m. on 4 August 1844 of yellow fever. R.J. Towns was the administrator of his estate, Brazoria county. In him, his country lost a powerful advocate, and its judiciary one of its most talented, popular and impartial judges. His brother, William Houston Jack departed this life on the morning of 20 August 1844 at the plantation of Gov. Runnels, on the Brazos. He had contracted the epidemic that prevailed in Galveston and died with the black vomit. The two brothers departed together -together they lived-together they struggled hand in hand in the great cause of liberty, and together they retired from the theater of action. *Par Nobile Fratrum*. Like the two Whartons, neither could survive the other. Both were lawyers. William H. Jack was one of the highest order of intellect. At the Bar, in the Senate, before the Hastings, he was a match for any man. He was the Calhoun of Texas. Patrick Jack's wife was Margaret E. Smith. He was a member of Holland Lodge No. 1 and was buried with Masonic Honors.

Albert C. Horton----A.C. Horton was born in Georgia on 4 September 1798. He came to Texas in 1835 from Alabama. He bought several leagues of land on "Old Caney" and settled at Matagorda. A reformed gambler, he joined the Baptist Church and married a daughter of Deacon Dent in 1828. He was elected to the first Texas Congress, the congress that framed the Constitution of the Republic of Texas. He was one of the commissioners appointed by President Lamar to select and locate the city of Austin. He joined the Masonic Lodge at LaGrange, Alabama. Going out of the Lodge room, he, with tears, said "This night I begin a new life. In this degree I see the beauty and the value of all my mother, my wife and her father have said. I am raised into a higher, holier life. I am a new man." He was a deacon at Matagorda, and trustee and patron of Baylor University. As a trustee, he gave $5,000, a magnificent bell, and the assurance that he would ultimately endow a professorship of not less than $50,000, but he died on 1 September 1865, after the cruel war crushed his great heart and wrecked his princely fortune. He owned nearly 300 slaves, a large number of them Baptist Church members, as Horton had built them a church and employed a preacher, Noah Hill. Noah Hill stated that it was the most touching scene he ever saw to see Gov. Horton and his wife reading the Bible and praying for their servants.

J.M. Denton----J.M. Denton was passed in Austin Lodge No. 12 in 1871 and he was affiliated with Rising Star Lodge No. 429. Denton died 7 April 1877.

George Ewing Burney----G.E. Burney was born 15 August 1814 in Robertson county, Tennessee. In Washington county, Arkansas, he married Sara A. Blair in 1837. He came to Texas from Carroll county, Arkansas, in 1847. In 1849, he introduced the bill which created McLellan, Bell and Falls counties. He was president of Waco Manufacturing Company. Burney died in Waco on 18 February 1878 and was buried in the First Street cemetery.

Peter W. Gray----P.W. Gray was born in Fredericksburg, Virginia, on 12 December 1819 and came to Texas in the winter of 1838. In 1839, he assisted with the removal of the Shawnee Indians from East Texas. He was a lawyer, District Judge, Houston City Alderman, legislator, and a devout Episcopalian. He died 3 October 1874. Gray county was named in his honor.

E.N. Goode----Edward Goode was born in Virginia about 1823. He was a prominent farmer of Bell county and was one of the pioneers that settled on Salado Creek. He was married to Mary Ann Denson, the daughter of Dr. and Mrs. T.C. Denson. Mary Ann's first husband was Robert F. Holmes of Arkansas. Edward Goode died in Bell county in 1881. His step-daughter, Julia Holmes, married Dr. J.R. Rucker.

Charles Coney----Charles Coney, who was a member of Austin Lodge No. 12, died 1 May 1860.

James Childers----Dixie Lodge was called to meet 27 July 1869 for the purpose of burying James Childers, whose widow was Julia A.

W.G. Engledow----W.G. Engledow, First Past Master of Dixie Lodge, was buried 12 July 1879 by Dixie Lodge.

Aaron Moses----Aaron Moses was the first member of Bremond Lodge No. 350 to die.

W.C. Boone----W.C. Boone was among the first elected officials of Bremond Lodge 350. His burial was noted in the 1872 Lodge minutes. Also noted was that and he was their beloved and honored Chaplain.

Thomas M. League----T.M. League was a pioneer merchant of Houston and Galveston. He was born 8 March 1808 and died 25 November 1865 in Galveston.

Anthony Butler----Anthony Butler was United States Consul in Austin's Colony. He was a member of Milam Lodge No. 11.

Benjamin Rush Milam----B.R. Milam was killed at the seize and capture of Bexar in 1835. His was the first Masonic funeral in Texas.

Stephen Slade Barnett----S.S. Barnett was born 5 December 1807 in Madison county, Kentucky, and came to Texas in 1838. Barnett was in House of 5th Congress in 1840. Barnett was a charter member of Danville Lodge No. 101. In 1877, he died in Gregg county.

John Smith Davenport Byrom----J.S.D. Byrom, a native of Hancock county, Georgia, was a signer of the Declaration of Independence. He moved to Jasper county, Georgia, with an uncle and guardian, John Byrom, where he married Nancy Fitzpatrick on 17 March 1818. After their divorce, he married Mary Anne Knott and they came to came to Texas, at Brazoria county, in 1830. He was in the Battle of Velasco in 1832. Byrom died 10 July 1837 in Washington county. He was a member of Holland Lodge No. 36 and St. Johns No. 5.

George W. Capron----G.W. Capron was in the Army in 1836. He was a member of Holland Lodge No. 1 and Grand Tiler in 1863.

Josiah J. Crosby----J.J. Crosby, a Colonel in the Army and First Master of Phoenix Lodge No. 8, died 13 July 1850.

Valentine Bennett----Major Bennett was born in Massachusetts in 1780 and came to Texas in 1825. He was a Quartermaster and Commissary in Texas Army, and was severely wounded in the face and hip at Battle of Velasco on 26 June 1832. He was also in Battle of Concepcion in 1835 and seize of Bexar in 1835. His wife, Mary Kibbe, died before he came to Texas. Their children were Miles S. and Sarah. Bennett died at the home of his daughter in Gonzales on 23 July 1843.

Thomas Jefferson Callihan----T.J. Callihan was born 10 May 1817. He arrived in Velasco in 1836, and married Polly Talbort on 7 January 1838. They settled near Liverpool, Brazoria county. He married second Johanna Bishoff, who was born in Germany. Callihan fought at San Jacinto and served in the Civil War. He was a member of St. Johns Lodge No. 5. He died 31 May 1880.

William Jones E. Heard----W.J.E. Heard was born in 1803. He was Captain of Company F, first regiment of Texas volunteers at San Jacinto. His second wife was a sister of Postmaster General John Rice Jones. Heard died on 8 August 1874 in Chappell Hill and was buried there at the Masonic cemetery.

L.N. Cassady----L. N. Cassady was born in Knox county, Tennessee, and died 24 December 1879. His wife Laura died 15 September 1876. They were buried in the First Street cemetery in Waco.

C.C. Herbert----C.C. Herbert, a citizen of the Republic of Texas, was a member of Caledonia Lodge No. 68. He died in 1868.

William P. Massie/Massey----W.P. Massie or Massey, who fought at San Jacinto as a member of Captain John Smith's company on Galveston Island, died 8 March 1876.

B.R. Thomas----B.R. Thomas was born 19 February 1807. He died 2 October 1880 and was buried in the Masonic cemetery in Chappell Hill. His age at the time of his death was seventy-three years, seven months and thirteen days.

Joseph Worthington Elliott Wallace----J.W.E. Wallace was born in Pennsylvania on 8 April 1796 and came to Texas in 1830. As Lieutenant Colonel, he was second in command at Battle of Gonzales in 1835. In 1839, he was a delegate to a convention at Richmond to consider the location of a railroad. He was a member of the militia at the Plum Creek Fight in 1840. Wallace died on 24 August 1877 in Columbus, where he was a member of Caledonia Lodge No. 68

E.C. Tinnin----E.C. Tinnin died 20 July 1876 at the age of fifty-three years, five months and eighteen days. He was buried in the Kaufman cemetery, Kaufman county.

James Aeneas E. Phelps----J.A.E. Phelps was born in Mississippi and educated as a doctor. He came to Texas as one of the Old Three Hundred in 1822. He was in charge of a hospital unit at San Jacinto. Santa Anna was held prisoner in Phelps home, and Phelps saved Santa Anna from suicide. Phelps, who helped organize the Grand Lodge, died in 1847.

Edward H. Tarrant----E.D. Tarrant was born in North Carolina in 1796. Soon after, his family moved to Tennessee. Tarrant came to Texas and was in the Army of 1835-36. He represented Bowie county at the Convention of 1845. He lived near Italy in his later years. He died 2 August 1858 and was buried in Pioneer Rest cemetery. Tarrant county was named for him.

William Barrett Travis----W.B. Travis was born 9 August 1809 near Red Banks, Edgefield county, South Carolina. He studied law and began practice in Calaiborne, Alabama. He was married to Rosanna Cato, one of his pupils, in Alabama. They had a son and daughter and were then divorced in November 1835. He moved to Texas in about 1832. His letter of 24 February 1836 addressed "To the people of Texas and all Americans in the world" has been described as the most heroic document in American history. He died at the Alamo on 6 March 1836. Travis was raised 13 August in Lodge No. 3, Clairborne, Alabama.

Josias Power----Josias Power was born 27 August 1824. He died 20 December 1876 and was buried in the Burkett cemetery in Lavaca county.

Charles Edward Travis----C.E. Travis was the son of William B. Travis, who died at the Alamo. He was born in August 1829 in Alabama. After his parents divorced, his custody was given to his father. His father visited him in February 1836 on his way to San Antonio. His sister, Isabella, married John Grissett. C.E. Travis was a lawyer and a Texas Ranger. He died at his sister's in Washington county on 8 December 1860. Both children of William B. Travis were buried at the Masonic cemetery in Chappell Hill. A monument was erected for Susan by her son-in-law, Thomas G. Davidson. She died at the age of thirty-six years.

James W. Moore----Dr. J.W. Moore died at the age of fifty years on 20 June 1882. He was buried in Old Shiloh cemetery, Lavaca county.

Samuel S. Adams----S.S. Adams was born 29 January 1832. He died 11 March 1872 and was buried in the Mossy Grove cemetery, Lavaca county.

L.T. Nash----L.T. Nash died 16 March 1863 at the age of thirty-eight years and five days. Nash was buried in the Kaufman cemetery, Kaufman county.

Joseph H. Eubank----J.H. Eubank was born 12 December 1825. He died 24 January 1865 and was buried in the Old Burnet cemetery in Burnet county.

James W. Moore----Dr. J.W. Moore died at the age of fifty years on 20 June 1882. He was buried in Old Shiloh cemetery, Lavaca county.

James Moore----James Moore died 15 October 1867 and was buried in the Masonic cemetery in Chappell Hill.

A.M. Pharis----A.M. Pharis was born 7 January 1846 and died 23 February 1878. He was buried in Rockvale cemetery in Burnet county.

Charles Cornelius Nash----C.C. Nash, the son of William and L.A. Nash, died 13 January 1878 at the age of forty-four years and ten months. Nash was buried in the Kaufman cemetery, Kaufman county.

J.B. Arnett----J.B. Arnett was born 20 January 1820. He died 30 January 1879 and was buried in Bear Creek cemetery, Burnet county.

Francis Kellog----Francis Kellog was born 6 April 1835. He died 28 February 1863 and was buried in the Wheelock cemetery, Robertson county.

Samuel S. Adams----S.S. Adams was born 29 January 1832. He died 11 March 1872 and was buried in the Mossy Grove cemetery, Lavaca county.

TEXAS MASONIC DEATHS WITH SELECTED BIOGRAPHICAL SKETCHES

Robert M. White----R.M. White, M.D., was born 11 January 1836. He died 21 September 1880 and was buried in the Masonic cemetery in Chappell Hill.

William Harrison----William Harrison was born 3 January 1813. He died 17 December 1878 and was buried in Magill cemetery, Burnet county.

E. Luter---- Capt. E. Luter, an old Texan, and for over twenty years a worthy citizen of Goliad, died at St Mary's, Sunday, 6 December 1868. He left a wife and several small children.

Amasa Turner----Amasa Turner was born 9 November 1800 in Massachusetts. In 1825, he moved to Mobile, Alabama, where he married Julia Morse in 1827. He came to Texas in 1833 for his health. Turner participated in the siege and storming of Bexar, was Captain of a company at San Jacinto and during the Civil War, and was Provost Marshall of Lavaca county. He was a member of Harmony Lodge No. 6 and Gonzales Lodge No. 30. He died at Gonzales on 21 July 1877 and was buried in the Masonic cemetery.

Fletcher Watts Hubert----F.W. Hubert was born 11 September 1803. He died 18 June 1848 and was given a Tribute of Respect by Graham Lodge in June 1848. At the time of his death he was forty-four years, eight months and twenty-seven days old. He was a citizen of the Republic and was buried in the Masonic cemetery, Chappell Hill.

B.M. Smart----B.M. Smart was born in Monroe county, Indiana, 8 February 1816. On 1 January 1880, he died and was buried in Mahomet cemetery, Burnet county.

William Morton----William Morton came to Texas in 1822, as one of Austin's Old Three Hundred. When Robert Gillespie, who he did not know, died at his home in 1825, he built a brick monument to a fellow Mason, located in Richmond. This is the earliest mention of Masonry in Texas. Morton drowned in a flood of the Brazos in 1833.

S.W. Snodgrass----S.W. Snodgrass was born in West Virginia on 6 May 1846. He died on 16 June 1880 at the age of thirty-four years, one month and ten days. Snodgrass was buried in the Hoover Valley cemetery, Burnet county.

Robert Gillespie---Robert Gillespie came to Texas in 1825 from Franklin county, Alabama. He was waylaid, assassinated, and robbed shortly after arriving. He died at the home of William Morton.

Herman Aiken----Herman Aiken died in Bell county in 1860 at the age of fifty-two years. He was buried in the Salado cemetery. Aiken, who was in the Civil War, wrote about his life experiences in a booklet named "Fireside Tales."

Jacob Haller----Jacob Haller died on Saturday, 24 September 1853, at Chappell Hill of yellow fever contracted at Houston. Haller, with his wife, Mary Hargrove Haller, founded Chappell Hill. Haller was a charter member of the Masonic Lodge. He was the first buried in the Masonic cemetery in Chappell Hill.

J.E. Ferguson----J.E. Ferguson bought Chalk Mill, in Bell county, in 1867 and his family operated the mill until 1876.

Samuel May Williams----S.M. Williams came to Texas as Stephen F. Austin's secretary and later as partner. He arrived in San Felipe in May 1824. He wrote and spoke Spanish and French. He had charge of all maps, charts, and clerical work of Austin's colonies. In 1834, he became a partner with Thomas F. McKinney, and in 1837 they moved their business to Galveston, where Williams died 13 September 1858.

George Washington Poe----G.W. Poe was born about 1800 and came to Texas in 1834 with his wife, Frances E. He was in the Battle of San Jacinto. He also was Paymaster, Adjutant General and, temporarily, Secretary of War. He received a league and labor for his military service in Montague county. He died in 1844.

James L. Partain----J.L. Partain was given a Tribute of Respect from Tarrant Lodge No. 91 in February 1859.

Robert Emmet Bledsoe Baylor----R.E.B. Baylor was born 10 May 1791 in Bourbon county, Kentucky. He was an eminent pioneer, preacher, scholar, lawyer, and statesman. Baylor, who came to Texas in 1838 from Alabama, was District Judge of Supreme Court of both the Republic and State of Texas. He was in the Battle of Plum creek. Baylor University was named for him. Baylor's death occurred on 30 December 1873 in Independence. He was a member of Baylor Lodge No. 125 and he was Chaplain of the Grand Lodge of Texas Masons in 1843, 1846, and 1847.

John H. Day----J.H. Day, an old Texan, died at Brenham on 20 April 1861.

John A. Winn----J.A. Winn died at the age of fifty-four years, three months and nine days on 30 November 1870. He was a member of the Masonic and I.O.O.F. fraternities, and served with the CSA. His wife, Eveline A., who died 30 May 1864 at the age of forty-one years, three months and twelve days, was buried with him in the First Street cemetery in Waco.

R.J. Jackson----R.J. or E.J. Jackson was given a Tribute of Respect from Llano Lodge No. 242 in October 1862.

R. W. Chappell----R.W. Chappell was born 24 December 1831. He was a Pvt Wauld's TX Legion CSA. Chappell died 17 January 1876 and was buried in the Masonic cemetery in Chappell Hill.

John Belden----John Belden arrived in Texas on 25 October 1835 as a member of W.G. Cooke's "New Orleans Grays." He fought at San Jacinto and was at the fall of Bexar. After the revolution, Belden moved to Houston, where he died 15 September 1841. The administrator of his estate was J. DeCordova. He was a member of Holland Lodge No. 1 and was buried with Masonic Honors.

James H. Thompson----J.H. Thompson was born 8 December 1804. He died 26 May 1871 and was buried in the Masonic cemetery in Chappell Hill.

Stephen H. Everett----Dr. S.H. Everett was born 26 November 1807 in New York. Everett came to Texas in 1834, and was a signer of the Declaration of Independence. His and his wife, Alta Zera Williams, had three children. He died in late July or early August 1844 at the St. Charles Hotel in New Orleans, where he was on a business trip.

Gideon Keesee----Gideon Keesee was born in 1839. He was a Pvt Co. F 5 TX Cavalry CSA. He died in 1881 and was buried in the Masonic cemetery in Chappell Hill.

Joshua Hadley----Col. Joshua Hadley was born in North Carolina and for many years a citizen of Montgomery county. He met his sudden death by a fall from his horse in July 1845. Hadley had been married twice and had eight children. He joined the Army 30 June 1836 and served until 30 September 1836. He was a charter member of Orphans Friend Lodge No. 17 and served on a committee to secure a warrant and dispensation from the Grand Lodge of the Republic of Texas.

Alonzo Beeman----Alonzo Beeman, a Union man, settled on Stampede creek, Bell county, in 1852. He was a charter member of Leon Lodge No. 193, Bell county, and First Master of the Lodge. Beeman died 31 December 1869 and was buried in the Moffat cemetery, Bell county.

Isaac N. Moreland---Hon. I.N. Moreland came to Texas in 1834. He was Chief Justice of Harris county, and Commander of the Artillery Co. in the Battle of San Jacinto, where he commanded "Twin Sisters." He died 8 June 1842 in Houston and was buried there with Masonic Honors. He was a member of Holland Lodge No. 1 and Temple Lodge No. 4.

C.E. Childers----C.E. Childers was buried by Dixie Lodge on 15 January 1874.

Kindred Henry Muse----K.H. Muse was born 7 November 1804 in Camden, South Carolina. He came to Texas in 1837 and settled at Nacogdoches. He represented Nacogdoches county in the Third and Fourth Congresses and in the Senate of the Fifth, Sixth, and Seventh. While carrying the mail, he caught pneumonia and died 30 April 1845.

Warren D.C. Hall----W.D.C. Hall was born in Guilford county, North Carolina, in 1788. He moved to New Orleans in 1803. There, he was a member of Concorde Lodge No. 3. He first came to Texas in 1812 and emigrated with Col. M'Gee in his unfortunate attempt to revolutionize this country. Hall was the first white man on Galveston Island. Hall died 8 April 1867 at his place on the island about fifteen miles west of Galveston. He was with a fit of apoplexy on the night before and died before morning. Hall, who was near eighty years old, was a member of Holland Lodge No. 1 and was buried in Harmony Lodge plot in the Episcopal cemetery, where the Masonic emblem is upside down on his tombstone.

Richard F. Blocker----R.F. Blocker died 25 April 1861 at the age of thirty-five years. His wife, Mary A. Blocker, was born 2 October 1825 and died 1 March 1902. They were buried in at First Street cemetery in Waco.

T.W. Quarde----T.W. Quarde, First Master of Griffin Lodge No. 132, died at his home near Griffin, Texas, 7 January 1860. He helped organize and was Chartered Junior Warden of Mt. Enterprise Lodge No. 60 in the year 1850.

Anthony Martin Branch----A.M. Branch, died of yellow fever on 3 October 1867 at his residence in Huntsville, Walker county, Texas, in the forty-fifth year of his age. Branch was the son of Samuel Branch, Esq. and Winnifred Guerrant of Buckingham county, Virginia, and a native of said county and state. He graduated at Hampden-Sydney College at a period of life which gave earnest of his future prominence and usefulness. He came to Texas, settling in Huntsville, in 1847. He was elected to represent the people of his county, and senatorial district, in both branches of the Legislature. In 1863 he was called from the field, where he had made a gallant soldier, and sent by his constituency to the Lower House of the Confederate Congress.

H. Daniels----H. Daniels died at the age of thirty-four years on 1 December 1881 and was buried in the First Street cemetery in Waco.

Valentine Wesley Swearingen----V.W. Swearingen was born in Kentucky. He came to Texas in 1831 and settled in what is now Austin county. Swearingen, who was at the seize and capture of Bexar in 1835 and fought at San Jacinto, was a charter member of Lodge No. 67 at Chappell Hill. He was buried near Sealy in Austin county.

155

John Henry Moore----Col. J.H. Moore, born in Rome, Tennessee, 13 August 1800, and so long and so favorably known in the history of frontier warfare, had an announcement of his death in June 1842, but apparently he did not die until 2 December 1880. (death notice: Immediately after his return from the pursuit of a party of Indians that lately made a descent upon the settlements on Cummin's creek, he was attacked by an inflammatory fever, caused by fatigue and exposure he had undergone and so violent was the disease that it terminated fatally in about two days.) Moore came to Texas in 1818, returned home, and returned back to Texas in 1821. He was in the Army of 1835-36; in Battle of Gonzales; Vasquez Raid. Moore enrolled in Company F, Terry's Texas Rangers, but being too old to fight, he was appointed on a committee to secure bonds to finance the war. He was buried on his plantation nine miles north of LaGrange, where he was a member of LaFayette Lodge No. 34.

John Hansford----Judge John Hansford was cruelly murdered in Harrison county by an old gentleman named Mosely and his son-in-law, whose name was Bullard. John Hansford was born in Barren county, Kentucky. He was a member of the Third and Fourth Congress of the Republic. Hansford county was named for him.

Joseph B. Williams----J.B. Williams was born 14 October 1829. He was in the Civil War. He died 17 October 1875, and was buried in the First Street cemetery in Waco.

Robert Alexander----Robert Alexander was born 7 August 1811 in Smith county, Tennessee. He came to Texas in 1837 as a Methodist Missionary Minister. He arrived at Washington on the Brazos after riding horseback from Natchez, Mississippi. He was a minister at Howard and Belton, both in Bell county, as well as Waco and Galveston. Alexander's first wife, Eliza Ayers, died in 1878. His second wife was Mrs. Patience N. Wilson of Bryan. Rev. Alexander, nearly seven feet tall, served Texas forty-five years as an itinerant minister. His death date was 26 April 1882. He was a member of Graham Lodge No. 20, in Brenham, and Galveston Lodge.

Augustine Blackburn Hardin----A.B. Hardin was born 18 July 1797 in Franklin county, Georgia, the son of Swan and Jerusha Blackburn Hardin. He came to Texas in 1825 and was a signer of the Declaration of Independence. Hardin was a farmer and rancher in Liberty county, where he died 22 July 1871.

John Baylor Banks----J.B. Banks died in Galveston on 28 January 1874. He married Carolyn C. Browning on 22 January 1846 in Washington county. In 1853, he was a charter member of Colorado Lodge No. 96.

Joel D. Eidom----J.D. Eidom, of Troup, was buried by Dixie Lodge on 19 January 1874.

John Gilbert Love----J.G. Love was born 2 January 1788 in Davidson county, Tennessee. He entered Texas in 1825, settling about six miles northeast of San Augustine. Love was Alcalde, County Judge, Chief Justice, and in 1837, was appointed by Sam Houston as Collector of Customs on the Sabine river. His death occurred in September 1866. Love was a member of Red Land Lodge No. 3.

H.L. Little----Dr. H.L. Little was born in Owensboro, Davis county, Kentucky, in 1822. He was married to Nancy Catherine Wright in 1841. They had seven children. In 1854, Mrs. Little died, and Dr. Little arrived in Meridian, Bosque county in 1856. He married a second time to Rebecca Adams. Dr. Little was in the Civil War and his family has in their possession letters that he wrote to his wife describing the deprivation and suffering of the troops. Dr. Little died in 1876 leaving a wife with three young children.

Brooks Moon Willingham----B.M. Willingham was born in 1814. His parents were Cashwell Willingham, born about 1790, and Martha Moon. He, along with his wife, Mary Louisa Austin, and eldest son and grandson came to Meridian, Bosque county, from Charleston, South Carolina, by way of steamer to Galveston in 1860. Willingham, and his sons, operated mercantile stores in Morgan, Kopperl and Kimball. He died in 1871 and was buried in Kimball cemetery.

William A. Alley----W.A. Alley, an old settler of Texas, was born in Missouri about 1800. He emigrated from Missouri in 1822, and was one Austin's Original 300. He was at the storming and capture of Bexar. Alley settled on the Colorado at Alleyton (named for him), where he resided until he died at his residence on 15 August 1869 at the age of seventy years. He was a member of Caledonia Lodge No. 68.

Ben Milam Hamilton----B.M. Hamilton was born 23 October 1840 in Galveston. He was initiated 1867, passed 9 February 1867, raised 9 March 1867, was a member of Colorado Lodge No. 96. Hamilton married Catherine Tisdale in Travis county. He died on 4 August 1870 and was buried in Manor cemetery. Mrs. Hamilton was buried in the Bastrop cemetery.

W.D. Eastland----W.D. Eastland was born in Alabama on 22 March 1826. He died in Waco on 6 March 1877 and was buried in the First Street cemetery in Waco.

Alexander Michael Clingman----Dr. A.M. Clingman was born 15 May 1830. He was in the Civil War. He died on 15 June 1870 at the age of forty and was buried in the First Street cemetery in Waco.

Constantine W. Buckley----C.W. Buckley was born 22 January 1815 in Surry county, North Carolina. He moved to Houston in 1838. He was a farmer, a member of the Texas House, and a lawyer. Buckley drowned in the Brazos on 19 December 1865.

Matthew Cartwright----Matthew Cartwright was born 11 November 1807 in Wilson county, Tennessee. He came to Texas with his parents in 1825 to near San Augustine. Cartwright married Amanda Holman, the daughter of Isaac Holman, who came to Texas in 1835. From 1847 until 1860, he was active in buying and selling lands. Cartwright died 2 April 1870. His son, A.P. Cartwright, died 11 August 1873 of black jaundice at the age of thirty-three. Cartwright's other children were Columbus, Leonidas, Matthew, Anna W. Roberts, and Mary C. Ingram.

John N. Waitt----J.N. Waitt died 28 August 1876 at the age of thirty-three. He was buried in the Masonic section of the First Street cemetery in Waco.

James H. Gurley----J.H. Gurley died 17 June 1865 at the age of thirty-six years and five months. Gurley and his wife, Lucy B., who died 16 January 1869, were buried in the First Street cemetery in Waco.

Samuel Damon----Samuel Damon was a member of St. Johns Lodge No. 5. He was in the Army of 1835-1836. The town of Damon, located in northwestern Brazoria county, was named for him. He was a brick maker for many Brazoria county plantations.

Thomas Mason Dennis----T.M. Dennis was born 9 March 1807 in Georgia. He came to Texas in 1835, and fought at San Jacinto. Dennis moved to Rockport in 1871 and later to Karnes county. He died in Gonzales on 15 October 1877.

John B. Denton----Rev. J.B. Denton was born 28 July 1806 in Tennessee. He was an orphan by the age of eight. He was adopted by a Wells family. Denton married Mary Greenlee Stewart of Louisiana, who taught him to read and write. He became a Methodist Episcopal preacher and came to Texas in 1836-37 with another preacher, Littleton Fowler. He began the study of law and was licensed to practice. Denton was also an Indian fighter and was instantly killed by Keechi Indians on 22 May 1841. He was a member of Milam Lodge No. 40. Denton County was named for him. Denton's son, A.N. Denton, killed J.W. Curtis in Weatherford in June 1859.

Lemuel Dale Evans----L.D. Evans came to Texas in 1843, settling in Fannin county. He was a member of Congress, and a member of Temple Lodge No. 70. Evans died in Washington, D.C., in 1877.

J.L. Farquahar----J.L. Farquahar, a prominent farmer of Washington county, was a charter trustee of Baylor. He was Steward of the Grand Lodge.

George Fisher----George Fisher was born in Hungry in 1795. He was in the Texas Revolution, and was Collector of Customs at Port of Galveston. Fisher presented his papers, library and correspondence to the State of Texas in 1856. He was Grand Treasurer. He died in San Francisco on 11 June 1873.

Jabez Demming Giddings----J.D. Giddings was the son of Lucy Demming and James Giddings, both natives of Connecticut. James Giddings was in early life a ship captain, and in later years a farmer in Susquehanna county, Pennsylvania, where he died in 1863. Jabez was born on 8 October 1814 in Susquehanna county. His brother, Dewitt Clinton, was born 18 July 1827 in Susquehanna county. Jabez was married to Ann M. Tarver and they had two children. After Jabez came to Texas in about 1838, he was a lawyer, school teacher, district clerk, and a member of the Somervell Expedition. He was a prominent businessman in Washington county. He was Grand Master in 1846 and a member of Graham Lodge No. 20. Jabez died at Brenham on 25 June 1878. The town of Giddings was named for him.

Mirabeau Buonaparte Lamar----M.B. Lamar was born 16 August 1798 at Louisville, Georgia, the son of John and Rebecca Lamar, who were first cousins. On 1 January 1826, he was married to Tabitha B. Jordan at her home in Perry county, Alabama. In 1827, they had a son to die at birth, a daughter Rebecca Ann was born two years later. Mrs. Lamar died in Columbus, GA, on 20 August 1830, in the twenty-first year of her age, leaving her husband and two children. Highly educated and of a literary mind, Lamar, in 1835, in order to drown his sorrows, visited Texas with an idea to write its history, but decided to stay in Texas. Lamar, who was in the Battle of San Jacinto, was chosen vice-president and president of the Republic. Lamar's mother died, while on a visit to visit him in Houston, 26 July 1839, and Rebecca Ann died at the age of sixteen at Macon. In 1851, he was married to Henrietta, daughter of John Newell Maffit, at Galveston. Lamar died 19 December 1859. Mrs. Lamar died, near Santa Anna, Coleman county, 6 October 1891. They were buried in the Masonic cemetery at Richmond. Dr. Thomas B. Lamar of Macon, Georgia, brother to Mirabeau B., died 13 May 1858.

Jack F. Kaiser----J.F. Kaiser died from effects of a pistol shot received in Palestine on 10 December 1877 and was buried by Dixie Lodge on 14 December 1877.

Stephen J. Sparks----S.J. Sparks was born 13 March 1824. He died 20 March 1857 at the age of thirty-three years and seven days, and was buried at the Volo cemetery, Bell county.

John T. Miller----J.T. Miller, the son of John Benton Miller and Mary Roberts Miller, was born 4 April 1820 in Logansport, Cass county, Indiana. He was married twice, to Frances Cone and Eliza Ann Spencer. He came to Texas in 1838 from Washington county, Arkansas, and to Austin in 1855. He owned the Eclipse Stables located on the site later occupied by the Driscoll Hotel. He was an old and much respected citizen of Austin when he died 21 February 1882 at his home near Austin.

Beriah Graham----Dr. Beriah Graham, the only child of Thomas Graham, was born 15 January 1804 in Stokes county, North Carolina. The Grahams moved from Stokes county to near Russellville, Logan county, Kentucky, in 1805. Dr. Graham attended Transylvania University, Lexington, Kentucky, and St. Louis Medical College. In St. Louis, he was a member of Lodge No. 1 and was affiliated with Palestine Lodge No. 31 in June 1850. He was a SW in 1850 and was demitted 16 May 1853. He moved from Palestine to Austin after being appointed by Sam Houston to become superintendent of the insane asylum. In Austin, he was a ruling elder of the First Presbyterian Church. He died at his home in Austin on 25 August 1879 and was buried in Oakwood cemetery.

J.H. Kendricks----J.H. Kendricks, Secretary of Griffin Lodge, died near Griffin, 29 January 1860. His son was John W. Kendricks, Governor of Wyoming.

Simon Wiess----Simon Wiess of Wiess' Bluff, Jasper county, was born at Lublin, Poland, 1 January 1800. He was a Royal Arch Mason at Constantinople, 2 April 1825, and went to Asia Minor the same year, where he held a prominent position in the Masonic circles. In 1826, he visited the Mt. Lebanon Lodge, Boston, and in 1828, he was in San Domingo, where he was in the Masonic Fraternity. He was in various Lodges, in many parts of the world, including Harmony Lodge and Dewitt Clinton Lodge No. 129, Jasper county. He could read, write, and speak seven languages. In 1836, he was Deputy Collector for the Republic. On 6 January 1836, he married Margaret Sturrock at Natchitoches, Louisiana. Margaret was the daughter of William Sturrock and Ann Swan. Margaret was born in Scotland, near Dundee, 12 June 1814, and died at Wiess' Bluff, 17 May 1881. She was a woman of prayer and of the Bible. The Wiess family moved from Louisiana in 1836 to Nacogdoches. In 1838, they moved to Beaumont and in 1840 to Wiess' Bluff, where Simon Weiss died on 13 August 1868. Their children were Pauline Coffin, Napoleon, Mark, William, Valentine, and Massena.

George Patton----On 15 August 1863, Dixie Lodge was called to meet for the purpose of burying George Patton, member of Mound Prairie Lodge No. 173.

~~~~~~

PART 3

ADDITIONAL INFORMATION

PETITION FOR FIRST LODGE IN TEXAS

In 1877, an interesting incident in the early history of Masonry in Texas was brought to light. In 1828, eight years before Texas achieved her independence upon the battlefield of San Jacinto, Bros. Stephen F. Austin, the father of Texas, Ira Ingram, the first Speaker of the Congress of the Republic of Texas, H.H. League, Eli Mitchell, Joseph White and Thomas M. Duke met together at the little village of San Felipe, on the Brazos river, in the first Masonic Convention ever held upon the soil of Texas. These distinguished pioneers and settlers of this great State must hereafter rank Brothers John A. Wharton, Asa Brigham, James A.E. Phelps, Alexander Russell, Anson Jones and J.P. Caldwell as the earliest patrons and promoters of Masonry in Texas, and go down into history with this additional halo of glory around their memories.

In November 1877, Bro. Guy M. Bryan of Galveston, who was the custodian of the papers and archives of Stephen F. Austin, found a document among Gen. Austin's papers, containing the proceedings of this Convention, and he wanted them presented to the Grand Lodge. It was accompanied by a paper in Spanish which proved to be the form of a petition or dispensation for a new Lodge. Before removing to Texas, Bro. Stephen F. Austin was a member of St. Louis Lodge No. 3, holding a Charter from the Grand Lodge of Pennsylvania, at the town of St. Louis, in what was then the unoccupied Masonic Territory of Missouri. His status as an M.M. being established, there was no question of the authenticity of the documents, and they were deposed with the Grand Secretary in accordance with Bro. Bryan's request.

The convention met for the purpose of petitioning the Grand York Lodge of Mexico for Dispensation for a Lodge at San Felipe. About that time and afterwards, intense excitement existed in Mexico on the subject suppressing the Masonic Societies in obedience to a Bull fulminated against them by the reigning Pope. Indeed, in a short time, all the men of influence in the country were arrayed upon the side of one or the other of the political factions, which were said to be under the guidance of the several Scotch and English Lodges. The "Escoses," (or Scotch) Lodges were composed of large proprietors and persons of distinction, and were mostly men of moderate and conservative principles. The "Yorkanos," (or York Masons) were opposed to the Central, or Royal, government and were in favor of the entire expulsion of the Spanish from Mexico. Toward the close of 1827, Don Jose Montano published his plan for the forcible reform of the government, in order to counteract the growing influence of the Yorkanos. Civil War soon after raged, and in the struggle that followed, the rival Masonic bodies lost their power and prestige, and were rent into fragments. Disaster will always follow when Masonry goes beyond her legitimate sphere and enters into the domain of things which concern her not. Owing to this distracted state of affairs the enterprise of forming a Lodge in San Felipe was permitted to die out.

The document alluded to, being an important contribution to our history, was published in the proceedings of the Grand Lodge of Texas:

At a meeting of Ancient York Masons, held in the town of San Felipe de Austin, on the 11th day of February 1828, for the purpose of taking into consideration the expediency of petitioning the Grand York Lodge of Mexico for granting a Charter or Dispensation for organizing a Subordinate Lodge at this place, the following Brethren were present: Bros. H.H. League, Stephen F. Austin, Ira Ingram, Eli Mitchell, Joseph White, G.B. Hall, and Thos. M. Duke.

On motion of Bro. Ira Ingram, and seconded, Brother H.H. League was appointed chairman, and Thos. M. Duke Secretary. On motion of Stephen F. Austin, and seconded, it was unanimously agreed that we petition to the Grand York Lodge of Mexico for a charter or Dispensation to organize a Lodge at this place, to be called the Lodge of Union. " On balloting for officers of the lodge, the following brothers were duly elected: Bro. S.F. Austin, Master; Bro. Ira Ingram, Senior Warden; and Bro. H.H. League, Junior Warden. (Signed) H.H. League, Chairman Attest: Thomas M. Duke, Secretary"

Marcus Mott, Grand Master, wrote:

There is something peculiarly touching and interesting in this record. Those noble men, standing upon the confines of civilization, seeking to establish an Empire in the almost untrodden wilds of Texas, and looking forward was prophetic-ken to the time when the "wilderness would blossom as a rose," and tower'd cities and the busy hum of men usurp the resort of the Indian and the home of the wild beast--seemed to feel that masonry was a necessary incident to the civilization of the Anglo-American. They sought to invoke beneficent teaching and humanizing influences in aid of their grand undertaking. No higher tribute was ever paid to our Order. No nobler estimate to its wisdom and truth ever imprinted upon the records of time.

New England poets and orators have exhausted the flowers of poesy and the graces of oratory in describing the sublimity of the spectacle when the puritans first stood on the shore of the New World and thanked God that they could worship Him according to the dictates of their conscience.

To my mind the spectacle of Stephen F. Austin and his associates, in the village of San Felipe, in 1828, and that of John A. Wharton and his associates, in the grove of trees back of the town of Brazoria, in 1835, seeking to give direction to the vital forces of Masonry, and invoking its aid as a great lever of civilization in founding a new nation, are no less sublime and impressive. They will be dwelt upon with rapture by the coming orators and poets of masonry, who will embalm the scenes in the genius of eloquence and inspiration of poetry.

The sacrifices and achievements of such men as Austin, Wharton, Anson, Jones, Rusk, Houston, and others in founding the magnificent empire which we now enjoy, excite our special wonder and tempt the belief "that there were giants in the earth in those days." And when we reflect that contemporaneously there with they sought to establish Masonry upon a sure and firm foundation in this fair land, our wonder is converted into gratitude, and as was so well said by Grand Master Sayers, we find the strongest incentives to preserve and perpetuate the heritage they have transmitted to us."

~~~~~~

MASONRY AS EXPLAINED IN 1853

An article from the June 18, 1853 issue of the *Victoria Texian* :

Masons and Odd Fellows now form an integral portion of the population of La Grange, as they do most other towns and cities in the United States. Orders so wide spread and so universal in their influence, must certainly be based upon some substantial benefit they confer upon individuals and communities. Yet these societies have their enemies, and are regarded by some as institutions calculated to exercise a baleful influence upon society, morality and religion. But such hostility, when properly sifted, will be found to consist of nothing more than bare prejudice based upon ignorance and preconceived aversion.

Take one evidence of this fact. The chief objection, and the one most frequently urged against Masonry and Odd Fellowship, is that men are often admitted into their Lodges who do not act up to the rules and requirements of such societies, but sometimes behave in open violation of law and good order, yet are rarely expelled for their misdemeanors. But is not this the case with members of the different churches? How often are churchmen retained, though publicly guilty of immoral and unchristian conduct? And can a greater amount of perfection be expected in secret societies than in religious denominations, notwithstanding the latter professes to be guided by a far higher standard of duty? The grand object of Masonry and Odd Fellowship is not to make men perfect, but to improve, refine and elevate them, as far as possible; to develop those inherent impulses of benevolence, charity, friendship, sociality, and sympathy for each other, and for making in general-- impulses which often lie dormant most aroused and stimulated into actively by a solemn and mysterious compact entered into with these secret orders.-- Though all do not prove zealous and exemplary members, if not deemed beyond the pale of reformation, they are commonly retained for further trial, just as delinquent church members are retained, in order that a wholesome restraint may still be exercised over them.-- How idle and unreasonable then, are all such remarks as these: "Did I not tell you so.--That man is a Mason, and an odd Fellow too? Yet you see what he has been doing."

But though all such reflections are unjust, when aimed at Masonry or Odd Fellowship, as a body, they ought certainly to inspire every member of these benevolent and noble orders, who has any claim to self-esteem or self-respect, to show by his daily conduct that he cannot himself be fairly made the subject of such mortifying observations. He should aim to show that he has not entered into a binding obligation to practice all the high principles inculcated by these orders merely to cloak his immorality or dishonor from the world, but that he has done so from a generous desire not only to reform his own habits, and develop his own virtues, but also that he may exercise by his example, a like beneficial influence upon those who are bound in closed fellowship with him, and who are under similar vows to act ever in accordance to the dictates of "friendship, fidelity, and love."

~~~~~~

TEXAS MASONIC DEATHS WITH SELECTED BIOGRAPHICAL SKETCHES

WHERE TO OBTAIN MORE INFORMATION

To request information about a Texas Mason, visit the Masonic Grand Lodge at 715 Columbus, between 7th & 8th, in Waco, or mail your request to:

Masonic Grand Lodge
Library and Museum of Texas
P.O. Box 446
Waco, Texas 76703

Provide as much of the following information as possible: the Mason's full name; date and location of death; name and/or number of Texas Lodge (note: they do not have any out of state records); locations of residence in Texas (county, town/city, year); and any other information that may be helpful to locating the Mason's records.

Currently, there is no charge, however, donations are appreciated. The Masonic records include nine items of information: the Mason's name; lodge number; location of the lodge; dates of degrees-initiated, passed, or raised (if he received Degrees in Texas); an affiliation date with the lodge; a demission date or any suspensions for nonpayment of dues or un-Masonic conduct reinstatements, a death date official record of offices held in Texas Lodge. The records date back to 1837, when the Grand Lodge of Texas was organized.

The Confederate Military Lodge of Research is a research Lodge, dedicated to researching the involvement of Masons in the War for Southern Independence. If you are a member of the Sons of Confederate Veterans, you are eligible for membership. Currently, the fee for affiliation is $20.00 and annual dues are $10.00. Contact them at Compatriot and Brother Clifton W. Crisler, P.O. Box 776, Alexander City, Alabama 35011-0776, or by e-mail at comilor@lakemartin.net.

To obtain a copy of a booklet on Masonry, contact:

Masonic Information Center
8120 Fenton Street
Silver Spring, MD 20910-4785

~~~~~

GLOSSARY

Anno Lucis - Abbreviated A.L. Meaning "in the year of light" it is computed by adding the formerly supposed age of the world, 4000 B.C., to the present era. Therefore, the year 1865 is 5865 A.L.

Aprons - Like many artisans today, stonemasons centuries ago wore leather aprons to carry their tools--and to protect themselves from flying chips of stone. Their custom was adopted by the men who became Freemasons. Modern Masons wear a lamb's tone or cloth apron, sometimes elaborately decorated or embroidered to show their pride in being a Mason.

Degree - A degree is a stage or a level of membership. It is also the ceremony by which a man attains that level of membership. There are three, called Entered Apprentice, Fellow Craft, and Master Mason. The names are taken from the craft guilds. In the Middle Ages, when a person wanted to join a craft, such as the carpenters or the stonemasons, he was first apprenticed. As an apprentice, he learned the tools and skills of the trade. After proving his skills, he became a Fellow of the Craft. When he had exceptional ability, he was known as a Master of the Craft.

Entered Apprentice - Abbreviated E.A., is the first degree of masonry. It is in Freemasonry a preliminary degree, intended to prepare the candidate for the higher and fuller instructions of the succeeding degrees.

Fellow Craft - Abbreviated F.C., is the second degree of Freemasonry. Like the Degree of Apprentice, it is only preparatory in the higher initiation of the master. Yet it differs essentially from it in symbolism. For, as the first degree was typical of youth, the Second is supposed to represent the stage of manhood, and hence the acquisition of science is made its prominent characteristic.

Grand Lodge - The administrative body in charge of Masonry in some geographical area. In the United States, there is a Grand Lodge in each state and the District of Columbia.

Lodge - The word "lodge" means both a group of Masons meeting in some place and the room or building in which they meet. Masonic buildings are also sometimes called "temples" because much of the symbolism Masonry uses to teach its lessons comes from the building of King Solomon's Temple in the Holy land. The term "lodge" itself comes from the structures which the stonemasons built against the sides of the cathedrals during construction. In winter, when building had to stop, they lived in these lodges and worked at carving stone.

TEXAS MASONIC DEATHS WITH SELECTED BIOGRAPHICAL SKETCHES

Mason - A Mason is a member of a fraternity known as Masonry (or Freemason). A fraternity is a group of men who join together because there are things they want to do in the world; there are things they want to do "inside their own minds"; and they enjoy being together with men they like and respect.

Masonry - A fraternity of Masons of which religion plays a very important part. A man must believe in God to become a Mason. Meetings open with prayer, and a Mason is taught, as one of the first lessons of Masonry, that one should pray for divine counsel and guidance before starting an important undertaking. Masonry encourages every Mason to be active in the religion and church of his own choice. To join the Masons, a man must be sound in body and mind, believe in God, be at least the minimum age required by Masonry in his state, and have a good reputation. There are also less "formal" requirements such as he should believe in helping others, believe there is more to life than pleasure and money, and he should want to grow and develop as a human being. A man is not asked to become a Mason. For hundreds of years, Masons have been forbidden to ask others to join the fraternity. A man who wishes to become a Mason must ask a Mason for an application. His application is considered by the local Lodge and a vote is taken. If he is approved, the Lodge contacts the man to set a date for the Entered Apprentice Degree. Upon completion of all three degrees, the man is a Master Mason and a full member of the fraternity.

Master Mason - Abbreviated M.M., in all the Rites of Freemasonry constitutes the Third Degree. As an Entered Apprentice, the Freemason was taught elementary instructions which were to fit him for further advancement in his profession; as a Fellow Craft, he is directed to continue his investigations in the science of the institution, and to labor diligently in the tasks it prescribes; but, as a Master Mason, he is taught the last, the most important, and the most necessary of truth, that having been faithful to all his trusts, he is at last to die, and to receive the reward of his fidelity.

Symbols - Symbols are used because they communicate quickly. Masonry uses symbols as a way of communication and teaching. Some form of the "Square and Compasses" is the most widely used and known symbol of Masonry. The Square symbolizes things of the earth, and it also symbolizes honor, integrity, truthfulness, and the other ways we should relate to this world and the people in it. The Compasses symbolize things of the spirit, and the importance of a well-developed spiritual life, and also the importance of self-control--of keeping ourselves within bounds. The "G" stands for Geometry, the science which ancients believed most revealed the glory of God and His works in the heavens, and it also stands for God, who must be at the center of all our thoughts and all our efforts.

~~~~~~

NAME INDEX

Benge 109
Bennefield 84
Bennett 2, 13, 48, 65, 66, 92, 100,
    116, 149
Bennison 119
Benson 14
Bentley 56, 73
Benton 42, 53, 133
Beorns 12
Bernstein 109
Beroman 13
Berry 25, 44, 46, 79, 83, 92
Berryhill 69
Berthier 22
Betts 39
Bevens 17
Bevill 16
Bible 14
Billert 60
Billingslea 5, 86
Billingsley 117
Billingsly 132
Billington 30
Billips 32
Bills 82, 119
Bingham 44, 72
Binion 7
Binkley 8
Binns 118
Birdsong 32
Birdwell 21, 35, 73, 88, 111, 115
Birmingham 94
Bishoff 149
Bishop 8, 14, 25, 49
Black 16, 22, 29, 91, 99, 139
Blackburn 19, 27, 35, 54, 63, 64,
    156
Blackmon 17
Blackwell 24, 71, 98
Blair 3, 5, 67, 74, 148
Blake 77
Blakey 25, 50, 132
Blankenship 99
Blanton 13, 62
Bledsoe 27, 82, 87, 153
Block 77
Blocker 155

Blood 58
Bloodworth 72, 90
Bloomingdale 52
Blue 58, 86
Blum 44
Boardman 73
Bobo 32, 36
Bockman 105
Bodenhamer 79
Bogam 61
Bogarth 112
Boggess 85, 109
Boggs 65
Boirsean 22
Bolding 3
Boles 2, 85
Bolger 47
Bolinger 2, 57
Bolton 80
Boman 48
Bond 10, 44
Bonds 60, 98
Bone 46, 91, 103
Boness 110
Bonfoey 138
Bonner 13, 17, 19
Bonney 38, 127
Booker 95
Boon 133
Boone 65, 94, 148
Booth 105
Bordeaux 40
Border 116
Boren 18, 102, 116
Borlace 141
Bornefeldt 60
Borroum 23
Boswell 33
Bottom 33
Bottoms 95
Botton 80
Bouchelle 42
Bounds 98
Bourland 42
Bourne 18
Bovay 85
Bovey 85

Burge 31, 96
Burke 101
Burkham 104
Burkhead 13
Burks 75
Burleson 17, 82, 120, 129, 131, 138
Burleth 67
Burley 40
Burliegh 5
Burnett 90, 101
Burney 90, 91, 148
Burns 24, 45, 63, 96, 115
Burris 7, 10, 53
Burroughs 89
Burrows 14
Burton 57, 60, 87, 91, 92, 118, 141, 142
Bush 5, 120, 137
Busick 117
Bussey 60
Bust 36
Butler 4, 8, 15, 43, 82, 118, 148
Butrell 14
Button 33
Butts 31
Byars 88
Byers 37
Bynum 102
Byram 73
Byrd 114, 116
Byrom 149
Cabeen 75
Cabiness 77
Caho 108
Cain 38, 70, 121
Caison 110
Caldwell 26, 62, 71, 74
Calhoun 85
Callahan 43
Callanan 119
Callihan 149
Callison 49
Calloway 13, 60
Calvert 10, 24, 25, 119
Calvin 81
Camby 90

Cameron 16, 35
Cammack 49
Campbell 12, 15, 19, 21, 27, 36, 77, 85, 96, 103, 108
Cannon 4, 10, 17, 91, 94, 96
Cantrell 113
Cape 103
Caperton 50, 84
Capron 15, 149
Capshan 3
Caragin 111
Caraway 15
Cargill 114
Carlock 63
Carlton 17
Caro 98
Carothers 21
Carpenter 5, 64, 84, 112
Carr 20
Carrington 12, 74
Carrol 7
Carroll 12, 22, 38, 54, 67, 85, 101
Carson 33, 59, 137
Carswell 80
Cartar 115
Carter 26, 41, 49, 54, 64, 74, 105, 121, 122
Cartmell 29, 125
Cartright 47
Cartwright 13, 40, 59, 158
Caruthers 27
Carville 44
Case 21, 75
Casey 35, 102
Cassady 102, 149
Cassels 2
Cassidy 2
Casterline 113
Castillian 5
Castleberry 74, 102
Castleman 34
Caswell 80
Cater 4
Catlin 112, 113
Cato 87, 150
Caudle 36
Causey 93

Faucett 33, 88
Faught 17
Faulk 111
Faulkner 16, 39
Fawcett 29
Fay 109
Fearhake 74
Fearis 16
Fears 13
Featherston 89
Fedder 112
Feeney 16
Fees 100
Fennell 96
Fenner 109
Ferguson 37, 59, 75, 153
Ferrel 95
Ferrell 61
Ferret 61
Ferris 94
Fields 30, 58, 109
Filby 16
Files 75, 105
Finch 129
Fincher 116
Finlay 145
Finley 61, 81, 106
Finnin 116
Fisher 78, 88, 109, 159
Fisk 74
Fitch 61, 110, 111
Fitzgerald 111
Fitzgerrold 72
Fitzhugh 11, 92
Fitzpatrick 21, 149
Flaniken 23
Fleishman 21
Fleming 70, 99, 106
Flemming 42, 49
Flinn 110
Flint 18
Flood 132
Flournoy 79
Floynoy 79
Foley 27
Forbes 101

Ford 12, 15, 37, 59, 94, 101, 103, 111
Fore 16
Forehand 132
Foreman 10
Forester 83
Forgey 33
Forman 96, 103
Forrester 54, 83
Forsyth 32
Forsythe 61
Fort 2, 33, 43, 121
Foscue 35
Foster 5, 7, 13, 18, 30, 41, 42, 56, 60, 68, 82, 93, 120
Fotch 13
Founer 73
Fowler 10, 32, 117, 138, 141, 158
Fowlkes 104
Frabick 22
Frame 31
Francis 8, 95, 109, 114
Franklin 59, 99, 125
Franks 31, 120
Frazar 72, 120
Frazer 40
Frazier 22, 35, 55, 65
Freeland 13, 112
Freeman 9, 47, 117
Freeze 16
French 4, 22, 81, 102, 104, 136
Frost 50
Fry 63, 105
Fudge 38
Fulghim 52
Fulgium 63
Fuller 2, 27, 33, 36, 67, 93
Fullerton 8, 18, 31, 54
Fulton 62, 65
Furgerson 81
Furlow 16, 36, 47
Gage 7
Gainer 42
Gaines 19, 77
Gains 49
Galahar 103
Galispie 106

Texas Masonic Deaths with Selected Biographical Sketches

Hamilton 12, 25, 41, 57, 106, 112,
157
Hamitt 14
Hammett 41
Hammill 23
Hammond 76
Hammonds 13
Hamous 22
Hampshire 55
Hampton 2, 7
Hams 45
Hancock 15, 46, 82, 118
Hand 47, 76
Handley 83
Haney 65, 69
Hankins 18
Hanks 12
Hanley 42
Hannah 24, 36
Hanneman 75
Hansaker 18
Hansford 156
Harbison 118
Hardaway 52
Hardcastle 43, 48
Hardeman 139
Harden 45, 97
Hardew 12
Hardie 34
Hardin 24, 72, 82, 107, 156
Harding 55
Hardman 10
Hardy 61, 91, 99
Hare 33
Harefield 14
Hargrave 112
Hargrove 23, 153
Harington 112
Harlan 36
Harless 96
Harley 56
Harman 13
Harmon 5, 22, 51, 76, 86, 97, 113
Harms 42
Harper 12, 14, 15, 45, 80
Harrall 64
Harrel 44

Harrell 17, 19, 21, 38, 64, 89, 136,
144
Harrington 33, 81
Harris 12, 16, 19, 21, 25, 30, 41,
48, 59, 60, 70, 74, 79, 87,
98, 105, 113, 119
Harrison 5, 13, 31, 33, 37, 57, 64,
71, 93, 97, 102, 118, 124,
127, 146, 152
Harry 10
Harryman 99
Hart 18, 21, 50, 69, 82, 115
Hartgraves 3
Hartless 36
Hartranft 59
Harvey 13, 72, 112, 133
Harvick 64
Harwell 50
Haskins 62
Hassell 4
Hastings 93, 118
Haswell 104
Hatch 136
Hatcher 27
Hatfield 33
Hathaway 84
Hatley 2, 62
Hatter 90
Hatton 80
Haviland 21
Hawkins 23, 60
Hayden 65
Hayes 80, 119
Haygood 117
Hayherse 63
Hayhurst 32
Hayman 58
Haymond 103
Hayne 10
Haynes 36, 38, 43, 54, 87
Hayney 61
Haynie 8, 22, 76, 78, 136
Hays 59, 67, 99
Hayse 80
Hayter 13, 90, 94
Hazel 96
Hazelett 40

TEXAS MASONIC DEATHS WITH SELECTED BIOGRAPHICAL SKETCHES

Luper 67
Lusk 10, 119
Luter 30, 152
Lyday 33
Lynn 22, 54
Lyon 74, 94
Lyons 109
Lype 15
Mabert 13
Mabray 118
Mabry 33, 44, 64
Macdonald 18
MacFarland 10
Mack 21
Mackan 95
Maddox 13, 32, 79, 93, 118
Maffit 159
Magale 101
Magee 39
Maggard 26
Magill 95
Magruder 135
Mahaffey 24, 63
Mahanay 119
Majors 101
Malick 60
Mallard 5
Mallony 62
Mallory 114
Malone 63, 87, 100
Mamlok 67
Manker 18
Mankin 19
Mankins 110
Manley 75
Mann 5
Mannerlyn 19
Manning 14, 98, 100, 121
Manor 112, 144
Mapes 120
Marbut 22, 30
Marchbanks 68
Marchmann 138
Marcus 92
Maris 82
Markham 121
Markley 85

Markman 22
Marley 42
Marlow 44, 113
Marly 12
Marsey 86
Marsh 61
Marshal 95
Marshall 65, 82, 93, 134
Martin 2, 5, 15, 18, 21, 38, 49, 68,
    74, 76, 81, 84, 86, 92, 97,
    109, 118, 140
Mason 7, 31, 47, 49, 107, 158
Masongale 15
Mass 78, 90
Massa 2
Massey 8, 74, 86, 93, 150
Massie 57, 101, 150
Masters 89
Masterton 115
Matheney 117
Mather 92
Mathews 10, 58, 86, 96
Matlock 65
Maton 81
Matthews 12, 16, 21, 64, 67, 93,
    96, 107, 116, 140
Mattinly 62
Mattison 17
Mattox 13
Matzdorf 91
Matzorf 91
Mauk 68
Maupin 75
Maxwell 20, 104
May 16, 65, 153
Mayer 35
Mayers 55
Mayes 4, 62, 132
Mayfield 12, 68, 111
Mayier 24
Maynard 11
Mays 14, 48
McAdams 64, 118
McAlister 43
McAlpin 102
McAnulty 4
McAuley 21

McBeth 68
McBride 23, 63, 71, 101, 127
McCabe 15, 107
McCain 43, 60
McCaleb 48
McCall 12, 55, 79
McCamley 10
McCampbell 103
McCarley 73
McCarrty 71
McCarty 10, 39, 70
McCary 54
McCaskill 40
McCaven 23
McClain 71
McClanahan 71
McClane 41
McClellan 89
McClennon 21
McClosky 23
McCloy 46
McClure 18, 40, 118
McClusky 54
McCollock 21
McCollough 60, 96
McCollum 90
McComb 9
McCombs 70
McConnell 85
McCoombs 77
McCopping 86
McCord 53
McCorkerel 65
McCorkle 14
McCormick 15, 94
McCoulskey 81
McCoy 18, 88
McCrarie 49
McCrary 15
McCravey 71
McCraw 96
McCright 108
McCrocklin 116
McCrory 72, 139
McCullough 76, 115
McCurley 43
McCurly 79

McCutcheon 46, 114
McDade 23, 27, 136
McDaniel 50, 53, 54, 60, 63, 99, 122
McDavid 94
McDenna 7
McDonald 5, 32, 60, 65, 98, 103, 146
McDougal 110
McDougald 47, 90
McDowell 55
McDuff 41
McEacham 24
McEachern 5
McElroy 90, 97
McFarland 3, 16, 17, 21, 33, 55, 97, 142, 143
McGarity 65
McGaughey 36
McGauhey 54
McGee 5, 34, 39, 64, 76, 108
McGeehe 84
McGehee 82
McGill 98, 107
McGinnis 42
McGowan 94
McGown 43
McGregor 10, 11
McGright 108
McGuffy 7
McGuire 69
McIlhenny 6
McInnis 69
McIntosh 69
McIntyre 57, 120
McKain 14
McKamy 118
McKean 29, 101, 132
McKee 4
McKeen 101
McKellar 62
McKenna 108
McKenney 62
McKennon 83
McKey 64
McKimmins 35
McKinnan 83

Moore 2, 5, 15, 18, 21, 23, 24, 32, 33, 36, 41, 42, 53, 55, 57, 61, 63-65, 68, 73, 78, 80, 82, 86-88, 92, 93, 96, 97, 99, 100, 102, 113, 114, 118, 136, 151, 156
Moores. 30
More 18
Morel 9
Moreland 154
Morgan 14, 17, 22, 25, 29, 48, 50
Morison 119
Morphus 14
Morris 12, 30, 56, 63, 64, 69, 76, 82, 87, 104, 113
Morrison 106, 115
Morrow 5, 30, 109, 132
Morse 41, 152
Morton 80, 112, 152
Moseley 22, 37, 53, 95
Mosely 23, 156
Moses 58, 148
Moss 78, 80, 90, 109
Mote 41
Motley 51, 58
Mott 12
Mouldenhauer 101
Mouldon 19
Mowatt 5
Moxley 98
Muckleroy 67
Mullen 88
Muller 76
Mullhollon 25
Mullin 57
Mullins 30, 112, 117
Munden 77
Munger 50
Murchison 101, 108
Murden 77
Murdock 36
Murphey 76
Murphy 17, 46, 53, 115
Murray 15, 53, 59, 69, 70, 103, 110
Murrell 21
Murtland 75

Muse 59, 155
Mynatt 43
Myrick 83
M'Gee 155
Nabers 5
Nabors 54, 80
Nail 17
Nall 58
Nance 37
Nash 4, 7, 31, 86, 87, 133, 151
Nathan 101
Nathens 101
Navarro 140
Naylor 15
Neace 98
Neal 14, 18, 57, 95
Nealy 104
Nebbatt 2
Neblett 46
Neeley 119
Neely 97
Neighbors 4
Neill 97
Nelson 36
Nerts 21
Nesbett 49
Nesbitt 67
Nesmith 102
Nethery 27
Nettles 21
Neumann 85
Newburgh 69
Newdorfer 99
Newell 159
Newlin 16
Newman 90
Newton 10, 19, 44, 53, 67, 71, 78, 115
Ney 119
Neyland 12, 35
Nichols 12, 52, 55, 81
Nicholson 22, 136
Nicks 12
Niebours 13
Nix 68
Noakes 80
Nobles 75

Texas Masonic Deaths with Selected Biographical Sketches

Noel 108
Nolan 105
Noland 10
Nolen 108
Noler 111
Norman 43
Norris 4, 52, 86, 98, 119, 145
Northway 129
Norton 8, 50, 81
Norvell 61
Norwood 23
Nunelly 62
Nunn 79
Nunneley 36
Nutt 106
Nyegaard 22
O'Neal 8, 14
O'Quinn 38
Oaks 42
Oats 88
Obrecht 117
Ochiltree 25, 125
Odell 108
Oden 29, 85
Odom 19, 31, 56, 111
Ogbourn 68
Ogburn 24
Olde 67
Oldham 30, 41, 86, 112, 117
Olinger 82
Oliphant 4, 21
Oliphint 32
Oliver 16, 25, 31, 62, 73
Ollinger 82
Onstott 79
Orear 113
Orgain 117
Ormby 116
Orr 3, 118
Osburn 115, 119
Oswald 4
Oswalt 58
Oustott 79
Outhouse 18
Outlaw 21
Overend 110
Overstreet 47

Owen 8, 14, 15, 25
Owens 2, 12, 14, 47, 89, 118
Owings 23, 85, 116
Pace 29, 63, 94, 96
Paine 4
Palmer 12, 24, 37, 50, 60, 61
Pannell 85
Pannill 61
Panter 12
Paris 117
Parish 8, 30, 38
Park 5, 53, 62, 91
Parker 12, 24, 28, 30, 48, 54, 77,
      93, 101, 117, 119, 122
Parks 44, 78, 91, 134
Parman 87
Parmer 11
Parr 27, 30
Parris 49
Parrish 110
Parrott 31
Parsons 9, 46, 89, 91, 100
Partain 5, 153
Partlow 54
Pascal 86
Paschall 81
Past 37
Pate 80, 95
Paterson 99
Patillo 10, 22
Patrick 52, 87, 130
Patten 12, 83
Patterson 3, 8, 18, 19, 30, 51, 71,
      102
Pattillo 51, 52
Patton 17, 40, 54, 83, 89, 160
Paul 12
Paulk 78
Paulson 33
Paxton 17
Payn 43
Payne 13, 51, 77, 85, 95, 100, 108
Peace 47
Peacock 80
Peak 5
Pearce 17, 23, 69, 91, 96, 97
Pearson 69

Pearsons 26
Pebley 105
Pebly 105
Peck 100
Pederson 119
Peebles 40, 49, 78
Peed 114
Peeler 62
Peery 88
Pendavis 37
Pendergrass 23
Pendleton 102
Penick 53
Penn 52, 94
Pennington 81
Penrice 16
Penrod 15
Peobles 78
Pepper 109
Perkey 16
Perkins 7, 14, 25, 37, 52, 77
Perrie 46
Perrin 62, 96
Perrine 44
Perry 7, 39, 41, 66, 69, 71, 72, 92,
    110, 128, 136
Perryman 12, 32
Persch 52
Persinger 116
Pestole 17
Peters 76
Peterson 54, 64, 76
Pettit 3
Pettus 114
Petty 39, 48, 112
Pevyhouse 17
Phalen 103
Pharis 91, 116, 151
Phaton 103
Phelps 15, 91, 150
Philips 15, 91
Philleo 101
Phillips 33, 42, 50, 65, 82, 90, 92
Pickard 112
Pickering 43, 72
Picket 36
Pickett 19, 110, 116

Pickins 42
Pierce 97
Pierson 25
Pigman 111
Piles 57
Pinckston 55
Piner 111
Pinson 37, 53
Pipkin 47
Pipkins 91
Pistol 32
Pitman 25
Pitner 2
Pittman 56
Pleasant 87
Plemmons 105
Plummer 60
Poag 23
Poe 153
Poer 47
Poff 5, 99
Poindexter 40
Poiner 114
Poland 98, 104
Pollard 19, 104
Polly 14
Poole 92, 114
Pope 67, 80, 88
Porter 2, 16, 96, 110
Portwood 16
Posey 17, 50
Post 111
Potter 22
Potts 18, 35, 37
Powell 17, 30, 59, 93, 98
Power 81, 150
Powers 14, 32, 49, 69
Prather 48
Pratt 120
Prewitt 105
Price 4, 7, 12, 21, 26, 37, 44, 55,
    57, 59, 69, 77, 78, 85, 96,
    113
Priest 84
Prim 15
Prince 49
Prindle 11

Sandcliff 29
Sandel 117
Sandell 49
Sanders 2, 7, 17, 20, 32, 41, 52,
        60, 75
Sandifer 51
Sanford 31, 69
Sanger 44
Sansom 102
Santa Anna 150
Sarter 43
Saunders 4, 10, 47
Savage 71, 91, 106
Sawyers 103
Saxon 85, 102
Saycock 78
Scaff 46
Scales 78
Scarborough 13, 14, 81
Scarbrough 43, 103
Schaeffer 22
Schaffter 85
Schenck 51
Schmidt 93
Schonert 112
Schultz 12
Schwartz 78
Schwerien 53
Schwing 79
Scoggins 40
Scogin 69
Scott 8, 9, 21, 22, 25, 37, 38, 42,
        43, 56, 59, 96, 99, 100,
        110, 118, 135, 145
Scrivner 79
Scroggins 16, 38
Scruggs 23, 42
Scuggs 2
Seal 28
Seale 24
Seals 89
Seawright 65, 72
Secrest 41
Seeley 117
Seelhorst 67
Sego 90
Segui 5

Self 51
Sellers 4
Selman 22
Semones 75
Sentell 2, 35
Sevier 86
Sexton 109
Shackelford 79
Shackleford 18
Shadden 54
Shaddock 17
Shaddon 3, 5
Shanks 30, 109
Shannon 15, 18, 64, 146
Sharp 4, 12, 21, 101
Shaver 132
Shaw 18, 41, 53, 86, 92, 145
Shea 142
Shearer 119
Sheegog 105
Sheeler 49
Sheffield 48, 55
Shehan 109
Shelburne 113
Shellman 8
Shelton 15, 84
Shepherd 23, 36, 94
Sheppard 21, 40, 102
Sheridan 79
Sherman 41, 46, 72
Sherrell 12, 13, 38
Shetty 4
Shields 134
Shipman 114
Shipp 42, 56
Shirley 115
Shivel 121
Shiver 119
Shoaf 70
Shoemaker 86
Shook 52, 57
Shotwell 77
Shown 99
Shrigley 94
Shrock 105
Shropshire 22, 137
Shrum 24

TEXAS MASONIC DEATHS WITH SELECTED BIOGRAPHICAL SKETCHES

Taliaferro 21
Talley 53
Tally 21, 52
Talman 40
Tamplin 13, 96
Tanahill 32
Tander 96
Tandy 16, 78
Tankersly 13, 118
Tannehill 69, 133
Tanner 27
Tarrant 2, 150
Tarrence 65
Tartt 120
Tarver 8, 120, 159
Tate 13, 24, 27, 37, 43
Tatom 112
Tatum 25
Taylor 4, 5, 10, 12, 15, 23, 27, 30,
   35, 37, 38, 46, 50, 52, 55,
   60, 63, 71, 72, 86, 87, 97,
   125, 139
Teaff 53
Teague 120
Teat 62
Tedford 14
Telge 59
Tellison 65
Templeton 48
Tennan 79
Terrell 21, 88, 90, 114
Terrill 22
Terry 10, 108, 113, 143
Teters 24
Tevis 97
Thatcher 13, 23
Thein 47
Thigpen 13
Thomas 22, 27, 36, 39, 42, 44, 47,
   49, 50, 61, 66, 77, 95, 107,
   110, 121, 150
Thomason 56
Thomison 104
Thomma 69

Thompson 12, 14, 18, 22, 26, 27,
   42, 44, 48, 49, 55, 63, 67,
   68, 83, 87, 90, 95, 96, 100,
   116, 120, 154
Thomson 97
Thorbune 23
Thornton 5, 111
Threadgill 77
Threlkill 90
Thurston 141
Thweatt 37, 87
Tibaut 109
Tibout 115
Tidwell 67
Tiller 74
Timmins 4
Timns 53
Tinnin 79, 150
Tinnon 39
Tippen 104
Tippett 10
Tisdale 38, 157
Tittle 47
Titus 80
Todd 40, 91, 111
Tolbert 27
Toler 50
Tomlinson 13, 18, 80, 111
Tomlison 117
Tommins 112
Tompkins 109
Tompson 27, 90
Tonage 23
Torbert 74
Torrey 67
Touchstone 76, 106
Towles 53
Towns 147
Townsen 96
Townsend 78, 96, 117
Townsley 73
Trabue 33
Tracy 100
Trammell 102
Tramwell 7
Trant 65
Travelstead 67

~~~~~

www.ingramcontent.com/pod-product-compliance
Lightning Source LLC
Chambersburg PA
CBHW071120280326
41935CB00010B/1069